WHICH ? PAPER

Silvie Turner

estamp

A REVIEW OF FINE PAPERS FOR ARTISTS, CRAFTSPEOPLE & DESIGNERS

For Jake

Acknowledgements

Many friends have been extraordinarily kind and helpful in the preparation of this book. Mr R.K. Burt readily agreed to be advisor on my text and I am most grateful for his interest. Both his sons, and especially Clifford, showed courtesy and willingness to discuss anomalies and problems with me endlessly on the telephone and on my fact finding visits to Union Street. I chased John Purcell relentlessly and have to thank him for his insights, comments and welcome contributions. I always agreed with Stuart Welch's search for the best quality in papers and I thank him for sharing his experience and knowledge. Collecting accurate information is very difficult and to all the British, European and American papermakers, both handmade, mouldmade and machine-made, I should like to extend thanks for details of their makings sent so readily and also to all the international agents and suppliers for their samples, help and information also.

I am most appreciative of the articles by all the contributors who readily agreed to write on their specialist subjects. I should also like to thank the artists who sent me their paper preferences and comments, many of which I was sorry not to use because of lack of space. The initial research that Jacqueline Jeffries did in collecting the preliminary lists of retail papers was very helpful and I am grateful also to all the colleges and workshops who replied when I wrote to ask for their paper recommendations. To all the other specialists who have helped me by giving advice on the preparation of this book, I should like to thank them for their kind and professional direction. I should also like to thank all those who lent and gave permission for photographs to be reproduced.

I have relied on Lone McCourt, my designer, who always calmly and collectedly took everything in hand. Much love to my husband, who always supported this project, facilitating work for me in evenings , at weekends, taking children on trips, making Sunday lunches, etc.

Finally, I should like to dedicate this book to Jake Auerbach who, in searching for a present for Frank, finally convinced me that it was time for this research to appear in print.

© Silvie Turner 1991
Individual articles © individual authors 1991

Printed in England by BAS Printers Limited, Over Wallop, Hampshire
Designer Lone McCourt

First Impression 1991

Published by estamp 204 St Albans Avenue London W4 5JU

estamp would like to acknowledge and thank Townsend Hook Ltd. for their support in the production of this book.

A catalogue record for this book is available from the British Library

ISBN 1 871831 04 0

Papers used on the front cover (from top to bottom) - black *momigami*, pale blue cotton linter paper special making, deep purple iris plant paper, pale brown handmade paper from South India, *unryu-shi,chirigami*, white *Fabriano Esportazione*.

CONTENTS

ILLUSTRATION LIST

Preface *Jake* from *Seven Portraits 1989-1990* Etching by Frank Auerbach. Courtesy Marlborough Graphics Ltd.

1 Sheets of paper hanging to dry.

2 The surface of a sheet of paper at a magnification of 1000.

3 Sheets of hand- and mouldmade paper.

4 A Hollander beater with pulp.

5 Cotton linters before being used in the papermaking process.

6 The corner of a wove mould without deckle showing BG watermark of Barcham Green & Co. Ltd. Photo courtesy Barcham Green & Co. Ltd.

7 The corner of a laid mould showing the watermark device from Dieu Donné Press and Papermill. Photo courtesy Dieu Donné, USA..

8 Early Italian watermarks from Cartiere Miliano Fabriano.

9 A variety of papers showing various watermarks :
   Moosehead watermark in a laid paper from Tervakoski Osakeytiö, Finland
   Handmade watermark in a paper from the Tumba mill, Sweden
   The *Arches* watermark
   'Ceri Richards', the artist's signature as a watermark in a specially commissioned paper. Photo courtesy Curwen Gallery.

10 Weighing paper at an old Dutch mill

11 Part of a sheet of *Colombe* (Larroque Duchene, see p. 33)

12 Kathryn Clark forming a sheet of handmade paper at Twinrocker, Indiana, USA. Photo courtesy Twinrocker. Photograph taken by Todd Matus.

13 Forming a sheet of handmade paper at Wookey Hole Mill. Photo courtesy Wookey Hole Mill. Photograph taken by West Air Photography.

14 Making paper at Moulin de Larroque, France.

15 Paper drying at Moulin de Larroque, France.

16 Examples of inconsistencies in a handmade sheet
   Effects of crushing of wet sheets
   Mark caused by droplet of water on a wet sheet
   Peppering or wildness in a sheet
   Crushing in a sheet

17 Watermark in a sheet of paper from Sheepstor Handmade Papers.

18 Paper air drying on ladders at Handmade Plant Papers mill in Herefordshire

19 Ian Tyson working on an art project in John Gerard's Papierwerkstatt in Berlin. Photo courtesy John Gerard.

20 *Inclusions Florales* handmade at the Richard de Bas Mill, France.

21 Watermark used in a paper from Wookey Hole Mill.

22 The *su* - a Japanese mould cover.

23 Paper being made with the *sugeta* in a wooden vat in Kurodani, Japan

24 *Kozo* fibre, after stripping, being hung to dry in a Japanese papermaking village.

25 Black specks of the outer bark being picked from the *kozo* fibre whilst it is washed in the river.

26 Women sorting *kozo* fibres for papermaking.

27 Inside Paper Nao's shop in Japan. Photo courtesy Paper Nao and Atlantis.

28 Paper pulp being poured into the mould. Photo courtesy Nigel Macfarlane and Khadi Papers.

29 Cleaning and sorting of dried papers at Sri Aurobindo Ashram Mill in Pondicherry, India.

30 The character of *papyrus*.

31 Mouldmade paper passing onto the drying cylinder at St Cuthberts Mill, Somerset. Photo courtesy St Cuthberts Mill.

32 The vat area of a cylinder-mould machine at St Cuthberts Mill, Somerset. Photo courtesy St Cuthberts Mill.

33 Reeling up mouldmade paper at St Cuthberts Mill. Courtesy St Cuthberts Mill.

34 Paper maturing at the Zerkall Mill, Germany. Photo taken from *Die Geburt des Papiers* by Armin Renker produced for the Zerkall mill in 1952.

35 A selection of mouldmade papers.

36 A Fourdrinier papermaking machine.

37 The papermaking plant at Townsend Hook Mill in Kent. Photo courtesy Townsend Hook Ltd.

38 Storing Japanese papers.

39 Stack of papers made by Gillian Spires. Photo courtesy Gillian Spires.

40 Chinese papermakers laying wet paper on walls to dry in the sun.

41 The screen shop at Curwen Chilford printmaking studio with paper stacked ready for printing. Photo courtesy Curwen Chilford Studio.

42 Simon Green standing with packed paper in Hayle Mill. Photo courtesy Barcham Green and Co. Ltd.

43 A selection of Indian papers.

44 A selection of fancy papers.

45 Twelve Japanese craftspeople hand forming the largest sheet of handmade paper in the world in Kyoto, Japan.

46 A selection of extra rough surface papers.

47 John Purcell, David Dodsworth and Ian Mortimer making a 2x2 metre sheet at Meirat handmade paper mill in Madrid, Spain. Photo courtesy John Purcell.

PREFACE

Twice a year I am faced with the seemingly intractable problem of finding a present my father would both enjoy and use.

Two years ago, time running out again, I asked Silvie Turner if she knew of a book that examined paper in the way that Wisden looks at the careers of cricketers, the bare statistics tempered with illuminating insights. Strangely, it seemed that no such work existed and I bought some wine instead.

Paper is as varied, as specifically produced, as any tool of my father's trade and this year, due to Silvie's enthusiasm and expertise, he will receive an encyclopaedia that reveals the individual capabilities and range of this most basic of artists' materials.

Jake Auerbach

Jake from *Seven Portraits* by Frank Auerbach
Etching. Image size 18x15 cms, paper size 26x21.5 cms
Printed on Somerset White Textured, 300 gsm,
torn edges plus one natural deckle, left.
Printed by Marc Balakjian at Studio Prints, London

INTRODUCTION

1 Sheets of paper hanging to dry

Quite simply, this book is about sheets of paper. Paper that is unused, paper before it is drawn or painted on, written or printed on, cut up, torn or used in collage. There are already many books on paper - on the history and the techniques of papermaking, on deterioration of papers and on attempts to preserve and repair damaged papers. This book is unique in that it reviews a range of the finest qualities of paper available today. It aims quietly to guide the artist and the buyer of fine papers through the qualities and to assist in selecting a paper.

The idea of collecting information concerning fine papers that are for sale came partly from a genuine desire to know precisely what is in a sheet of paper. I wanted to be very clear what certain terms meant, what qualities certain fibres gave to a sheet. I also wanted to try to understand the aesthetic qualities of a sheet of paper and why the look and the feel of the paper was, in the first instance, so important.

I consider that artists have far greater control of their work when they have knowledge of the materials they work with even though it is not always essential or necessary; knowledge offers an opportunity to become better acquainted with a paper. For me this knowledge has extended to an interest in the contemporary craft of papermaking. A small amount of documentary information about the people who make and sell papers is also included in the book.

The best papers are those which have been developed by artists and papermakers working together, for specific uses, and not simply made by industry with a general market in mind. There are many examples of papers formulated in this way referred to in this book. Artists concerned about permanence and other qualities of the paper they use should not be afraid to consult manufacturers and suppliers for more information about specific details. Manufacturers are aware of the need for good quality products and of the factors that affect the paper, and many listed here maintain high standards and are glad to give assistance.

Setting out to explore the world of fine quality papers can be likened to tumbling down Alice's rabbit-hole - a total new world of discovery. Once you have experienced the joy of paper, you can spend a lifetime looking at and for it. I hope this book will serve to awaken newcomers to the delights of fine paper, that it will enlighten artists of all disciplines to the range of paper that is available to them and I hope it will encourage many to explore the beauty of fine paper.

NOTE TO READERS AND SUPPLIERS

If you do not find your favourite paper among the entries (possibly because a manufacturer or agent did not return the request for information in time), please let me know. Although I cannot answer individual requests for paper details, I will try and include them in the next edition. Also, while transactions between readers and suppliers are strictly between those people, I should like to hear comments concerning particular papers and their availability, indications on how useful you have found this sourcebook and any suggestions for future editions.

WHAT IS PAPER ?

2 The surface of a sheet of paper at a magnification of over 1000

Paper is a substance composed of fibres interlaced into a compact web, usually in the form of a thin flexible sheet, most commonly white. The earliest sheets of paper were reputed to be a mass of tangled silk made in China around 200BC. The paper of Ts'ai Lun, however, produced in AD105, was made from beaten hemp, rags, fishing nets and tree bark - a much superior sheet.

The earliest European papers were made at Cordoba in Spain around 1036 primarily from raw materials of linen or cotton rags which gave the paper great strength and permanence. As the demand for paper grew and the craft of papermaking spread throughout Europe, each country developed its own special papermaking skills and particular qualities of paper.

All paper up until the nineteenth century was handmade in a sheet form that often incorporated the best qualities of hand papermaking. As industry developed, spurred on by the need for cheaper papers, the change from the more expensive and harder-to-come-by fibres such as cotton rags, to ground wood as a raw material resulted in a weaker paper that was impermanent. Books, artwork, and numerous documents that were produced during this early expansion of the papermaking industry are decaying rapidly and require conservation to preserve them. As the causes of the breakdown of wood pulp papers began to be understood, various paper-refining techniques were developed by the paper industry and are being continually modified today. This book looks at the range of fine quality papers that are produced for artists of many disciplines.

WHY IS PAPER IMPORTANT?

The characteristics sought in a sheet of paper will be dictated by the particular use to which the sheet is to be put and the right choice of paper is imperative if the best results are to be achieved. As artists often produce highly individual and unique works, the same qualities should be sought in the materials and the support used.

   Although the principal role of paper is simply to act as a medium to support and hold together the printed, painted, written or drawn image, it has other functions too. Paper should be able to satisfy aesthetically and be able to withstand any rigours applied to it by way of the process being used. It should be economical to work with and the price should suit a particular pocket. Paper sets the limits as to how accurate a printing job can be; how a work is viewed. The shade and texture of a sheet adds to the impressions made by the final work. In addition to accepting the transfer of ink or paint properly, the surface of the sheet of paper has a direct bearing on how clearly a drawn or printed image will appear and on how strong the final colour(s) will look. Paper must also fulfil its finished function - to be folded, to be printed on, to be permanent in whatever environment is selected, whether bound in a book or mounted in a frame.

   The choice of which paper to use is often a difficult, arduous and time-consuming job. On the other hand, looking at papers can be a very interesting and often rewarding experience; this book aims to make life a little easier by giving some armchair information.

QUALITIES OF PAPER

3. Sheets of coloured *Roma* handmade paper by Fabriano, Italy.

When someone who does not have a detailed or technical knowledge on the subject of papermaking wants to buy a sheet of fine paper, it is often the aesthetic qualities, the look or the feel of the paper that determines the purchase. However, there are many other distinguishing features of a sheet and terms used to describe paper that it is useful to understand and to be conversant with. This section gives information about the qualities and characteristics of paper .

PAPER SPECIFICATIONS

Before you set out to purchase a sheet of paper, it is useful to understand certain terms which your retailer may use. Below is a table of specifications which lists the details of a sheet of paper. Every paper can be described in these terms. Each category describes a different characteristic of paper :

Name of paper *e.g. Saunders Waterford*

Descriptive name *(its purpose) e.g. Watercolour*

Type of paper *e.g. Mouldmade*

Furnish *e.g. 100% cotton linters*

Special properties *e.g. Internally and tub sized, acid free, long grain direction,*

Watermark *e.g Watermarked and embossed*

Deckle edges *e.g. Two natural deckles, two torn*

Surface finish *e.g. Rough, Not, or H.P.*

Weight *e.g. 150 gsm*

Thickness *in micrometers usually used for boards*

Size *(dimensions of the sheet) e.g. Imperial*
Whiteness or colour *e.g. White*
Quantity *e.g. Single sheets, mill pack, reams, etc.*
Instructions *e.g. For delivery (or shipping) should also be included, dates required.*

NAME

Readers who are looking for a specific paper by name will need to look it up in the paper index (see p.136) and find it in one of the paper lists. The majority of papers listed in this book use the mill brand name e.g. *Velin Arches*. Many paper agents and retailers in different countries give the papers different names, in some cases to make a difficult or foreign pronunciation easier in a mother tongue. For example *Velin Arches* is often called *Arches Cover* in the USA. Whenever there is any confusion about a name, consult your local retailer for advice.

DESCRIPTIVE NAME

This category describes the use that the paper is put to, e.g. *a drawing paper.* A whole section in this book is devoted to the uses of paper (see p.83 ff).

HANDMADE, MOULDMADE AND MACHINEMADE

The making of any type of paper today falls into one of three categories : handmade, mouldmade and machinemade.

Contemporary handmade paper is made by the same age-old traditions of scooping an amount of pulp up from the vat onto a mould by hand. Occasionally hand papermakers will introduce a new piece of equipment or modify a process to suit the late twentieth century's demands but basically the process of fine quality hand papermaking continues in much the same way as it did centuries ago, with variations in the process in different parts of the world adapted to suit local conditions. (See Handmade Papers, p.23ff)

Both mouldmade and machinemade papers are made on a machine but in each case the papermaking machine is quite different. The development of a machine to emulate the qualities of handmade paper was inevitable and the cylinder-mould machine allows the same basic raw materials to be utilised as in handmade paper but on a larger scale with a faster and more even production in a continuous roll. Called mouldmade, this type of papermaking is now a firmly established European tradition. The paper produced on a cylinder-mould machine is different from a handmade quality but is often considered to be half handmade and half machine-made. (See Mouldmade Papers, p.47 ff)

Machinemade paper is made on a flat bed Fourdrinier papermaking machine. Paper made on a Fourdrinier has a vastly heightened speed of making and drying to that of a cylinder-mould machine and utilises usually a different quality of pulp. Since the mid twentieth century, a lot of research and development has gone into making mass-produced papers specifically for the artists' and designers' market and the range is now large for every conceivable purpose. The quality of machinemade paper is quite different from the other two qualities. (See Machinemade Papers, p.67 ff)

It should be made clear that this book concentrates on looking in detail at handmade and mouldmade papers produced worldwide for artists' use. It also includes a number of machinemade papers but because the range is so great, those papers included are the personal choice of the author.

WOVE OR LAID

When paper is made, there are only two coverings to the mesh of a paper mould, these are termed 'wove' and 'laid'. Like a watermark, they are indicative of a certain quality when the sheet was formed. They can be distinguished when the sheet of paper is held up to the light. A wove mesh on a paper mould is similar in appearance to that of a woven fabric with warp and weft threads; this produces a very smooth paper with an evenly distribution of pulp. Unlike the older, more traditional laid mesh in which a series of strong parallel lines constructed in wire are held together with less heavy 'chain' wires running at right angles to them. These show as distinctive lines in the 'laid' paper. All papers were 'laid' until John Baskerville's invention of wove paper around 1757.

FURNISH

The furnish describes the basic ingredients of the paper, which when added together give a specific type of paper. The most basic of the ingredients is the fibre from which the paper takes its particular characteristics.

THE IMPORTANCE OF FIBRES

Paper is made from cellulose fibres derived from plant sources. These fibres are cells of varying length and width and are derived from a variety of plants. The best papers are made from plant cells that are very high in cellulose.

Each fibre has its own characteristic and lends certain attributes to the paper it is made from. It has its own shape, size and structure both before and after processing and an understanding of the type of fibre used is of great value in understanding the behavioral characteristics and life of the paper.

Before being used in any papermaking process, the fibres are treated mechanically in the presence of water, a process called beating. The oldest method of beating was to pound the fibres in a stone or wooden trough, or hammer the fibres on a flat stone.

In many papermaking practices this was later replaced by the 'Hollander' beater. The principle of the Hollander beater (and the modern beater) is to pass the fibres, suspended in water, through a controlled gap between a fixed and a revolving bar.

During this beating operation, cutting (shortening fibre length), fibrillation (shredding and bruising of fibre walls), and hydration (when fibres begin to accept water more readily) can all take place, adjusted by the papermaker. In addition to altering the strength of the paper, the beating also affects the type of paper being made. If the fibres are beaten with a minimum of fibrillation and cutting, the resulting paper has bulk, e.g. like blotting paper; where there is little cutting and a maximum of hydration, a dense, sealed, non-porous paper results, e.g. like greaseproof paper. The final quality of paper is a compromise between fibre selection and beating.

Where possible, a papermaker will select those fibres which have the properties he and the artist require in the finished product. This may not always be possible either because the fibres are not available locally or are not commercially viable. It is this latter fact which accounts for the reason why the vast majority of modern machinemade papers consist of a mixture of fibres derived from hardwood and softwood trees and that papers made from fibres such as esparto, cotton, linen, jute and ramie are of a different quality, more expensive and rather special.

TYPES OF FIBRES

Cotton differs from many other plants in that in its natural state the fibres freely yield a pure cellulose without requiring much preliminary treatment. Cotton linters and cotton rags are the two types of material available to the papermaker from the cotton plant. *Cotton linters* consists of the shorter fibres left behind after the ginning operation, which are not used in the thread

4 (Left) A Hollander beater filled with pulp
5 Cotton linters before being used in the papermaking operation

spinning manufacture.These are sold as blotter like sheets, already washed and boiled. Cotton linters is the principal fibre used in hand- and mouldmade papermaking today.

Cotton rags consist of the staple (or textile)cotton plant. These fibres, used in the manufacture of cotton thread, are longer, tougher fibres and the process of making them into threads imparts a certain hardening to the surface. The cotton thread is collected in the form of old rags and the papermaker must undo all the mechanical process of weaving and thread-making and must free the fibres from the tougher cell surface. Cotton rags, common in the past, are not used widely in the papermaking process today (except perhaps in India) but do impart a wonderfully strong paper. Many manufacturers describe their paper as 'rag' paper. A question to ask when buying such a sheet is whether the ingredients are linters or really rags.

Linen covers a wide variety of raw materials known as flax or linen. The fibres are long and tubular, thus imparting a hard, strong, firm to handle, often smooth and silky feeling to the paper. As in the case of cotton rags, linen rags represent a very good source for the papermaker. *Jute* is a plant native to India and the Far East but the fibres do not easily fibrillate, they are not naturally white nor do they bleach easily. *Hemp* is native to China and is one of the oldest papermaking fibres. It is a strong fibre with a tendency to longitudinal splitting which produces a hard, coarse paper.

Kozo, mitsumata and *gampi* are the three native papers of Japan; *kozo* is probably the toughest and strongest of all the papermaking fibres with long sinewy threads which neither shrink nor expand in use; The fibres of *kozo* are about 10 mms long; they are tough and mesh easily so that *kozo* papers retain their strength even when crumpled and folded. *gampi* papers are made from fibres that are long, thin and glossy, making the papers that are translucent and tough; they have a wet strength and an inherent resistance to insects. *Mitsumata* has a fibre length of about 4 mms and the papers have a soft, smooth surfaces and an elegant, glossy appearance and are also naturally insect-resistant.

The group of leaf fibres includes *esparto grass*(short, tubular smooth fibres), manila , known in the Philippines as *abaca*. Grass fibres include *bamboo, giant nettle, rice straw and rattan*; all are used in papermaking in many of the Far Eastern countries.

Today the vast majority of papers in the world are made from *woodpulp*. A new process for breaking down the wood pulp and isolating the cellulose fibres from the resinous substances in the wood has provided manufacturers with a High Alpha Cellulose wood fibre paper which promises to be comparable to most rag papers in its longevity.

In the manufacture of a fine paper, a quality fibre, even if an expensive one, represents approximately only 10 per cent of the total cost of the sheet. The qualities it imparts to the sheet are a definite advantage, outweighing those of many of the less expensive but also inferior papers.

SPECIAL PROPERTIES : SIZING AND ABSORBENCY

Sizing a paper makes it moisture- or water-resistant in varying degrees, i.e. it changes the absorbency of a sheet. The absorbency of a paper is controlled partly in the preparation of the pulp but mainly in the addition of size to the paper. The are two methods of sizing :

Internal sizing
If the size is added to the wet pulp in the beater before the final sheet is formed, the process is called internal sizing (or beater- or engine sizing).

Tub sizing
If the size is added to the paper surface after it has been made and dried, by passing the sheet through a tub full of size, re-drying the paper and hardening the size, it is called tub sizing or surface sizing.

Most printmaking papers are beater sized, whilst watercolour papers are tub sized to reduce the absorbency of the surface.

Many manufacturers today are aware of the need for purity in papers and are careful of the acidic effects which some sizing agents can cause. Although rosin or gelatin size have been much used in the past, a common size today is 'Aquapel'. Other surface sizes include glue, casein and starch.

WATERLEAF
This is the term used to describe paper that does not contain any size. Waterleaf paper is naturally absorbent as a result of the cellulose fibres which are water-loving by nature. Any liquid applied to the waterleaf surface, initially wets the fibre and then is absorbed into the sheet by capillary action between the fibres.

SPECIAL PROPERTIES : ACID FREE

Apart from the price and supply, the aspect of paper often most discussed today by artists and conservationists alike is permanence. There are many ideas about permanence and many papers are listed as 'long life', 'permanent','acid free' or 'neutral'. What does this mean?

The presence of acids in paper has been shown to contribute towards deterioration and consequently paper that claims to be 'acid free' or 'permanent' has become desirable. Most discussion centres on the questions of the neutrality of paper and of its yellowing with age caused by oxidation. For permanence, the paper fibres have to be as pure cellulose as possible. Cotton is 100 per cent cellulose; cotton rags supply longer fibres than the more commonly used cotton linters but each is high in cellulose. Wood pulp varies in cellulose content but High Alpha Woodpulp can be up to 93 per cent cellulose, is almost as pure as cotton pulp. However the fibres are shorter and it lacks characteristics in the finished sheet desired by many artists.

The pH value is a measure of the strength of the acidity or alkalinity of any paper. The measure of availability of free hydrogen ions representing, in lay terms, the balance between acid and alkaline components of a material is what is actually measured. 0 pH is very acid, 14 pH is very alkaline, 7 pH represents a situation of balance between the acid and alkaline components and is a 'neutral' solution, hence the measure of an acid free paper.

The majority of artists' papers made today carry the quality label 'acid free'. This doesn't necessarily mean that they have a pH value of exactly 7 but probably close to it, close enough for the paper to withstand the ravages of time and last without yellowing or becoming brittle. Most papers claim to be acid free are of a neutral pH at their time of manufacture or even slightly alkaline. However, many conditions (including adverse environmental conditions) can affect this neutrality well before the artist buys the paper, and subsequently. Because of this, many papers have a 'buffering' agent added to their making. This means that an alkaline substance, usually calcium- or magnesium carbonate, either occurring naturally in a water supply or purposely added by the papermaker, will help to protect a paper.

Paper has existed for centuries without a pH of 7; printed papers in the paper museum at Fabriano in Italy which have a pH rating of 4 are still beautifully preserved. It is wise to accept that manufactures vary and note that the papers listed in this book have not been independently tested.

SPECIAL PROPERTIES : GRAIN

Grain is a characteristic of all papers made on a machine i.e. mould- and machinemade papers. It results primarily from the alignment of fibres during the formation of the sheet. Long grain describes fibres running parallel with the longest side of a sheet, short grain along the shortest side. The grain direction has many effects on a sheet of paper :

• Paper tears more easily along the grain direction than across the grain.

• Papers fold more readily parallel with the grain direction than against it but folding endurance is greatest against the grain.

• Paper is stronger and stiffer across the grain direction.

• When the paper absorbs or gives off moisture with the changes in atmospheric humidity, it expand or contracts more in the cross direction than in the grain direction.

• Paper should be printed with the grain direction running across the printing machine as paper stretches much less in the grain direction. This is an important point when estimating how much paper is needed for a job, especially in offset printing and it is extremely important to converse with your printer and/or your paper merchant about the grain direction if it is relevant, so as to avoid unnecessary hassle, reprinting and wastage; the cross direction should be the smaller dimension, thus giving the possibility of greater stability and consistent registration.

The majority of Eastern and Western handmade papers are 'roughshake', a term used to indicate that the fibres are distributed at random, i.e. have little or no grain direction. This characteristic is peculiar to handmade papers and is a distinctive asset, allowing the paper to remain stable and strong in variable conditions.

WATERMARKS

A watermark was defined in 1708 as a 'distinguishing mark or device impressed on the substance of a sheet of paper during manufacture, barely noticeable except when the sheet is held up against the light'. The watermark in a sheet of fine quality paper today should act as a recognition of the quality and standard of manufacture and as a guarantee of the authenticity of the sheet of paper.

The introduction of watermarking in Europe is almost certainly credited to the Italian papermakers at Fabriano. It is widely assumed that papermaking was established there around 1268 and fourteen years later the first watermark, a very rough cross with small circles at each end and a larger one in the middle, appeared from a known mill. These basic devices were thought to assist in the recognition of moulds belonging to papermakers who were illiterate. By the fifteenth century, most papermakers used some watermark or other. Various studies of the history of watermarking devices have been made and Dard Hunter suggested a classification of the types of design into four categories : The earliest, representing simple shapes of crosses, circles, triangles, knots: Man and the works of man: Trees, flowers, grasses, etc: Wild, domestic or legendary animals. Although this is a very general list, it appears to be fairly representative of the types of watermarks. A fifth group would be letters and numbers as many papers today carry the designation of a particular sheet, country of origin, etc.

MAKING A WATERMARK

Termed in French *filigraine* and in the USA *papermark*, the watermarking process is a feature of Western papers. The design is formed initially out of bent copper wire and attached as a mirror image to the flat surface of the mould. The design requires close collaboration between artist, mouldmaker and papermaker as the limitation of the process must be understood and acknowledged. Where the watermark device is attached to the screen of the mould a raised surface occurs. Because the actual quantity of pulp is less over the raised part than over the rest of the sheet as the paper is made, when dry, it appears as a slightly thinner layer of paper than the rest of the sheet, though this is only discernible when the sheet is held up to the light.

Many intricate designs are produced today with thousands of thin wires mostly soldered (and not stitched as was usual in the past) into place.

Historically, because many of the papers were manufactured for bookmaking, one, or repeated, watermarks were placed either directly in the centre of a sheet of paper or in suitable positions for the paper to be subsequently folded in half, quarters, eighths, etc. and cut.

 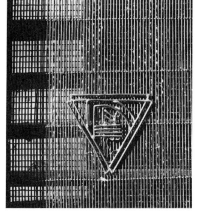

6 The corner of a wove mould without deckle showing BG watermark of Barcham Green

7 The corner of a laid mould showing the watermark of Dieu Donné paper mill

Today the placing of watermarks in large sheets of paper is generally confined to the edges of a sheet of paper so as not to interfere with the process for which the sheet is being used.

CHIAROSCURO WATERMARKS

In this method of watermarking, an image in the paper is expressed in terms of tone (light and shade) as opposed to simply a line mark. Initially a watermark artist carves his image into a wax block approximately only 0.5 in. thick. A plaster cast is taken from which a die and matrix (male and female) are produced. This relief is then impressed into the wire cloth of the wove screen before it is attached to the mould, thus forming undulations in its surface. When the sheet of paper is formed, heavier and lighter deposits of pulp are distributed in the relief areas of the mould, which when dry and pressed, can only be seen by holding the sheet of paper up to the light. Cartiere Miliani Fabriano is notable for its skill and widespread use of the chiaroscuro watermarking method. Many other mills use similar techniques especially those manufacturing banknote papers including Portals in Britain, Tervakoski Mill in Finland and Tumba Bruk in Sweden.

SPECIAL WATERMARKS

Many commissioned papers contain a special watermark which is often the name of the artist, an event, date or place of making. Most hand papermakers incorporate their own watermark devices into each of their sheets, quickly recognisable if you are acquainted with their papers, intriguing if you are not. A false watermark is created by stamping the sheet when wet.

8 (Far left) Early Italian watermarks from Cartiere Miliani Fabriano
9 (left to right, top to bottom)
   A variety of papers showing watermarks :
   A moosehead in a laid paper from Tervaoski Osakeytio, Finland
   A 'handmade' watermark from the Tumba Mill, Sweden
   The *Arches* watermark
   'Ceri Richards', the artists's signature as a watermark in a special making.

SURFACE FINISH OR TEXTURE

The texture of a sheet can be the result of the quality of certain types of fibre, a certain type of beating, of the natural drying processes, or of a contrived pattern impressed on the paper's surface during or after its formation. Three terms are used to describe the surface of hand- and mouldmade papers :

Rough

This is the natural surface of a handmade sheet when it is dried without any smoothing or pressing and is reminiscent of the surface of the felt that is used in its making. Note that mouldmade paper surface finishes are not produced in the same way as handmade paper finishes; for mouldmade papers, the rough surface is made by using a rough felt. Other terms used to describe the Rough surface include coarse, antique, felt, irregular.

Not

The 'Not' surface, derived from 'Not Hot Pressed', is the result of parting and repressing of handmade sheets *without* any intermediary felts or boards. This gives a surface finish in between the H.P. and Rough. To produce a Not surface on a mouldmade paper, the felts used are of a slightly finer texture than the Rough felts. Other terms for Not include cold pressed, dull, eggshell, matt, medium, regular, satin, slightly grained, unglazed, velour.

Hot Pressed or H.P.

If hand- and mouldmade paper has a smooth finish it is described as 'Hot Pressed'. The term is not perhaps accurate on all counts. Although some manufacturers do press their sheets between hot glazing rollers, some pass them through cold, highly polished metal rollers with pressure to obtain the smooth surface effect. Historically a surface that is H.P. was obtained by polishing with a smooth hard object, calendering, or coated and then polished. The H.P. surface can also be described as glazed, high, sheen, smooth or super-calendered.

Note that the terms for these surfaces are general and they are not consistent to different manufactures.

Although many handmade papers appear to have the same surface on either side, there is a wire side (the side the pulp is closest to the mesh of the mould) and a felt or top side. Any additives in the paper may, if heavier than the pulp, sink to the bottom of the thick pulp in the mould and so become more apparent on the wire side than on the felt side.

With mould- and machinemade papers, it may be the case that the bottom of the paper web closest to the wire is more porous than the top or felt side. Thus the finish can be said to be 'two-sided'. The wire side is more 'open', contains less size, has shorter fibres and a more pronounced grain. The felt side, on the other hand, can have a closer formation, have less grain because of better crossing of the fibres, and is usually better for the printing side. Some (often mouldmade) papers are made with two distinct surfaces to provide a choice for the artist.

In Japanese handmade paper (often called *washi*) it is easier to differentiate between the top *omote* surface which is smooth and the underside *ura* which is more uneven.

DECKLE EDGES

The deckle edge is that natural, slightly wavy edge, often uneven in thickness that is found only in a handmade or mouldmade sheet of paper. Until paper began to be made in continuous lengths, the distinctive deckle edge of a handmade sheet was considered to be a defect and was trimmed away for the most part. During the nineteenth century, a deckle edge became a snobbish symbol of the handmade product. The deckle is, in fact, the name of part of the papermaker's mould which he holds onto while making the sheet. It determines the edge of the sheet and ensures that the sheet of paper is of consistent thickness during the making.

A full sheet of handmade paper has four true deckle edges, whereas mouldmade paper only has two true deckles, parallel to each other, formed at each side of the web of paper on the cylinder-mould papermaking machine. The other two edges are made when the paper is torn in sheets from the roll along a line where the fibres have been made less dense (formed by a raised wire or tape across the mould).

10 Weighing paper in Imperial style
at an old Dutchhandmade mill

WEIGHT

All papers are made to a weight. Traditionally, this weight has been measured in pounds (lbs) weight per 500 sheets of a certain size of paper. For example, a common size/weight of a handmade paper is 'Imperial 140lb' which means that 500 sheets of paper of Imperial size (22x30in.) will weigh 140lb.

Confusion has arisen because of the fact that two different sizes of paper of the same basic weight can be referred to by two different weights, e.g. Imperial 140lb is the same basic weight as Double Elephant (40x27in.) 246lb or Royal (20x25in.) 106lb.

Metrication of the basis paper weights has meant that, to a large extent, the anomalies of the Imperial system have been overcome by referring to the basis weight of a single sheet of paper in grammes per square metre weight, expressed as 'gsm' here but also as gm^2 and g/m^2. The weight of a sheet of paper is now referred to as the 'grammage' which is the weight in grammes of a single sheet of paper one square metre in area.

Examples of appropriate conversions are

Substance in gsm	approx. equivalent in pounds	
150-160 gsm	Imperial 72lb	Royal 54lb
180-200 gsm	Imperial 90lb	Royal 68lb
240-250 gsm	Imperial 120lb	Royal 90lb
285-300 gsm	Imperial 140lb	Royal 106lb
410-425 gsm	Imperial 200lb	Royal 150lb

BULK

The bulk of a sheet is distinct from its weight. Bulk should not be equated with strength either. Bulk is dependent on how well pressed a paper is and the same amount of fibre can produce a thin compressed sheet or a thick porous sheet; this in turn depends on the amount of processing the fibres have been subject to. The individual fibres of a bulky paper are further apart than in a compressed sheet and contain more air pockets, rendering the paper light weight and not particularly strong.

SIZE

Sizes and weights are intricately and traditionally linked and the appendices (see p.113 ff) describe the systems of measurement in detail - the older, more traditional Imperial system of measurement and the newer, standardised metric system.

WHITENESS OR COLOUR

White is a term commonly used to describe the colour of a sheet of paper. There are enormous variations in the shades of 'whiteness' and they are dependent on a number of factors : the basic fibre colour, fibre cleaning and bleaching, drying and sizing operations, etc. With the discovery of bleaching practices (chlorine was first used in 1774) it has become possible to make white paper from various coloured and even poor-quality materials. But bleaching can have a distinct disadvantage; papers become yellow, brittle and deteriorate quickly if traces of bleach are left in the fibres.

19

Water also affects the shade of whiteness and any impurities such as silt, chemicals, fertilisers contained in the water during the papermaking process will be imparted into the pulp if the water is not strictly monitored.

The colour of a Western handmade sheet is quite different from that of an Oriental white sheet. The best papers in Japan are made in the winter time when the coldness keeps the water free of impurities and bleaching by the sun and reflections from snow impart a special crispness and cleanness to a sheet.

During this century there has been a tendency to increase the whiteness of papers artificially by adding chemicals known as optical brightening agents. These contain fluorescent bleaching agents which absorb ultra violet radiation and re-emit it as blue light. While they may initially produce a whiter sheet, the colour changes markedly with age and eventually the sheet will turn yellow. This will not happen to a paper made with the natural shade of a basic fibre.

QUANTITY

Although it is possibe to buy single sheets of paper, it is often cheaper to buy a pack of paper - a quire of 25, a millpack of 100 or 125 sheets, or a ream of 500 sheets. The quire and ream are traditional measures of quantity and many references have been made to the antecedents of these terms; the Arabic *risma* was and still is used, relating to clothes and textiles tied in a bundle; it probably applied to a parcel of paper in the same way and derivatives of this include Italian *risma*; English *ream*; Danish *rills*; French *rame*; German *ries*.

Occasionally papermills will sell direct to artists but on the whole not in single sheets or small quantities. Most buying is normally done through a paper agent or retail supplier.

OTHER QUALITIES OF PAPER

Occasionally, other qualities in paper need to be understood and below are listed some of the characteristics that may puzzle a paper buyer.

DRYING

Pole and loft dried papers (common to handmade sheets) are dried without the tension that occurs during the machine drying of mould- and machinemade papers. This allows them to be more stable in different atmospheric conditions. If the web of paper in mould and machinemade production is dried under tension, the stresses produced can become fixed or frozen, constituting a part of the paper's structure.

HARDNESS AND SOFTNESS

The comparative hardness and softness of a sheet of paper is reasonably easy to ascertain by feeling. The factors determining the hardness or softness are varied. Surface hardness if often a result of sizing plus a certain amount of calendering or pressing; the absorbency and drying potential of a sheet is affected by the particular method and amount of sizing.

BRITTLENESS

Brittleness, a property causing cracking and breaking, is often the result of the pulp being overbeaten which drastically reduces the length of the fibres. If the paper has a 'rattle' it may be a hardness caused by the addition of alum during the making.

DENSITY

Dense papers are are hard and compact, their fibres are strongly bonded together so that the sheet will expand and contract as a whole with any moisture changes. In soft, bulky, porous papers, the fibres can shrink and swell without so much change in the overall dimensions of the sheet.

Density is closely related to the dimensional stability or 'expansivity' of a paper. It is also related to the paper's tendency to curl.

OPACITY

Opacity is concerned with the extent to which an image can be seen through a sheet of paper. Opacity is important when considering the appearance and legibility of an image especially when printing a book, organising a series of sheets to be viewed together or working on both sides of a sheet of paper.

The terms used when talking about opacity are *show through* (the view through the preceding page) and *strike through* (the view from the back of the same page). Opacity depends to some extent on the quality of beating given to the fibres and the weight or amount of fibres in any given sheet.

Opacity is also linked to the quantity of loading agents and fillers in a sheet of paper whether added to the 'stuff' or applied directly to the paper surface. The principal use of loading agents is to make the paper more impervious to ink, although other agents may be added to the pulp e.g. buffering agents. Size (not the dimensions of a sheet but gelatine, glue, starch, etc.) is a loading agent.

LOOKING AT A SHEET

Buying a sheet of paper one one's own without access to an experienced retailer can be difficult. However, many distinguishing features of a sheet can be ascertained by careful and intelligent examination. Below are listed some of the ways to identify the characeristics of a paper :

• By loosely handling the the paper between thumb and forefinger and gently shaking the sheet at one corner, an appreciation of the softness and crispness of the sheet can be obtained :
• By rotating one's thumb lightly over the top surface, the texture can be ascertained, although a more efficient way is to hold the sheet up to eye level and look along the top surface.
•By tilting the sheet at various angles against a light source, the amount of light reflected off the surface can be judged.
(It may be necessary to ask for a sample of paper for the next four tests as they will damage the paper.)
• The absorbency of a sheet can be tested by applying an amount of moisture(often from the tongue) to a small part of the surface, or better, by applying a drop of water and noting the number of seconds the shine of the water takes to disappear.
• By tearing the sheet, the comparative strength between different grades of paper can be judged, and if the paper is mouldmade it should be torn in

Colombe

two directions; the easier tear will be found in the 'grain direction' (often parallel to the longest dimension of a sheet and called the 'long grain' of a sheet). Handmade papers do not normally have a grain direction but occasionally there might be a slight difference in the tearing strength between directions. The fibre length can be seen from a close examination of one of the torn edges with a magnifying glass.
• Both surfaces of the sheet should be carefully scrutinised under a light source to determine if there is any difference between the top and the undersides of the sheet.
• By bending, folding or creasing a part of the sheet, the hardness or tendency to crack can be judged.
• In most cases the watermark should read the correct way round, thus indicating the top or correct side of the sheet.

Handmade paper is more prone to have inconsistencies and this may not impair its use in certain cases. 'Good' sheets should be ordered, not 'seconds', when requirements necessitate absolutely evenly produced papers.

12 Kathyrn Clark forming a sheet of handmade paper at Twinrocker paper mill, USA

HANDMADE PAPERS

THE HANDMADE CHARACTER

........I hoarded the stuff (Crisbrook)

buying seconds and mill packs from

which I could find plenty of good

parts of sheets torn for small prints. I

am still printing on Crisbrook from

my stocks and will despair when they

are finally depleted....

Jo Winkleman

President, Royal Society of Painter Etchers and Engravers

The hand process of making a sheet of paper today remains basically the same as many hundreds of years ago. The basic fibres must first be freed from all the substances which, although indispensable to their plant life, impair their value as a papermaking material. Thus the plant is subject to various sorting, cleaning, chopping and soaking operations before its use as a fibre in papermaking. Many professional hand papermakers today, however, use an already prepared fibre base, such as cotton linters, for ease of production.

A thorough beating in a Hollander beater is one of the most important operations in the manufacture of a good quality paper, in which the fibres are parted and bruised and put into a condition in which they will intertwine with one another or 'felt' when submitted to the vibratory shake of the vatman. These beaten fibres are then added to a large tub (vat) filled with water in approximate proportion of 1 per cent pulp to 99 per cent water.

The apparatus for papermaking by hand is called a mould and deckle. In the Western tradition of papermaking, the mould consists of a sturdy, often mahogany, frame covered with a fine wire mesh, over the top of which fits a second frame, the deckle. A sheet of paper is made by the action of the craftsman (called a vatman) dipping this sieve-like mould into the steam-heated vat and pulling up the mould with a shaking action, front to back and left to right, thus aligning the fibres in four different directions, which is called a 'roughshake'. As the excess water drains away, a thin, even, compact sheet of interlocking fibres is formed on the surface of the mould. To prevent the pulp from falling off the ends of the mould, the deckle is held on the top while the sheet is being made and gives the edge to the wet sheet. This skilled action of a vatman, although it takes only about four seconds, is vital to the formation of a perfect sheet of paper. The vatman then removes the deckle and passes the mould to the coucher who upturns and tips the wet pulp onto a damp felt blanket. This process of making the sheet is repeated numerous times until perhaps a hundred sheets (a post) of paper have been made. The pile of wet sheets, each interleaved with a felt, is then removed and the excess water squeezed out under pressure. After further pressing and drying, the compressed papers are separated by a layer and hung or laid often in natural air in a special, open loft to dry.

The sheets may take up to four to five days to dry completely, although today large mills employ a heated cabinet or hot cylinders for drying operations. The sheets are then ready for the sizing and finishing rooms.

Between two to five reams of paper per day can be made at one vat mill depending on the size and weight of the sheet under manufacture, the whole process from beginning to end taking approximately three week to complete. The best papers in a good 'make' have resisted the used of chemicals and additives, except possibly for size and colouring, and are free from agents which might harm the paper in future years.

It is impossible to make a quantity of hand made paper without defective sheets. These were first termed 'Broke Sheets' and were graded as B, BXXX or XXX and were packed at top and bottom of a ream before despatch. Occasionally termed 'Retree' ('retry' means try over again) or 'outsides', or more likely now 'seconds' and graded XX, they still represent the defective sheets in a pack. Damage or defective paper often discarded during manufacture is usually re-pulped.

HANDMADE PAPERMAKERS

Handmade papermaking is a traditional craft. The vast majority of papermakers today are individuals who, with insight and vision, possess the natural manual skills either to continue production or to set up new operations. Such people are rare and should be valued for their sense of dedication and their talents in producing unique and often beautiful papers that can be made in no other way.

Very few of the small, one-man operated mills working today can trace their history back to past centuries as a working paper mill and even fewer papermaking families can state that their mill is maintained in working order. Even the location of handmade mills and workshops has tended to change. No longer is it necessary to site a mill by a stream, nor is it obligatory to be reliant on locally grown raw materials, on nearby transport or a local labour force. In the Western world, the majority of mills today are small operations (1-6 people). The workshop is often sighted in picturesque old buildings, almost always linked with domestic accommodation, indicating that the whole family may be involved. Many of today's oldest hand-

13 Forming a sheet of handmade paper at Wookey Hole Mill

made mills in Europe are museums with a small output in many cases linked to a large commercial paper factory whose management has had the insight to preserve and restore this old machinery and equipment.

What is significant is that in many of the countries over the Western world, each individual maker, working often in isolation, strives and often succeeds in making papers that are individual and personal, even when the basic ingredients and the processes are the same.

Raw materials have undergone a revolution. Since the early experiments with wood pulp, commercial producers have utilised it in its many forms. However, wood pulp, even in its acid free form, is not a popular basis for a handmade sheet, imparting qualities that an experienced papermaker distrusts immediately. The hand papermaker in the West has turned to a form of cellulose found in abundance in cotton linters which now represents the basis of much handmade paper in Europe and the USA, although many papermakers offer paper made from different fibres such as linen, hemp, sisal, jute and mixtures. Handmade quality is the only type of paper in which such a variety of papers from different bases can be found.

The market for handmade product has also changed. In the past governments, lawyers, banks qualified for the best-quality 'makes' and the rest of the manufacture was available for domestic everyday use.

15 Paper drying at Moulin de Larroque, France

14 Making paper at Moulin de Larroque, France

Today the machine can produce paper products to suit the majority of these markets and so that individual papermaker is left with reduced sales. Many hand papermakers have opened up their mills to tourists who are most interested to see the continuance of the age-old craft; many have turned to 'decorative' production such as handmade paper for letters, envelopes, boxes, cases, small personal books, etc. A more important development of recent years stems from the awareness of paper not only as a vehicle but also as a medium for artists and designers coupled with the increasing use of handmade paper by museum conservationists and restorers. Each of these possibilities exerts an influence on the hand production of today and has helped to maintain an aspect of this craft that was underexploited and in danger of becoming extinct. By maintaining and increasing the demand for the handmade sheet, the hand fabrication of paper will be able to continue to delight not only those who take a simple pleasure in the beauty of paper but also those who appreciate its uniqueness as a basic material on which to draw, to paint or to print.

INCONSISTENCIES IN A HANDMADE SHEET

Many people make the mistake of regarding inconsistencies in a sheet of handmade paper as defects. Small inconsistencies are often an inherent part of a sheet of handmade paper, though they are much less likely in mouldmade papers which are subject to more rigorous technical controls.

The majority of faults in a handmade sheet are often due to mechanical rather than chemical factors :

• Signs of poor beating are revealed as lumps of unevenly distributed pulp when a sheet is held up to the light.

• Knotting is common with certain types of fibre which may cause lumps or bumps in the surface.

• Extraneous matter, hairs, dust or dirt may have dropped unnoticed into the vat and eventually become embedded in the sheet.

• Uneven thickness in the body of the sheet is either a result of the vatman's action or unevenness of fibre distribution in the vat.

• Small spots or light patches are not uncommon as a result of drips or splashes of water into the wet sheet during the making process.

• If, while the wet sheet is being turned onto the felt, the mould has slipped, a thick deposit of wet fibre may accumulate at one edge.

• The coucher must take care of the felts which, if they become worn or damaged, will disfigure the texture of the surface.

• Variations of up to half an inch may occur in sheet size (caused by loosely fitting deckles).

• Sheets should show no indication of how they were dried. Occasionally marks of clips used to hang the sheet up or a string mark along the middle of the sheet indicate the drying method.

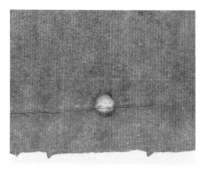 

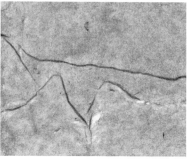 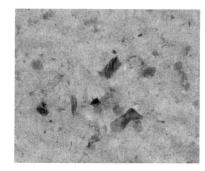

16 Examples of inconsistencies is a sheet :
(Top) Droplet of water marking the sheet
(Bottom) Effects of crushing of wet sheets

(Top) Crushing in a sheet
(Bottom) Peppering or wildness in a sheet

HANDMADE PAPER MILLS

Europe can boast a fair number of hand papermakers. In Britain about six individuals, all with small, specialised output, are practising their craft. The makers that have an established production are listed in the *Handmade Papers List* (see p.30 ff). Other smaller makers include Gillian Spires who works in Devon :

I make paper from plants which grow locally near my home in Devon. The process I follow uses primitive Oriental methods. The fibres are all beaten by hand on a granite block, therefore my production is relatively small, and I concentrate on quality. Over the last seventeen years my waterleaf papers have been used for printing with oil based inks in the West and for painting with water based inks in the East. ...The raw material is collected and the process chosen according to the purpose for which the paper is to be used. Uses are as diverse as for rare books, embroidery, furniture and large screens as well s my own art work. I prefer to use natural dyes for coloration whenever possible. The colour range can be extensive, dyeing the fibres to suit the project.... The surface is suitable for the discerning printmaker who is aware of the fibre length and texture of the paper, a favourite feature being the frayed edges by making without the use of a deckle.

An individual papermaker, Nigel Griffiths, set up his papermaking operation in 1980 in Kent and has continued to make a small specialised manufacture ever since :

...my paper conforms to the best traditional practice e.g. 100 per cent best white cotton rag, hand-made, pressed, air-dried, tub-sized in gelatine and air-dried again. No chemicals are used and the colour is natural. Individualistic enough not to be confused with other makes of paper, but consistent in quality, finish and perform-ance, and of large dimensions...

Sheepstor Handmade Papers set up and run by Tim Powell has continu-ing handmade production :

I have been making paper since 1969. My production is now mostly Watercolour paper, but I also make other handmades. Watercolour is usually from stock while other papers tend to be special orders. The furnish is entirely cotton linters, sized with with aquapel or gelatin. The latter is of course more expensive and takes a lot longer

and is usually by special order. Most of my paper is a natural white, almost a cream compared to commercial paper. For tinted papers I use inert mineral pigments. My weight range is 100 - 600 gsm.... Special watermarks can also be arranged.

17 Sheep watermark in a sheet of paper from Sheepstor Handmade Papers

Bob Partridge, a papermill engineer, initially owned the Two Rivers Paper Company based at Rosebank Mill, Ramsbottom but the mill was sold on his retirement in 1985 to Paul Ritchie, an engraver and printmaker. The present owners, Lynne and Jim Patterson, bought the business in 1988 and relocated it at Pitt Mill in Somerset. Jim Patterson has a papermaking family background with twenty-seven years mill experience in the UK and abroad. Pitt Mill is an ancient corn mill, probably 300 years old, which ceased working at the turn of the century, became dilapidated and was used as a chicken loft and a store for the farm house to which it is attached. The house and mill were bought in 1986 by the Pattersons. After restoration, production began in April 1988 and has steadily grown until now when it is producing a standard range.

Plant Papers Mill founded and run by Maureen Richardson is a small mill in Herefordshire, making a wide range of papers from plant bases. The Griffen Mill set up by Christine Laver in 1987 has developed a new range of handmade papers called the *Studio* range in addition to the other archival quality handmades they already produce as standard sheets. Wookey Hole

Paper Mill is the only museum of papermaking in Britain that professionally produces a small standard range of handmade sheets for printmaking, drawing and watercolour.

Many small mills continue to make handmade sheets in Europe. Enzo-Gutzeit OY is a large and important paper manufacturer which continues to support the small-scale but very high standard production of handmade sheets at its Tervakoski Mill in Finland including writing and a number of drawing papers for artists in its range. In Sweden, the Lessebo Handpaper Mill started to make handmade paper in 1693 and now, part of the large AB Klippans Finpappersbruk in Sweden, continues to produce handmade writing sheets, envelopes and some artists' papers. The first paper mill at Tumba also in Sweden, was built in 1755 and only handmade paper was made up until 1939 when a cylinder mould machine was installed. The company AB Tumba Bruk have at present no commercial output of handmade papers although a small amount is produced in the museum attached to the mill.

Aided by a long tradition of book making, in France there are at least six mills practising serious standard production; the most well known is Richard de Bas mill set in a country area in the Auvergne which combines a papermaking museum; Jacques Bréjoux continues his fabrication at the Moulin du Verger du Puymoyen; Georges Duchene runs both Moulin de Larroque and Moulin du Pombie; Moulin de Pen Mur and Moulin Vallis Clausa produce handmade papers and the paper museums at Canson and Montgolfier and the L'Atelier-Musee du Papier in Anglouême continue to attract visitors.

In Italy, Cartiere Miliani Fabriano handmade papers have been enthusiastically praised throughout the ages by artists and users alike; this mill has achieved remarkable control over its production so that it is able to continue to produce superb quality handmade papers in a uniform standard that is hard to beat. The Magnani family in Pescia continue to maintains small specialised production of handmade and some mouldmade papers for writing and drawing at their Cartiere Enrico Magnani mill and the museum of papermaking at Amalfi Museo della Carta keeps the papermaking tradition alive and provides much information for study.

In the Netherlands, The Middelste Molen has started handmade production supported by the Schut paper company. In Spain, Capellades Paper Museum has been making papers since the thirteenth century and has been renowned for its excellence for many hundreds of years. A small range of paper is made using 100 per cent rags and the age-old equipment that was restored in the 1940's. Following European tradition, Augusto Aviles, the papermaker/owner of Papel Hech a Mano Meirat, makes a range of characterful papers made of flax; each paper is individually handmade and carefully crafted and this mill is particularly known for its unique large sizes, range of weights and surfaces.

18 Paper air drying on ladders at Handmade Plant Papers mill in Herefordshire

In USA, the well known papermills such as Twinrocker, HMP Handmade Papers, Dieu Donné continue to increase their standard production and it is a pity these handmade ranges are not more widely available in Europe.

In Canada, La Papeterie St Armand, founded by Dave Carruthers in 1979 in Montreal, specialises in the production of quality handmade papers for artists and bookbinders. St Armand is distinguished by its attention to quality and fibres such as 100 per cent linters, flax and cotton rag are used to produce high-quality watercolour and drawing papers such as Dominium watercolour paper.

Little standard handmade production is available in Australia although individual makers continue.

In Israel, a project that started at the Beer Sheba Visual Art Centre, the Uncle Bob Leslie Papermill has become a papermaking centre for Israeli hand papermaking where paper is made from the local plant, *negev* or *mitnan*.

MADE TO ORDER

A special order of paper that a mill makes to a specific recipe, size, shape or colour, etc. for a client is called a special or custom making. Custom ordering is not a complicated process requiring a large volume order. It is in reality a simple process; a dialogue takes place between artist, paper-maker and often paper agent to achieve a certain combination of paper qualities. The majority of the mills listed above will undertake custom makings with pleasure, while some only produce custom work. A special making allows for a special watermark - the artists' name, a commemorative insignia and many other changes producing a special paper that is often not like any of the standard ranges. A typical example of a handmade special making is two thousand sheets but less is often negotiated for instance Moulin du Verger requires no more than 500 sheets to render a making worthwhile.

THE PAPER WORKSHOP

Papermaking studios exist that do not make any standard production at all. They often specialise in working with artists on paper 'art' projects where the paper forms the expression and not simply the support. Studios include Paper Art run and owned by Fred Siegenthaler in Muttenz, Switzerland. His expertise and studio facilities are available for many types of custom making and he does not hold any standard range. In a similar manner, Otavio Roth runs his paper workshop Handmade Papel, Texto e Arte LTDA, in Sao Paulo, Brazil. This is a two-man operation catering exclusively for special projects with orders of over 200 sheets; they produce a large amount of

cotton rag paper for small press publishers. In England, Jacki Parry runs The Paper Workshop in Glasgow along the same lines. This workshop aims to explore and develop the craft of papermaking across the broadest possible spectrum of art and design by providing facilities for artist craftspeople and designers using the studio for a variety of projects and has been very successful in promoting papermaking along these lines in Britain. In Britain also, the Nautilus Press and Paper Mill is an educational facility, community project and a business producing crafts from custom handmade papers, paper art, book arts, designer bookbinding, letterpress printing, printmaking and related photography.

19 Ian Tyson working on an art project in John Gerard's Papierwerkstatt in Berlin

In Berlin, John Gerard's Handgeschöpfte Papiere not only makes custom papers for artists and small publishers but also works extensively on collaborative projects with artists making unique and multiple paper works.

HANDMADE PAPERS

Handmade papers are extremely individual papers; often aesthetically astonishing in their beauty, available in a vast range of colours, weights, surfaces and textures and presenting a myriad of experiences to the user. However to compile an accurate list of handmade papers is difficult - not all mills produce sheets on a continuous basis and much handmade production is a making for a specific retailer, client or agent. It is possible that the paper's characteristics can vary with each making but the handmade papers listed here have, on the whole, an established production and are reliably available from a range of agents and retailers, occasionally throughout the world. It is worth noting that this list is concerned with papers made in the Western tradition and is compiled alphabetically by mill name. It does not identify the papers which have the biggest market from those that only have a small retailing or national sales. As many mills produce custom makings for specific agents or retailers, it is important not just to look at one source when searching for the right paper. If you are interested in handmade papers whose specifications are not listed here in detail, contact the mills yourself for information or ask your local retailer or paper agent to do it. Look also at the section on *Handmade Papermakers* (see p.24). Addresses can be found in the appendices.

To distinguish the papers from the mills, we have introduced • before the name of each paper.

DIEU DONNE HANDMADE PAPERS

This mill founded (in 1976) and run by Susan Gosin and Bruce Wineberg has gone from strength to strength. Situated in New York City, Dieu Donné provides custom-designed archival handmade papers for artists and for book/paper conservators. It also makes its workspace available for artists to create works of art in handmade paper plus many other teaching and assitance schemes. The papers are made from a variety of mixed fibres, unusual blends including linen rag, silk and cotton and all are neutral pH with four deckles and no watermark. Papers include *Agate Brown, Blue flack, Carribean Blue, Charcoal Grey, Dark Grey Swirl, Dark (brown) Linen, Emily Dickenson, Evergreen, Falco (with flecks of wool and feathers), Germanicus, Hot Pink Swirl, Irides, Li Tai Po, Wall Street Grey, White Linen* and many others. They are available from specialist paper suppliers particularily in America. Write to the mill for more information.

FABRIANO HANDMADE PAPERS

Cartiere Miliani Fabriano is a uniquely famous, Italian hand papermaking mill and only a small part of the massive papermaking empire producing banknotes and security papers for the Italian goverment. Fabriano produce a range of hand-, mould- and machinemade papers which are listed separately in each different section. The handmade sheets are very densely formed and are couched onto several different grades of felts which offer a wide range of surfaces. This manufacture is widely available in many countries throughout the world.

• FABRIANO ESPORTATZIONE

A paper still manufactured by hand with 100% cotton fibre and a neutral pH. It has four deckles and a localised watermark. It is internally and vat sized with gelatine. It is available in white only and the Rough finish is a good, solid, heavily textured sheet.

Specifications
Handmade
100% cotton
Tub sized
Neutral pH
Acid free
Watermarked CMF
Four deckle edges
Not (*Fina*) and Rough (*Grossa*) finishes
Weight 200, 315, 600gsm
Size 56x76cm
Creamish white only
Suggested Applications
Drawing
Crayon
Inks
Watercolour
Tempera
Charcoal
Pastel
Printmaking

• FABRIANO ROMA

A handmade sheet with a neutral pH guaranteeing its permanence. It is available in eight, wonderful Italian strong tones and white, in one size and one weight. This sheet carries two watermarks - bottom left hand corner CM Fabriano and bottom right hand corner the She-wolf of Rome suckling the two twins plus the Roma name. Sheets show chain and laid lines.

Specifications
Handmade
100% cotton
Watermarked
Laid
Acid free
Four deckle edges
Not surface only (Cold pressed)
One size - 48x66cm

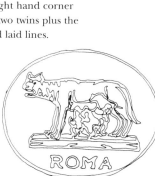

One weight 130 gsm

Nine colours

Suggested Applications

Pencil

Chalk

Inks

Watercolour

Printmaking

Letterpess

Book binding

Drawing (dark shades excellent for Chairoscura)

Pastels

• FABRIANO PERUSIA

A laid handmade paper with a Not surface and includes the Griffin watermark. The production of this paper was discontinued by the mill for general markets and is now being made especially for New York Central Art Supply Inc.

• FABRIANO UMBRIA

A paper of great beauty. Made by hand is has four deckle edges and is available in white (*Bianco*) and cream (*Gialletto*) in two sheet sizes and one weight - 150gsm. The sheet includes the crown and sceptre watermark.

Specifications

Handmade

100% cotton

Neutral pH

Acid Free

Internally soft sized

Watermarked in right hand bottom corner

Four deckle edges

H.P. (Satinata) and Not (Fina) finishes

Sizes 32x45 or 51x71 cm

White and cream

Suggested Applications

Crayon

Pastel

Inks

Acrylics

Watercolour

Intaglio

Lithography

Screenprinting

Lino and woodcuts

Drawing

Calligraphy

GRIFFEN MILL HANDMADE PAPERS

Griffen Mill was founded in 1987 by Christine Laver. Output was centred around the production of three papers designed for use by archivists, paper conservationists and bookbinders but also able to be used for printing techniques possibly including laser printing. These are relatively thin papers; each sheet has four deckle edges and is available as a laid or medieval laid sheet. Its archival nature is indicated by the watermark which is an infinity symbol with a small 'G' underneath. Traditional fibres are used and the papers are internally sized and buffered to a pH range of 7-8. All papers are neutrally sized with Alkyl Keytene dimer emulsion and buffered with magnesium carbonate (also acts as inhibitor of catalytic oxodisation of trace elements). Polymide-epichlorohydrin resin is used as a wet strength agent to minimise weakening of cellulose fibre to fibre bonds at higher humidities. The Griffin Mill has recently moved premises and for new paper ranges and information, contact the mill direct.

• GRIFFEN LYNX

A light-brown paper, rather rich and creamish; again as many of the other papers it is produced in three lightweights. A rather subtle paper.

Specifications

Handmade

Cotton/linen/unbleach manilla mix unbleached

Neutral pH

Buffered with magnesium carbonate

Not surface finish

Wove, laid and mediaeval laid

4 deckle edges

Royal size

Weights 55, 80 and 115 gsm

Light brown

Suggested Applications

Drawing

• GRIFFEN PHOENIX

A lightweight, buff toned paper with a subtle, matt surface finish.

Specifications

Handmade

Cotton/linen/unbleach manilla mix in varying proprtions

Unbleached

Neutral pH

Buffered with magnesium carbonate

NOT surface finish

Four deckle egdes

Wove and laid and mediaeval laid papers

Royal size, 51x64.6cm

Weights 55, 80 115gsm

Toned

Suggested Applications

Drawing

• GRIFFEN STUDIO RANGE

This is a lovely new range of handmade drawing papers for artists launched in June 1990 from the Griffen Mill. They have been introduced as an 'art paper of archival quality'. These are available as laid papers, 180gsm in a small range of pastel colours. With the exception of pre-ageing tests which have not been done the technical specifications of these papers complies with those recommended by the Society of Archivists, BS 4971 part 1 '88 and ANSI/ASTMD 3290-

76. They are suitable for a wide range of drawing media. Besides being an exclusive and subtle range, an added bonus to these papers is the degree of wet strength present which gives excellent dimmensional stability in a variety of atmospheric conditions.

Specifications
Handmade
100% Cotton fibre
Acid free
Neutrally sized with medium to hard strength
Four deckle edges
Royal size 51x64.6cms
Weight 180 gsm
Studio Grey (with black flecks), Cream (whitish) and Buff
Applications
Drawing
Watercolour
Pencil
Crayon
Pastels, etc.

• GRIFFEN UNICORN

The lightest tone of the cream shades of paper, called 'Old White'; again a subtle paper with intrinsic character.

Suggested Specifications
Handmade
Cotton/linen/unbleach manilla mix in varying proportions
Unbleached
Neutral pH
Buffered with magnesium carbonate
Not surface finish
Four deckle edges
Wove, laid and mediaeval laid papers
Weights 55, 80 115 gsm
Old white

HMP HANDMADE PAPERS

This mill, begun in 1973 at the home of John and Kathy Koller in Woodstock Valley Conneticut,USA, continues production mostly being involved collaborations with artists and print publishers. A longstanding connection with New Central Art Supply Inc. has led to a large range of white and coloured handmade papers being developed for their personal customers from cotton and linen pulp with some of the coloured papers being created naturally from cloths and fibres. Write direct to the mill for more information.

LESSEBO HANDPAPPERSBRUK PAPERS

Lessebo mill continues its handpapermaking facility as part of the AB Klippans Finpappersbruk in Sweden making papers of archive-quality making five tonnes annually. Lessebo manufacture a fine range of papers mainly for the Swedish market. The majority of the papers are white and available in H.P., Not and Rough surfaces. Lessebo Aquarelle is one of the best known papers manufactured with a neutral pH in varying sizes and weights. Lessebo paper is also used for elegant stationery, guest books, etc.and include *Bikupan, Post, Havamal, Biljett, Visitkort, Kort,* etc. For availability and information, please contact the mill direct.

MEIRAT HANDMADE PAPERS

Handmade in Madrid by Augusto Aviles at Papel Hech a Mano Meirat, this small range of lovely papers is made from flax. Available in a natural ivory white, cream plus a series of 'marbled' papers which actually means short coloured fibres inserted into the pulp- *Jaspeado azul* (blue fibres), *crema* (red), *gris* (grey) and *verde* (green). This mill offers papers which are specifically noted for their unique sizes - possibly the biggest Western handmade sheets are produced in maximum size of 2x2 metres. Besides producing smooth papers, Meirat 'Rough' papers are made from flax and left to dry in the mould giving a very heavily

textured Rough surface. There are two standards - sized (Velasquez) and unsized (Goya). Take special note of the Meirat blacks. The sizes in the smooth surface are restricted to 50x70 and 70x100cm, the sizes of the Rough papers are 1x1, 1x2 and 2x2 metres.

• MEIRAT GOYA

An ivory white paper, available in 'board' weights up to 1000gsm. Either side is useful and comes in a range of weights with two surfaces - Smooth and Textured.

Specifications
Handmade
Unsized
Not surface
Acid Free
Neutral pH
Fast tints
Four deckle edges
Colours include Ivory, cream plus grey, cream, green and blue speckled(fine threads)
Suggested Applications
Printmaking
Embossing
Casting

• MEIRAT VELASQUEZ

This paper is also available in the very heavy board weights suitable for many techniques; a fine paper with a strong black sheet as well as the more subtle, soft tones of the marbled grey, cream, blue and green.

Specifications
Handmade
Aquapel (synthetic) sized
Not and Rough (very stucco) surface
Four deckle edges
Five colours- ivory, cream, black, blue and green marbled.
Rough surface available in ivory and black only
Suggested Applications
Watercolour

Charcoal
Oils
Pencil
Typography
Printmaking
Engraving

MOULIN LARROQUE HANDMADE PAPERS

Georges Duchêne owns and runs two paper mills in France in the Dordogne area, the Moulin de Larroque and the Moulin du Pombie. The impetus for new and energetic production can be attributed to Georges Duchêne and here at the Larroque mill sheets are made in the traditional age-old manner.

• LARROQUE DUCHENE

This paper, whose real name is *Colombe*, is a grand, beautifully rough-surfaced, soft, natural coloured sheet which can be made up to 600 gsm weight and is made by hand and dried on the mould by master the paper-maker himself. The Larroque mill produces a range of handmade papers besides *Colombe*, including *Calcaire, Dessin, Garance, Gris Souris, Lys, Mais, Muguet, Nature, Pompeii, Thè.*
Specifications
Handmade
100% cotton
Aquapel sized
Four deckle edges
Various sheet sizes including Imperial
Soft
Very Rough top surface
Soft white colour
Suggested Applications
Drawing
Chalk
Pastel
Crayons
Printmaking

• LARROQUE FLEURS

A paper of gentle beauty, handmade in a soft white colour with inclusions of local petals, grasses and leaves.
Specifications
Handmade
100% cotton
Four deckles
Smooth Not surface
180 gsm standard weight plus several others
Royal and Imperial sizes
Natural white
Applications
Decorative uses
Drawing
Printmaking

MOULIN DU POMBIE HANDMADE PAPERS

This mill run and owned also by Georges Duchene in France produces a range of more decorative papers (often with flecks or speckles in them) than those produced at Moulin Larroque. The manufacture employs some mechanical processes to accelerate production - the papers are almost half handmade and half machinemade to reduce costs. Papers include *Moutarde, Litho, Sable, Salt & Pepper, Marbre, Linorg, Mouchetes* and are suitable for bookbinding and letterpress as well as drawing, printmaking and collage.

MOULIN DU FLEURAC HANDMADE PAPERS

This small mill in the Charante area of France produces a range of handmade papers in the age-old traditions of hand papermaking. All sheets are made from 100% cotton rag with four deckles and are vat sized and line dried. They are suitable for all drawing and printmaking techniques and the papers named by colour include *Warm Grey, Rustique, Chestnut, Peach and Sienna.* Atlantis Paper Co. in London can supply all of these papers to order.

MOULIN DU VERGER HANDMADE PAPERS

Production began in 1539 and this mill is now run by master papermaker Jacques Bréjoux who has experimented with various new fibres to produce an interesting range of different quality papers. One of the mill's strengths lies in Jacques Bréjoux's ability to hand-make virtually any paper to order that matches the customer's specification of fibre, mould, weight or colour, requiring no more than 500 sheets to render a special making worthwhile. Note also that besides the papers listed below, 100% linen and 100% manilla 'Chine' papers are made plus a flower paper. There is a new straw pastel paper with a rough, gritty surface in a lovely brownish colour available now from Atlantis Paper Co. in Britain.

• MOULIN DU VERGER HEMP PAPER

A veriety of handmade papers from hemp, some with 100% hemp, soft, translucent, absorbent and unsized, others internally clay sized to create a soft sheen, plus various textured surfaces too.

• MOULIN DU VERGER AQUARELLE

A variety of watercolour papers, some 100% rag, others 100% cotton; heavy, white watercolour paper.

• MOULIN DU VERGER LIN-COTTON

Cotton and linen mix with Not surface. Pale grey colour with black specks.

• ATLANTIS MOULIN DU VERGER

Atlantis Moulin du Verger restoration paper is especially designed to be sympathetic for paper repair of old books, drawings and manuscripts. It is made for the British paper company Atlantis by Jacques Bréjoux, using mixed cotton, linen and manilla fibres in the traditional manner on single faced 18th century moulds. Atlantis regularly produce special makings of paper for customer's requirements from this mill and previous making have included 170gsm buff endpapers, Islamic blue calligraphy papers and lightweight repair papers, etc. all made to archival standards.

Specifications
Handmade
Mixed fibres: cotton, linen and manilla
Neutral sized
Acid free
Laid mould
Four deckle edges
Watermarked if required
Stock papers not watermarked
Weights 50-120gsm
Sizes lighter weight 56x33cms, stock size 56x66cms
Two shades of antique off-white
Suggested Applications
Paper conservation
Bookbinding
Printmaking
Drawing
Calligraphy
Drawing

NIGEL GRIFFITHS HANDMADE PAPERS

Nigel Griffiths is a small British papermaker (See before). His paper are made form 100% best white cotton rag and the resulting sheet colour is a natural white. The are tub-sized with high grade gelatine and have a neutral pH. The weight is 330gsm on an Imperial size but Double Elephant is also available. Contact the mill for details.

PLANT PAPERS MILL HANDMADE PAPERS

A wide range of interesting coloured and textured handmade plant papers are made by English handpaper maker Maureen Richardson at her Plant Papers Mill in Herefordshire. Reflecting the natural beauty of the plant base that they are manufactured from, the papers offer a wide range of applications and

20 *Inclusions Florales* made at the Richard de Bas mill, France

uses. This mill has samples of over one hundred flowers, leaves, vegetables and stalks which yield the fibre and cellulose necessary to produce a piece of paper. Some are as thin as tissue, some very fibrous and thick. The papers include *Bracken paper, Cotton paper, Mulberry aand Manilla Paper, Onion paper, Rush paper, Straw paper, Vine paper, White flax paper*, etc. Contact the mill for deatils.

RICHARD DE BAS HANDMADE PAPERS

At the Richard de Bas mill, situated in the hamlet outside the town of Ambert in the Puy de Dome, parts of the original mill built some six hundred years ago are still are used to make their handmade papers. Papers are made mostly of cotton rag and linters and are still beaten by wooden stampers that pound away

(although this is not the only form of beating that takes place), powered by water from the local river which incidentally is slightly acidic. A wide range of printmaking, letterheading (small size sheets including envelopes) and restoration papers are made here plus several fancy and coloured sheets in a range of subtle tones - greens, browns, maroons, blues. This mill is renowned for its *Papier à Inclusions Florales* in which small petals and ferns of local flowers are dropped into the pulp whilst making. Several papers include fragments of wool from local sheep, and others small pieces of silk. The makings here are renowned for their consistency and durability and are available from stockist all over the world.

• RICHARD DE BAS AQUARELLE

This paper is a durable sheet, made with great consistency. R. K. Burt and Co. Ltd. in Gt Britain has a special making of this sheet in which an H.P. and Rough surfaces are made while the mill standard is only a Not surface.
Specifications
Handmade
100% cotton
Four deckle edges
Internally sized
Not (H.P.and Rough) surfaces
Sizes 57x78, 51x66cm
Applications
Watercolour
Specially good for carborundum etching
Mixed media such as wood block and screenprinting

• RICHARD DE BAS INCLUSIONS FLORALES

A beautiful paper, handmade in the mill and during the making local petal, grasses and ferns are dropped into the pulp.
Specifications
Handmade
100% cotton

Internally sized
Four deckle edges
Sheet sizes 25x33, 51x66, 59x78cm
Inclusions Florales
White
Applications
Decorative paper

RUSHCOMBE VALLEY HANDMADE PAPERS

No lists were available about the handmade papers by Chris Bingham at the time of going to press but information can be obtained from JvO Papers.

SHEEPSTOR HANDMADE PAPERS

A small mill producing mostly custom made papers. Some watercolour papers, all made entirely from 100 per cent cotton linters (see p. 27). Contact the mill direct for further information .

TERVAKOSKI OSAKEYHTIÖ HANDMADE PAPERS

A wide range of consistent handmade watercolour and printmaking papers from the two vat operation mill in the large paper empire of Enso Gutzeit in Finland. A range of sizes and weights are available.This mill produces a watercolour grade sized with PVA which is somewhat unusual but further information concerning this and other specifications should be sought from the mill direct.

TWINROCKER HANDMADE PAPERS

Another well-known American papermaking couple, Howard and Kathryn Clark, who enjoy a well-earned reputation in the handpapermaking field. The professional hand mill which was established in 1971 specializes in making artist papers to custom order. It boasts quite accurately that it makes the largest possible variety of papers, each in a comparatively small amount. Both traditional and innovative methods are used in their paper manufacture and all papers are made from natural fibres with a neutral pH; surface size is with gelatine and internal size is alkyl ketene dimer. They make papers for drawing, printmaking watercolour, calligraphy, pastel, pen and ink and non-silver photography. Sizes vary from small note sheets to 34x48" plus a jumbo sheet 48x96". Papers are made in all shapes and sizes and the variety is enormous. They run a subscriber service to keep customers up to date with paper samples, monthly listings, discounts, etc.

TWO RIVERS PAPER CO. HANDMADE PAPERS

This small hand papermaking concern, Two Rivers Paper Company, now firmly established under the directorship of Jim Patterson in Watchet in Somerset has developed a new range of handmade papers. All the papers are sold by direct mail as well as through agents.

• TR WATERCOLOUR PAPER

The paper is 100% cotton watercolour paper, size Imperial with a substance of 250 and 175lb. Imperial, in white and 175lb. only in five soft tints: cream, sand, oatmeal, green and grey. One finish (Not), air dried and traditionally tub-sized with gelatine. Each sheet is watermarked TR HAND MADE in the bottom left corner. All papers are neutrally sized with a promoted AKD, slightly wet strengthened, and loaded with approx 4% Ca CO3. Chalk loading ensures a pH neutral extract but because of alum in the gelatine the paper will 'spot test' acidic. Early experiments with neutral gelatine were disastrous but they are addressing the problem again! A paper with its own beauty, softly toned but strong in use.
Specifications
Handmade
100% cotton
Air dried
Gelatine sized

NOT finish
4% calcium carbonate buffered
Watermarked TR HAND MADE
Two weights-175lb and 250lb
Imperial size
White plus five soft tints- cream, sand, oatmeal, green and grey
Suggested Applications
Watercolour
Pencil
Charcoal
Pastel
Ink

21 Watermarks used in a paper from Wookey Hole mill

WOOKEY HOLE MILL HANDMADE PAPERS

A range of watercolour, printmaking, calligraphy and stationery papers are still made at Wookey Hole although the mill is also a museum. The stationery the sheet papers are identified by their size names - *Pott, Demy, Single Medium, Royal,* etc. The pulp for these sheets is 100% cotton linters with internal starch size, a pH of 7 and use of vegetable dyes. Contact mill for current stock.

HANDMADE PAPERS OF JAPAN

For just under fifteen hundred years, Japan has been producing handmade paper in a volume and variety which far outstrips those of any other country in the world. Handmade paper is used for every conceivable purpose - for writing, printing, calligraphy, conservation papers, letter paper, envelopes, fans, dolls, clothing, decorative papers, postcards, notebooks, as a primary element in the construction of houses in the form of *shoji* which function as windows and in the opaque room dividers known as *fusuma*.

Clearly when we speak of Japanese paper we imagine a paper which is made from finest quality fibres of plants indigenous to Japan, carefully and traditionally made without machinery, without chemicals and which possesses a certain *kansei*, which roughly translated means the paper is imbued with the maker's character, his perceptions, his attitudes, his feelings, his outlook and his generations of inherited skills.

Today, this quality of papermaking in Japan is not as widespread as in former years. Competition from machinemade papers has precipitated a decline in the production of handmade paper with the machine papers having made considerable advances in simulating the qualities of the handmade sheets. As with all handmades, the higher price of these special sheets and lessening availability of the best qualities encourages a lessening of knowledge and appreciation even by the Japanese themselves. It is difficult even in Japan to find shops which sell a range of the best qualities of papers. The Japanese government has designated as an 'Important Tangible Cultural Property' certain crafts people practising the making of paper by hand, with the hope of ensuring transmission of the skills of the papermaker to future generations.

When buying Japanese paper, be aware that there are lots of varieties and many qualities. If you wish to seek out the best Japanese papers in their traditional handmade qualities ask your agent, dealer or retailer supplier about the quality they are supplying (look for guaranteed conservation quality), as in reality many Japanese papers are not always accurately described.

COMPARING EASTERN - WESTERN MANUFACTURE

There is a long tradition in the Far East of papermaking using the inner fibre of the mulberry and other local trees to produce the extremely light and translucent papers of exceptional purity and great individual character.

Nagashizuki, the traditional practice of the Japanese papermaker, differs from that of the Western or European papermaker (called by the Japanese *tamezuki*) in many respects :

• In the Far East, bast fibres are used compared to the seed (mainly cotton) fibres of European makers.

• The Japanese papermaking method relies on the addition of *neri*, a glutinous, starch-like substance, to the pulp which increases the viscosity and restrains the seeping of the water so that a very complex sequence of making can occur. European papermakers make no such addition.

• The Japanese use a flexible bamboo or reed screen held in position over a bamboo frame/mould. This flexible screen is lifted off the frame to couch the sheet. European paper makers use a rigid mould and deckle.

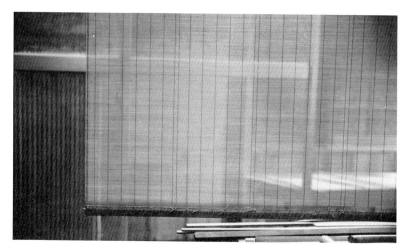

22 The *su*, the Japanese flexible mould cover

• They scoop an amount of pulp, distribute it over the screen and throw off the excess back into the vat whereas in the West, the papermaker scoops exactly the amount of pulp required for the weight and size of each sheet being made.

• The papermaker is a solo performer in Japan, compared in the West to the two- or three-man operation of a vatman, coucher and layer.

23 Paper being made with a *sugeta* in a wooden vat in Kurodani, Japan

• Moreover, due to the presence of *neri*, the Japanese sheets are couched directly from the reed screen (which is taken off the frame) on top of each other without any interleaving felt as is customary in the West.

• As in many Eastern methods, drying is a slow process of gradual and often natural draining, compared to the more drastic expulsion of water by heavy pressing as in Western manufacture. At its best and most traditional, drying takes place outdoors in Japan, with papers pasted on boards to dry in the sun rather than over heat.

GENERAL CHARACTERISTICS OF JAPANESE PAPERS

Because of the long fibres from *kozo, mitsumata,* and *gampi,* the three traditional papermaking fibres and the addition of *neri* to the pulp, Japanese papers have quite a different quality from the majority of Western papers. Although in the West it is the complicated patterned papers of Japan which are often thought typical, it is actually in the fine, plain papers, which are made in enormous variety and range, that the true heart of Japanese papermaking is revealed. These pure papers possess an inherent beauty, attributable to the care taking in their making, the result of centuries old traditions. The papers are often delicate, wafer thin, translucent, soft and absorbent. They are receptive to the black ink and the soft brush of the calligrapher and are excellent for the printing of coloured woodblocks for which they have been traditionally used. Because of their strength and purity many of the lighter weight sheets are used extensively for paper restoration.

The purest of papers have a glossiness which can harden with age and the life of a traditionally-made sheet withstands and often improves with age, its true qualities only becoming apparent centuries after it has been made. The length of the fibres and their interweaving is inherent in the making, producing papers of incredible strength no matter how thin they are.

In choosing a Japanese paper for use, its qualities need to be evaluated as with any paper and the most expensive paper will not necessarily be the best for a particular use.

As in the case of Western paper, Japanese paper should be examined against the light. This will reveal the evenness of making, the presence of fibres that may detract from its use and any extraneous matter that was not removed at the time of *chiri-tori* or sorting. If the paper looks fresh and crisp and has a slight rattle it was probably made at the best season in winter. If not and it is limp and flaccid, it may have been made during the summer months. The making of the best Japanese papers does not include bleaching except by the natural process of sunlight, so that many papers retain the natural colour of the fibre and pale buff papers are not uncommon. This expression of the natural materials from which the paper is made is much prized by connoisseurs of Japanese handmade paper.

SELECTION OF JAPANESE HANDMADE PAPERS

• AMIME

This white *kozo* fibre paper is made in Gifu Prefecture. It Incorporates a 'net curtain' pattern of holes made when a strong jet of water is forced through a screen onto a newly formed sheet. This paper is mostly used for decorative purposes and bookbinding. Delicate lace patterns also avaliable are waves (*Kanesui*), maple leaves (*Momiji*), squares (*Ohgoshi*), lines (*Sudare*), fans (*Seikainami Sho*), windows (*Koshido*), etc.

• BANSHI

From mediaeval times until recently, *banshi* represented the most popular paper in Japan. The name denotes a half-size sheet measuring approximately 25x25cms which was practical for many uses. Every province has its own type of *banshi* such as the famous, high quality *Sekishu- banshi* made by papermakers Kubota in Shimane Prefecture. *Banshi* today is normally made from *kozo* with other pulp added.

• CHIRIGAMI

A paper made from the discarded, black outer bark of the papermaking fibre. Until recently it was used for toilet paper and handkerchiefs but is now much valued for its tone and texture. Particles of this black bark are used in combination with other fibres in some papers. *Chiri Unryu Totori* is a paperr with long kozo fibres plus bark flecks.

• COCHIN-GAMI

A soft, translucent *kozo* paper used to cover lanterns and made widely in the Mino area of Gifu.

• GAMPI-SHI

A paper made from pure *gampi* fibres, sometimes known as *usuyo*. It is usually made with the wove silk screen on top of the normal bamboo screen on the *su* , thus producing an exceptionally fine and strong paper. Formally used widely for copy stencils, also suited to writing and calligraphy as it takes fine brush stokes really well, it is often used today for conservation and repair of paper. Usually formed in very thin sheets, gampi paper is often mounted onto heavier paper after printing. Some *gampi* papers are dyed to soft tones of pinkish beige; buttery cream; pale green. In some cases the fibre is dyed in the pulp, in others the colour is brushed onto the finished sheet.

• GASENSHI

A traditional Chinese-style drawing paper used widely in calligraphy and *sumi-e* brush painting. Made in the Tottori and Yamanashi Prefectures in large quantities.

24 *Kozo* fibre after stripping, hung to dry in a papermaking village

• HOSHO

This paper has traditionally been made with high-quality *kozo* fibres. The Echizen area in Fukui Prefecture has specialised in the manufacture of this paper ever since the fourteenth century. Today, other fibres are occasionally added to the *kozo* in the manufacture of this paper; true *kozo* paper is referred to as *kizuki hosho*. The best and most traditional *hosho* is prepared in the village of Otaki in Echizen in the workshop of the late Ichibei Iwano. *Hosho* is a very fine quality paper, thick, rich to touch, strong, fluffy, often creamy white and absorbent, the finest paper for woodblock printing as it does not shrink (and thereby impair registration) or tear easily.

• HOSOKAWA-SHI

A traditional name for paper manufactured in the Ogawa area of Saitama Prefecture which was very much in demand in the Edo period. *Hosokawa-shi* has been named an 'Important Tangible Cultural Property'.

• INOMACHI

A paper made from 100% *kozo* fibres with a smooth surface embedded with swirling fibres.

• IZUMO MINGEI-SHI

A designation of 'folk-art' paper has been given to this paper made by Eshiro Abe's mill at Iwasaka in Shimane Prefecture. The paper includes many different types of plain and coloured papers and is mainly used for decorative and artistic purposes.

• KANESEMIZ

Made in the Gifu Prefecture, this *kozo* paper is made with a fine stream of water played in waves along the length of a newly formed sheet of paper giving the effect of swirling fibres. Mostly used for decorative purposes and bookbinding.

• KOZO-GAMI

This is an inclusive term for all papers made of 100 per cent pure *kozo* fibres. Very many varieties exist in various weights and finishes from thick to thin, rough to smooth. It is used for a host of applications including clothing, umbrellas, *fusama, shoji,* woodblock printing and etching.

25 Black specks of outer bark being picked from the *kozo*.

• MINO-GAMI-SHI

This is the common term for all plain *kozo* papers made in the province of Mino in Gifu Prefecture. *Hon Mino-shi* is still made by Kozo Furuta at the village of Warabi in Gifu by the traditional methods.

• MITSUMATA-SHI

This is the common term for all papers manufactured entirely or mostly from *mitsumata* fibres. The paper quality is smooth and fine grained with a natural lustre and it is used mainly for stationery, visiting cards and as a decorative paper. *Mitsumata-hanshi* is a fine quality, soft-white paper made in Ehime Prefecture partcularily suitable for cursive calligraphy. Undyed *mitsumata* has a slightly pinkish hue, giving it a warm feeling. Heavier sheets are often composed of two layers laminated together.

• NISHIMOUCHI-SHI

A pure *kozo* paper, dark cream in colour, originally prepared by the *tame-zuki* method. Although the manufacture has declined in recent years, it is still made by the Kikuchi family at Yamakata in Ibaraki Prefecture. For *shoji*, woodblock printing and book production.

• OMI-TORINOKO

A fine quality *gampi* fibre thin paper, cream in colour, made in the Shiga Prefecture used for calligraphy, conservation and repair of paper. Production by the Naruka family from Shiga Prefecture has been designated an 'Important Intangible Cultural Property'. This paper is also made by Eshiro Abe.

• SEKISHU-HANSHI

This is one of the oldest of the pure *kozo* papers made in the Iwami area of Shimane prefecture. It is still made today at Isumi in Iwami and its production has been designated an 'Important Intangible Cultural Property', entrusted to Yasuichi Kubota. It is a strong, crisp, deep-coloured cream paper used for *shoji*, stationery and high-quality book production.

• SHIROISHI-GAMI

A pure *kozo* paper made by Tadao Endo in the village of Takanosu in Miyago Prefecture. Used mainly in conservation, folding-screen manufacture and for poetry cards.

26 Women sorting *kozo* fibres for papermaking

• SHOJI-GAMI

This represents the generic term for the translucent paper that is used to paste onto the wooden framework of sliding screens, doors, windows, partitions or *shoji* in a traditional Japanese house. A standard-size sheet measures approximately 51x56 cm and is cut into lengths to cover the standard apertures of the *shoji*.

• TENGUJO

A fine gossamer-type of paper made from pure *kozo* fibres which is very pliant in use. Principally made in Ino-cho in Kochi Prefecture by Sachio Hamada where its manufacture has been designated an 'Important Intangible Cultural Property'. It is used commonly for conservation and repair of works on paper and for paper collages.

• TORINOKO

This paper is traditionally made of *gampi* fibres and has a lustrous eggshell finish. This paper was in the past much prized for official documents. It is a strong, thick paper, white and smooth and is manufactured from *gampi* or *mitsumata* fibres.

• UNRYU-SHI

This paper, meaning literally 'cloud dragon paper', is made by the addition of long, swirling fibres to a basic *kozo* pulp at the time of manufacture. It is suitable for writing, decorative and cover paper. *Kawari unruyu* made in the Gifu Prefecture has dyed fibres added to the base payer of pulp; *Kinka unryu* made in the Kochi Prefecture is an exquisite, silky-soft cream paper with a curdled look which is caused by adding alum to the pulp in the vat. *Unryu* paper is also available with long *kozo* fibres plus flecks of gold and silver leaf. *Tanbata Unryu* has gold and silver flecks.

39

OTHER TYPES OF JAPANESE PAPERS

Many vegetable dyes such as barks, roots, fruit skins, leaves, flowers - are used to give dyed Japanese papers their very strong-hued colours; powdered mineral red iron oxide is also used extensively. The indigo *kon-shi* paper is a strong and durable dark blue paper.

Kata-zome is the stencil dyeing technique found on many coloured papers and sold in folk-art shops all over the world (also called *Mingei* and *Ume*). *Shibori-zome* is the Japanese tie dyeing art done using *minogami* papers because of their strength; they are often wrinkled by hand. *Itajime-zome* is the Japanese fold and dye technique in which the paper is folded into a concertina in certain patterns, wetted and the edges dipped into dyes, often one colour on top of another. The art of *sumi-nagashi* or marbling is another specialised Japanese technique, perfect for end papers, book covers and other decorative uses.

Wrinkled *momigami* papers are part of a group of papers that are treated with protective agents giving increased strength and resistance (even after being crumpled by hand many times) to wear, water and insect damage. *Danshi* is the paper that looks like a type of crepe paper; it is made by pressing a number of wet *kozo* papers on top of one another and creating deep furrows as they are pulled off the drying boards in a semi-wet state; the top sheet only is used and the rest are repasted again in the *danshi* process (also *Kakoh-shi*, and *Kysosei*).

The veneer papers, sometimes called *kiri*, *sugi* or *mokume*, are made from extremely thin slices of the core of various Japanese trees. The ends of the veneer papers are butt-jointed and bonded together on a thin base paper.

GLOSSARY OF JAPANESE TERMS

Keta hinged wooden frame, normally with handles attached, into which the *su* fits.

Nagashi-zuki the traditional method of Japanese papermaking in which the excess pulp is discharged from the mould on termination of the shake.

Neri vegetable mucilage used to retard the draining of the water, through the screen; normally derived from the *tororo-aoi* root.

Sha a fine silk gauze placed over the bamboo or reed *su* to create a 'wove' finish to the paper or to hold the watermark. Often used when making fine *gampi* paper.

Shi paper. As in *washi* which means Japanese paper.

Su the loose, flexible bamboo or reed screen covering the frame of the mould.

Sugeta the combined mould.

Tame-zuki the method of papermaking in which the scooping and draining of pulp takes place quickly without the addition of 'neri' to the stock. Similar to the Western practice of papermaking. Only occasionally used in Japan, sometimes in combination with *nagashi-zuki*.

Washi Japanese paper, as distinct from '*Yoshi*' - Western style or, more usually, machinemade papers.

SPECIALIST PAPER SHOPS

Specialist paper shops are hard to find. New York Central Fine Papers, Kate's Paperie in United States, Falkiner Fine Papers in England, Papper för kunst in Stockholm are examples of such shops run by special people with a passion for paper, who stock and sell a uniquely-assembled collection of quality papers; serious papers which are reliable, behave well in use and can be unquestionably beautiful. In Japan, Paper Nao is a shop, specialising in the unique quality, traditional Japanese handmade papers to suit all tastes and interests. Run by Naoki Sakamoto (known to customers and friends as Nao-san), his involvement with *washi*

27 The interior of Paper Nao shop in Japan

dates back more than seventeen years (the shop was opened in 1984). He stocks only Japanese papers for which he has seen the production process, although he carries some papers from Nepal, France, England and Denmark but no Chinese paper (the Chinese refuse to show the production of their finest paper - a paper that cannot be duplicated outside China - to outsiders). Having discovered in a visit to the conservation department at the Louvre, that Japanese papers marketed in Europe and USA were not properly labelled, Nao-san now personally and properly describes all the papers that he sells according to fibre content, processing, etc. and holds stocks of many of the best qualities of Japanese papers.

紙 舖 直
PAPER NAO

INDIAN AND HIMALAYAN HANDMADE PAPERMAKING

Artists all over the world now have the opportunity to use papers manufactured in India and the Himalayan kingdoms of Nepal and Bhutan for many applications. The papers are aesthetically pleasing, in subtle colours from the use of natural fibres, and all have their own strong characteristics reflecting the base material and the methods of making, drying and in some cases transporting Bhutanese sheets occasionally arrive already folded having been carried on the backs of porters many miles over the hillsides before reaching the shipping stations.

Paper has been made in the Himalayas for over twelve hundred years, traditionally to supply the Tibetan Buddhist monasteries with paper for woodblock and manuscript books. It is still made in a very simple traditional way high in the woods where the raw materials are to be found. In India the production of handmade paper very nearly became extinct during the British colonisation but was revived in the 1920s as part of Mahatma Ghandi's 'khadi' or village industry movement and there are many mills manufacturing handmade paper in India today. Well known in India is the Khadi and Village Industries Commission which has been responsible for sponsoring the handmade paper industry over the whole of India. The Sri Aurobindo Ashram Mill is another of the now famous papermills in Southern India. In Nepal, Chhema Debbi papermill attracts many travelling papermakers.

Nigel Macfarlane, in this whole section, outlines methods of Indian hand papermaking and the range of papers that his company 'Khadi Papers' imports. 'Khadi' have been importing papers from India for just over ten years. They began with the object of simply introducing some of the Indian handmade papers they had found to the Western market. Soon they were bringing back to India ideas and suggestions from artists in the West and they found themselves getting more and more involved in production. They now work closely with papermakers in India, Nepal and most recently Bhutan, and have built up a range of Asian handmade papers which for the first time is accessible as a medium for many disciplines including painters, printmakers and graphic designers.

INDIAN PAPERS

The rag papers are made from khadi, a long-fibred, handspun cotton which gives the papers exceptional strength. Unbleached khadi rags are used and the colour of the white papers is the natural colour of the raw cotton.

The 'rag and fibre' papers are given colour and texture by mixing cotton rag with organic fibres. Gunny paper is made with recycled jute sacking. Tropical crop waste is used in bagasse paper (sugar cane fibre), banana paper (banana leaf fibre) and the rice straw and rice husk papers. Other rag and fibre papers are made with tea, algae and wool fibres.

The papers are made in Maharashtra and Pondicherry, both in South India. There has not been a long tradition of papermaking here and there are European as well as Asian influences in the manufacturing process. The paper is made by pouring the pulp from a jug onto the mould which rests just below the surface in a vat of water. The papermaker spreads the pulp over the surface of the mould with his hands, forming the sheet in the water. This is an adaptation of the Nepalese floating mould method. The mould itself however is like a European wove mould and a deckle is used which gives the papers their characteristic deckle edge. The sheets are couched onto woollen felts, hung to dry and tub sized with gelatine as in traditional European papermaking.

NEPALESE AND BHUTANESE PAPERS

These papers have developed from a long tradition of Himalayan papermaking. They are bast-fibre papers, made from the inner bark of the so called 'paper tree', known as Lokta in Nepal and Deyshin in Bhutan. These are from the thymelaeceae family and are closely related to the Japanese mitsumata. The papers have a similar silky texture.

The fibre used in these papers is cut without killing the plant at ground level and then sprouts again and can be reharvested after four years. The papers are made without environmental damage to the increasingly threatened Himalayan forests.

There are now two ways of making these papers in Nepal. By the traditional Baglungi method (from Baglung in Western Nepal), the paper is formed in water by pouring the pulp onto a mould floating in water. The mould is placed on end in the sun and the sheet is peeled off when it is dry. The sheet made in this way has a cloud-like fibre formation.

The rest of the Nepalese papers are made using the Japanese Nagashizuki technique. The sheet is formed on a silk-backed 'su' mould by a dipping and layering method and brushed onto a zinc sheet for drying which gives the paper a very smooth surface.

The Bhutanese papers are both traditional papers. The Resho paper is made like the paper from Baglung by pouring the pulp onto a floating mould and has a wove surface. The Tsasho paper is formed on a dipping mould made of split bamboo and has a strong laid pattern. Both Bhutanese papers are darker and somewhat 'wilder' than the Nepalese.

APPLICATIONS

All of these papers, the South Indian, the Nepalese and Bhutanese, have been used by artists in every conceivable way, working in the widest variety of media. Therefore the applications suggested are intended as a guide only and should not limit the artists' creative use of the papers.

The khadi rag papers are internally sized and tub sized with gelatine. The surface size means that watercolours will stay on the surface well and can be moved along with the brush without penetrating the paper fibre. This resistance to absorbency is especially desirable in a watercolour paper. The sizing also gives considerable strength to the papers. This has been exploited by artists working in mixed media. Surface-sized rag papers are also recommended for etching, and the lighter weight rag papers (40-75 gsm) in particular for relief printing.

The Nepalese and Bhutanese papers are traditionally used for woodcut prints. Even the lightest weight Nepalese papers have considerable strength because of the length of the fibres and they can stand up to a good deal of handling. These papers have a natural size and can also be used for watercolour. They are especially recommended for work with ink. Recent additions to the range of rag papers are the small deckle-edged sheets, the smallest about the size of a post card, which can be used for small prints where a deckle edge is important or can be made into improvised sketch books. If there is one characteristic the South Indian and Himalayan papers have in common it is their striking physical presence, 'their object-like quality'. The papers never remain entirely in the background.

28 (Left) Paper pulp being poured into
     the mould

29 (Right) Cleaning and sorting of good
     sheets at the Sri Aurobindo Ashram Mill,
     Pondicherry

INDIAN AND HIMALAYAN PAPERS

• COTTON RAG PAPERS FROM SOUTH INDIA

A series of soft, intimate, natural papers with the details of their making seen in individual sheets. There are no watermarks in these sheets but options on personal watermarks (made with copper wire or sheeting) are often available. This paper is also available in a beautiful rich ash grey, beater dyed (a colour idea which initially came from printmakers at Wimbledon School of Art in London).

Specifications
Handmade
100% cotton rag
4 deckle edges
Rough (felt texture), Smooth (Not or Cold Pressed)
Internal size Rosin soap, tub size gelatine
6.8 - 7.2 pH
Wove paper
Sizes from 135x185mm to 69x102cm
Main sheet size 56x76cm
Weights from 135-640gsm
Natural white
Applications
Watercolour
Etching
Watercolour
Drawing
Pen and ink
Also strong enough for oil and pencil mixed media

• RAG AND FIBRE PAPERS FROM SOUTH INDIA

A fascinating series of papers with interesting inclusions giving added excitement to the sheets. The colours range from a rich browny ochre (gunny), yellowy, strawy cream, white with small black (used tea) spots, oatmealy (banana) grey, yellow (bagasse) ochre, pale (water weed) green and red/ blue 'Ingres type' hue from the wool paper.

Specifications
Handmade
Cotton rag mixed with Gunny, Straw, Husk, Tea, Wool, Algae, Bagasse, Banana. (Gunny is jute, Bagasse is sugar cane fibre, Banana is banana leaf fibre)
4 deckle edges
Rough (felt texture) and Smooth (Not or Cold Pressed)
Internal size Rosin soap
6.5 - 6.9 pH
Size 56x76cm
Weight 190gsm
Colour as found in raw material
Applications
All forms of printmaking
Book arts
Endpapers
Special projects
Decorative papers

• LIGHT WEIGHT RAG PAPERS FROM STH. INDIA

A series of delicate but characterful papers with lightness and strength. Colours are rich in natural whites and 'double Devon creams'.

Specifications
Handmade
100% cotton rag
4 deckle edges
Surface called Medium (lightly pressed)
Internal size Rosin soap, tub size gelatin
6.8 - 7.2 pH
Size 205x255mm to 46x60cm
Weight 40-75gsm
Available in natural cream and white
Applications
Relief printing
Calligraphy
Pen and ink
 Book arts

• HIMALAYAN PAPERS FROM NEPAL AND BUH TAN

This is a range of papers with special qualities of Himalayan makings. A quality different from the above papers; translucent, shades of pale, browny grey reflecting the amount of fibres per sheet. One edge of of one side is folded (roughly 1 cm.) when the sheet is wet to facilitate the handling. These fibres are hammer beaten and consequently some have fibres more visibility, others less so, some papers (notably *Baglungi*) are cloudy in the making and one (*Tsasho*) is a prominent laid sheet visible from one side.

Specifications
Handmade
Paper types include *Nagashizuki, Baglungi, Resho* and *Tsasho*
100% Thymelaecae bast fibre - Nepalese : *Loktha* (plus Hibiscus root), Bhutanese : *Deyshin*
Edges are uncut (*Nagashizuki* has one folded edge)
Surfaces- *Nagashizuki* has one side glazed, *Baglungi* is unglazed, *Resho* is unglazed wove and *Tsasho* is unglazed laid
Sized
7 - 7.2 pH
Weights from 10-45gsm
Sizes approximately 52x80cm
Range of pale browns, the natural colour of the fibres
Applications
Relief printing
Calligraphy
Pen/brush and ink
Decorative papers/Book arts

• KHADI DECORATIVE PAPERS

This is a small but expanding range of special papers from Khadi, including a beautiful black paper sheet (beater dyed) mottled with white pulp thrown into the mould. This particular sheet is made from 100% cotton internally sized with similar specifications to the other Khadi papers.

THAI PAPERS

Paper has been made in Thailand for many centuries and, in the past, it was often a family craft practised in the villages for many generations. By the 1930s, however, there were only twenty three hand mills left and today the craft only survives in the north. The north of Thailand is a largely mountainous area with Burma, China and Laos and the infamous 'Golden Triangle' known as Lanna as its neighbours. Papermaking owes its survival largely to another small industry - the paper parasol industry - and it was the use of handmade paper sized onto a wooden parasol frame that sustained the craft of papermaking in the northern villages.

Paper is made from the bark of the mulberry tree (*Thai-sa*) and the pulp is poured into the mould, and as it dries it leaves the distinctive imprint of the mesh of the mould on the back of the sheet. The paper is left to dry in the mould in the air. A noticeable feature of Thai paper is its long, narrow shape. This links back to the traditional folding manuscripts used to record Buddhist texts and medical treatises. The paper up to 60x80in. long called *Khoi* paper, is concertinaed when in use. Many paper agents and retailers throughout the world import Thai papers because they are cheap although it is wise to check their specifications if longevity is one of your requirements.

Handmade papers are still produced in many other Far Eastern countries - China, guarding the intricacies of its processes, exports some papers, as does, Taiwan and Korea. The availability of these papers depends on the retailer.

Watermarks from handmade papers :

44

PAPER THAT ISN'T PAPER

There are various sheets that look like paper that in fact are not paper at all and papyrus, *tapa, amate, huun*, rice paper, vellum and parchment all fall into this category.

PAPYRUS

Papyrus is the oldest writing material that is in existence today and the oldest of the discovered written papyrus rolls dates back nearly five thousand years. The words for paper - *paper, papier, papel* - are all derived from the Greek and the Latin words *papyros* and *papyrus.*

The papyrus is a perennial, non-woody aquatic plant growing up to a height of eighteen feet in the shallow rivers and lakes in many parts of Africa. It has a delicate tassle-like flower head. Out of the whole stem, on average only two feet, cut from the lower part, are used in papyrus sheet making.

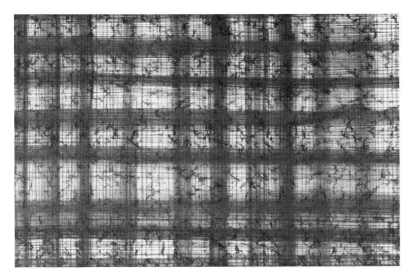

30 The character of a *papyrus* sheet showing the crossing of the strips of pith

The rind is first uncovered by means of a sharp knife and the pith is then cut in the longitudinal direction of the stalk in parallel layers of thin strips of equal thickness. These then undergo a rolling on a flat block of wood to get rid of all soluble materials. After soaking in a tank full of fresh water, the wet strips are laid out and cut to the required size. The first layer of the sheet is formed by laying strips at the top end of a felt in a horizontal line with a small overlap; the second layer is laid on top vertically at right angles to the first layer in a crosswise direction from left to the right edge of the sheet. A stack or 'post' of about fifteen sheets, individually felted, are then placed under a press and excess water squeezed out. After about two hours under the press, they are removed for an exchange of dry felts. The felts are changed (two to three times) for ten hours until the sheets are dry.

Papyrus paper sheets have better mechanical strength than many modern papers of the same weight and they can be used for any kind of writing, drawing and painting and in typewriters with great success.

TAPA

Tapa is a paper that looks like a fabric. The name is derived from the Polynesian for bark paper and is made from the mulberry, fig or breadfruit trees. After mature growth, the trees are cut down and divided into conveniently-sized pieces. The bark of the trees is softened in running water and the outer bark is scraped away to reveal the white inner bark. Using a long sharp knife, a slit is made in the inner bark and a very thin slice is sheered off. These 'slices' are laid to dry with the concave side outwards which helps them to straighten. Beating the slices (first softened with water) expands the size of this 'cloth' by about five times its origina length.

AMATE AND HUUN

Huun is also a beaten bark material made in a similar way to both *tapa* and *amate* and often polished to a fine smooth surface with a stone. It was used by the Maya peoples for writing and painting. The Aztecs of Central America, and more recently the Otomi Indians, are still making their own bark paper, amate. Thin strips are cut from the inner bark of their native trees but they boil the bark in a lye of wood ash for several hours and rinse it well before beating. The strips (which are cut in the Spring time and stored until needed) are laid out on a board and pounded until they felt together to form a sheet of the required size.

RICE PAPER

Rice paper is a misnomer. It is a paper-like material but it is made from the pith of the branches and trunk of the rice paper tree *Tetrapanax papyriferus*. It is a white, soft type of sheet made in small sizes only. The pith of the tree is pushed out after soaking in water for several days. It is dried and when required for use a small slit is made with a sharp knife and the pith is forced against the knife on a board which slices out a long strip.

It is a name often used mistakenly for a type of Japanese paper made from the mulberry tree which has been described as being made from rice stalks or rice paste - in fact it is the Chinese that actually manufacture a paper from rice stalks, also called rice paper.

VELLUM AND PARCHMENT

It is another common misnomer to call the many and various types of paper manufactured on a machine 'parchment' or 'vellum'. A more accurate description would be parchment- or vellum-like.

Vellum is a writing surface traditionally preferred by scribes for many centuries; making vellum is a slow procedure which allows little mechanisation and has changed little over the centuries. Vellum is prepared from calfskins (and sometimes goatskins) which are soaked in lime for anything up to fifteen days to clean them; the fur is scraped off by passing through a machine with blunted knife blades and then they are soaked again; the fat and flesh is then scraped off from the underside and they are returned to the soaking lime-bath again. The clean skin is stretched on a wooden frame with adjustments which pull the skin taut, and heat-drying is often employed except if the weather is fine. To prepare the writing surface, a craftsman individually shaves each skin with a semi-circular blade which removes the grain and smooths the surface. The skins are finally treated with pumice. Depending on the finishing processes and the original fur and skin colour, vellum can differ in type (coarse, fine, etc.) and tone (light to brownish mottled).

Parchment is made from the inner layer of a sheepskin in a similar manner to vellum preparation. The skin is limed and split and the scraping, soaking, stretching and degreasing procedures are carried out. Parchment is different in character from vellum in that it is naturally oilier and has a tougher, hornier surface; it is an alternative to vellum not a substitute.

WOOD VENEER

Wood veneer 'papers' could also fall into this section, being made from very fine slithers of bark, often laminated onto a paper base.

31 (Right) Mouldmade paper passing onto the drying cylinder at St Cuthberts Mill

MOULDMADE PAPERS

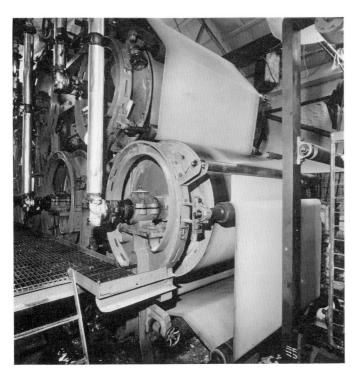

WHAT IS MOULDMADE PAPER ?

Although the basic process of papermaking has remained unchanged for two thousand years, machinery has now usurped much of the hand work formerly carried out by craftsmen. Even so, the traditions of the craftsman and his skills are still of fundamental importance when combined with modern methods of papermaking.

Two methods, Fourdrinier and cylinder-mould, are responsible today for the main types of paper produced in a continuous web and for clarity we have termed them 'machinemade' and 'mouldmade' paper respectively.

Of the machines producing paper in a continuous web, the cylinder-mould machine is the one responsible for making what is termed 'mouldmade' papers. The paper produced on these machines closely resembles handmade paper; the initial pulp preparation is similar to the handmade process right up until the the formation of the sheet where the machine then takes the place of the vatman, coucher and layer.

In the mouldmade process, a large cylinder, covered with a metal screen (either wove or laid), revolves half immersed in the pulp. By means of a partial vacuum created on the inside of the cylinder, the pulp adheres to the wire screen on the outside, consequently forming a layer of paper. As the cylinder revolves, a layer of wet fibres emerges at the top and passes through a pressing section. This consists of two cylindrical rolls which mechanically squeeze the water from the sheet. On the cylinder-mould machine, both top and bottom rolls are covered by a woollen felt or blanket. This gives a surface to the sheet which is very similar on both sides. If a rough surface is required, then special rough marking felts with a pronounced weave are used; for a Not surface, the felts are of a slightly finer texture. If an H.P. surface is required this is produced by passing the sheets through a series of metal polishing rolls, called calender rolls, at the end of the machine. The paper is finally dried by passing round a series of steam-heated cylinders.

TUB SIZING

St Cuthberts Mill in Somerset produces the Saunders Waterford series, a watercolour paper which is both internally and gelatine surface sized. The internal sizing agent is applied to the fibre prior to the sheet of paper being formed, whilst the gelatine surface sizing takes place after the sheet has been formed and partially dried. In the latter process the sheet is totally immersed in the gelatine solution and quickly becomes saturated. The saturated sheet then passes through a pair of press rolls and excess gelatine is squeezed out, after which the sheet then passes through further driers which both dry and set the gelatine. The paper is usually hand torn into sheets (making soft edges to the paper) which are then individually hand checked for quality. Representative samples of all papers are tested at all stages of production in the quality control laboratory to ensure consistency of weight, surface, degree of sizing, strength, pH and aging properties. Only after the paper has passed all these tests is it packed and ready for despatch.

MOULDMADE VERSUS HANDMADE

Many mouldmade papers have certain aspects in common with handmade papers. They are made from a similar base pulp to a very high quality by the manufacturers. The essential nature of a handmade sheet is that it is made by hand and, as such, is less consistent than any sheet made on a machine. This can be desirable or not depending on the requirements of the job. However, because the production of mouldmade paper is on a machine, many of the controls are mechanical with the result that a mouldmade sheet is very evenly made and more technically perfect and, as such, this paper is normally very reliable, and consistent. For many printing jobs, a mouldmade paper will be used because of this consistency.

One of the major differences in the manufacture of mouldmades and handmades is that the four-way shake of the vatman in the handmade operation cannot be copied by a cylinder-mould machine; this results in handmade paper having little or no grain direction giving more stability to the paper. As the wet mouldmade paper fibres travel down the web, the slight shaking action aligns the fibres in one direction and gives the resulting paper a grain direction.

32 The vat area of a cylinder-mould machine at St Cuthberts Mill, Somerset

The four deckle edges produced on a single sheet mould by the hand papermaker cannot be manufactured on the endless web of a cylinder-mould machine. In a mouldmade paper, two deckles are true (being the natural, parallel edges of the web) and two are always simulated even when the description states 'four deckles'.

It must be noted that retailers of mouldmade (and handmade) papers do not always admit to, or openly describe, the chemical constituents and treatments which their fibres have been subjected to, and to the uninitiated, they are not always apparent. Note especially the use of the term 'all rag' papers. This term indicates that the papers are made from cotton rags suitably treated, inferring also that they have been made to a neutral pH, etc. In fact 'rags' are only used today by a very small number of (normally hand-) papermakers and 'all rag' in a mouldmade paper description probably means that the paper is made from cotton fibre. Common sense and some knowledge (or experience) are needed when buying papers and buyers must be astute!

One important factor contributing to the past decline in the use of handmade papers was the size limitation of the handmade sheet. It is almost impossible to effectively or evenly form a perfect sheet exceeding 36x50in. mainly because of the difficulty in handling a mould of such a size without lifting tackle. Meirat in Spain actually make very large paper sizes, and Japanese papers too are made in large sizes, but most handmade sheets are of an average size. By contrast almost any size of paper can be made on a machine and current fashion for large sheets has encouraged many mouldmade manufacturers to produce paper in rolls.

If a comparison between a similar quality, size and weight paper from each type of manufacture is made, the handmade sheet will cost approximately double the price of the mouldmade sheet, which in turn will cost approximately double the price of the machinemade sheet.

MOULDMADE VERSUS MACHINEMADE

Machine papers in general are manufactured in quantity for industrial and commercial use and their properties and ingredients vary according to their applications. Many of the machinemade papers are not as pure as hand- or mouldmade and are many are not manufactured to withstand the ravages of time. Several machinemade paper manufacturers, however, concentrate on quality machinemades giving their papers a quality furnish and a neutral pH. It is possible to find the same basic fibres in use in both machine- and mouldmade papers (usually either cotton linters or High Alpha Cellulose

woodfree pulp in quality papers). It is the quality of the particular fibre, the proportion in which the different fibres are mixed together combined with the type of beating (a detail which few manufacturers disclose) that give the papers many of their characteristics.

A mouldmade paper is a quality paper, made and designed often in collaboration with artists, to help achieve a desired end product.

33 Reeling up mouldmade paper at St Cuthberts Mill, Somerset

The cylinder-mould machine is a slower-running machine than the faster Fourdrinier and hence the papers are more slowly made which gives them more stability and less grain direction. Mouldmade sheets are less directional than machinemade sheets. One aspect of this can be seen in their rolling up capacity - mouldmade sheets are easier to handle, easier to roll up.

Many intricate watermarks will be found in a mouldmade sheet because the watermarking practice on a circular cylinder-mould offers advantages that a Fourdrinier cannot. The surface characteristic of a mouldmade paper is made when the wet pulp passes directly onto the papermaking felt and is pushed up against the characteristics of that felt, whereas in a machine-made paper the felt does not pick up the wet pulp until it has gone through several stages of draining and drying. Mouldmade papers tend to have more bulk perhaps because of the longer time they take to dry, and are generally softer to the touch than machinemade papers. The making and drying processes of mouldmade papers are generally on a much smaller scale, with much hand testing and overlooking than is common for machinemade papers. This has the result that a mouldmade paper is generally of different quality altogether than a machinemade paper. The simulated, soft deckle edge made with a wire or tape across the cylinder-mould cannot be copied exactly by a Fourdrinier. In a machinemade paper, a soft edge is usually made with a jet of water sprayed onto the pulp at an angle during the making thus creating a thinner line of pulp where the sheets are torn.

As it takes more time to make a mouldmade sheet, hence it costs more.

MOULDMADE PAPER MILLS

The majority of the world's mouldmade papers are manufactured in Europe. The production of artists' papers on a cylinder-mould machine is limited to a few specific companies who often have a heritage in the trade.

As early as 1492, paper was recorded as being made at the town of Arches. Today the fabrication of first-class, mouldmade papers still takes place in the town of Arches for the Arjomari paper group, where production is geared to stringent control to ensure guaranteed quality. Although the Arjomari company manufactures a multitude of different types of papers with many applications, in the context of fine mouldmade papers, it is probably the largest manufacturer in the world. The papers are prepared under strict conditions which can be traced back to original methods handed down through the centuries. The *Arches* range of papers contain only cotton, linen and esparto fibres and are manufactured by a neutral process and buffered to ensure longevity. The Arjomari concern for purity and permanence has led to the inclusion of the symbol for infinity being introduced into many of their standard mouldmade ranges to denote that the quality corresponds to that required by conservationists.

Arjomari is an example of a forward looking and developing paper company and is listed on the Paris Bourse. It operates twelve mills in France, one in Spain (Guarro Casas) and one in Brazil through a joint venture. It has connections with various companies such as Canson & Montgolfier (who distribute the *Arches* watercolour range throughout the world), and Conté (who distribute the *Arches Perrigot* range). Their paper production is focused on five areas - coated papers used by printers and publishers (35 per cent production turnover), graphic art papers, including a range of fine papers for books (*Centaure, Valopaque, Yearling* and *Rives Color*), stationery papers (*Marais-Mèdaille, Vélin*), superfine papers for artists (*Arches, Johannot, Rives*) plus other synthetic and office papers (24 per cent production). Fine art and drawing papers (*Aquarelle, Arches and Canson*) accounts for 9 per cent turnover, technical and industrial applications papers accounts for 26 per cent production and fiduciary and security papers accounts for 6 per cent of production turnover. The company has invested in its own sales networks in the Netherlands, Germany, Switzerland, Australia and Japan and at the time of writing is proposing a merger with Wiggins Teape Appleton in Britain. The Arches mill always has product developments aimed at end-user satisfaction and these developments are often headed by artists, one of them being the famous painter Ingres who developed at Arches the Ingres laid drawing paper now sold worldwide. On 28 April 1990, 250 sheets of *Velin Arches* paper were flown aboard the space shuttle 'Discovery'. On them was printed an etching by artist Antonio Andivero. These prints, having been to the moon and back, were then offered to heads of state and individuals involved in the conquest of space.

Many of the mouldmade mills have a wide production range. Not only do they produce fine papers for artists, graphic art papers, printing papers or stationary ranges but also include a range of other specialist papers such as security and banknote papers.

In the sixteenth century, Charles III witnessed the installation of the Lana Papermill in the town of Docelles. The mill has passed through the hands of various owners since its inception and its fortunes have varied. Today Groupe Lana is a privately-owned, developing company with two factories employing around 400 workers. Its production includes a range of standard fine quality cylinder- mouldmade papers having that slightly unique character that differentiates them from the makings of its competitors; difficult to describe, this Lana range of papers are of a consistent standard, with firm but soft feel and especially suitable for watercolour, printmaking, bookbinding and for fine printing. Lana also produces several other categories of papers including an 11gsm paper (almost the thinnest paper in the world!) traditionally used for cigarettes but occasionally utilised in art-orientated projects.

As with many of the best quality mills, Zerkall, Renker and Söhne care about the quality of their mouldmade papers. A large production range is geared to consistency and evenness in sheet formation plus stability and quality in their range of papers. This company manufactures papers directly related to the needs of the fine art, printing and publishing communities and has developed a large range of fine papers which are neutrally sized and alkaline buffered. These papers meet the requirements described in ANSI Z 39.48-1984 (Permanence of Papers for Printed Library Materials)

34 Paper maturing at the Zerkall Mill. Photo taken from *Die Geburt des Papiers* by Armin Renker

Zerkall papers come in four separate ranges : light weight printings, board weights, Ingres papers and a new series of printing papers. Uses include offset, intaglio, screenprinting, lithography, artists' drawing and a fine range of mouldmade stationery. The papers are classified by a reference number and not a name, so it would be wise to ask your local dealer or paper agent for swatches before deciding on which paper to use. One of the largest markets at present involves supplying papers to private presses for fine book work. The Zerkall mill is well-known for producing special makings.

Two other mills in Germany produce mouldmade papers - Büttenpapierfabrik Hahnemühle and Schoellershammer. The Hahnemühle mill produces a range of mouldmade papers plus Hahnemühle Ingres, a range of textured, coloured Bugra Bütten and Hahnemühle 'Medieval Laid'. The Schoellershammer mill, situated in Duren, has manufactured paper for over two hundred years. It has reputation for fine quality in Europe and manufactures a wide range of machinemade papers for graphic design, technical drawing and printing plus a smaller range of machinemade papers for artists which includes drawing and painting papers and boards. It makes only three mouldmade papers specifically for watercolour.

St Cuthberts Mill, situated in the West of England, is renowned for its fine quality artists' papers. Since the 1700s and the days of handmade paper, St Cuthberts has built up a reputation for quality that has grown with the years. The production of artists' papers in Wells, Somerset originated at the neighbouring Wookey Hole mill which specialised in the manufacture of superior watercolour paper. This tradition continued when St Cuthberts took over Wookey Hole mill. Demand for the mill's papers increased and the production was transferred to St Cuthberts mill where artist's grades are now produced. Now part of Inveresk Ltd., St Cuthberts Mill produces the Saunders Waterford series, Bockingford Drawing and Watercolour paper and the range of Somerset Printmaking papers. The mill also offers artists the opportunity to commission their own paper. In keeping with St Cuthberts tradition of quality, all the artist's papers are archival, mouldmade and acid free. St Cuthberts artist's papers have been selected for many prestigious projects. In the spring of 1990, the Somerset paper was selected for fund raising lithographs based on watercolour paintings by HRH Prince of Wales. Each lithograph was produced on a sheet of Somerset 300gsm that carried not only the Somerset watermark but also the Prince of Wales' own crest. Today, a combination of traditional craftsmanship, modern technology and computer control has allowed St Cuthberts mouldmade artist's papers to become one of the finest ranges in world.

The Whatman paper company is the other British company with a mouldmade production, producing a small range of mouldmade papers for artists. Alan Witt, of Whatman, gives an introduction to Whatman mill mouldmade production :

The year 1990 marked the 250th anniversary of the founding of the company which is now Whatman Paper Ltd. In 1740 James Whatman commenced manufacture of handmade artists and document papers in Maidstone and within a few years had established Turkey Mill as the foremost in Britain, perhaps in the world. By introducing wove papers and discovering that the use of blue dye would neutralise the naturally yellow hue of rag papers, Whatman was able to offer, for the first time, a white paper without lines in it. In 1805, the company now run by William Balston built Springfield Mill also in Maidstone. This was the first paper mill in the world to be entirely powered by steam.

The growth of the company corresponded to the development of the English watercolour school which demanded a white paper to reflect light through the translucent colours. It was this feature which Whatman Paper Ltd bore in mind when, in 1983, after a market absence of twenty years, it reintroduced a range of Watercolour and Printmaking papers. Produced from a particularly pure cotton linter, these papers are mouldmade, internally sized with neutral agents, deckle-edged and identified by the famous Whatman watermark.

In order to retain the whiteness, external gelatine sizing is not used. This means that the papers are softer than some but they have carved themselves a niche in this international market. Now available in over fifty countries, the fairly limited range is also buffered with a little calcium carbonate (chalk) to absorb atmospheric acidity. As well as the deckle edge sheets many distributors around the world are licensed to produce Whatman Watercolour blocks, pads, boards, etc, but always from paper made in Maidstone in England. The watercolour paper is versatile and is used for other artists' techniques as well. The printmaking paper is more absorbent to eliminate set-off and is suitable for most printmaking methods.

It has often been stated, though quite erroneously, that the company producing Whatman paper had gone out of business. Nothing could be further from the truth. In the early part of this century the company started manufacturing laboratory filter paper which demanded even higher purity than the artists' and document papers. As time went on these papers developed into a range of filtration and scientific products. In the early 1970s it was recognised that the company which previously had been run

by the Whatman and Balston families needed a new impetus and it merged with its sole-selling agents to form the publicly-quoted Whatman Reeve Angel group. New products and markets were developed and in 1990 the group became Whatman plc with sales of over £50 million, 80 per cent of which is exported to most countries in the world.

However, the company has never forgotten its origins. Most of the original 1805 buildings still exist and the same pure waters, which gave the spring field its name and on which Springfield Mill was built, are still used to produce the paper.

Fabriano in Italy is another large paper manufacturing organisation renowned for its superior manufacture. It was at Fabriano that some of the first machines for commercial production were installed at the beginning of this century. Papers from Fabriano have been enthusiastically praised for centuries for their particularly high quality. Today the same is true and its mouldmade and handmade production for drawing, watercolour and printmaking papers holds a special character and beauty.

Watermarks from mouldmade papers :

Papierfabrik Schut has made papers for artists since the beginning of this century in the Netherlands. The old Van Gelder mill at Apeldoorn and the Schut papermill both now belong to the group Gelderse Papiergroep N.V. They manufacture a wide range of papers including security and loan paper, filter papers, old Dutch papers with the well-known *Pro Patria, beehive* and *Fleur de lys* watermarks, museum grades of paper plus a range of artists' papers; however they are all now machinemade papers with the cylinder-mould machine largely used for commissions, though some standard ledger and drawing papers are produced. The reason that these papers are included in this mouldmade section is that the machine making the artists' papers is unique - the web conforms to the same production speed as a cylinder-mould, the base pulp is of high quality, continuous production can be maintained because of the advantage of a continuous pulp supply, and the hybrid machine shares its drying end with the cylinder-mould machine. So this range of watercolour papers, although technically termed 'machine-made', are actually much closer to mouldmade papers.

Located in Barcelona in Spain, Papel Guarro Casas is one of the leading manufacturers of mould made papers for artists in Spain. Now part of the Arjomari paper group, it makes a wide range of coloured, Ingres, drawing and technical papers as well as a range of mouldmade papers for drawing, watercolour, printmaking and printing.

In Switzerland, the Sihl paper company has a long tradition of papermaking and today manufactures a wide range of machinemade artists' and designers' papers. It has one mouldmade paper in its range - a fine water-colour paper. Most of the art papers made at Sihl consist of the purest cotton, very carefully prepared at the company's plant. The water comes from the clear Swiss mountain streams and the company prides itself on having close contact with artists in the development of its ranges.

Cylinder-mould machines are not in widespread use in the United States. The majority of American artists' papers are machinemade.

'FEBRUARY PAPER' AND SPECIAL MAKINGS
Some time ago, Marlene Schiller wrote a story about Ken Tyler, President of Tyler Graphics in New York. He was looking for a special paper, something no one else had. He went to the Arches mill in France and asked to see

their samples. They all sat down around a table and the mill manager showed them some six hundred samples of different paper runs. Tyler insisted on a paper which has the weight of one sheet, the texture of another, the absorbency of a third, the feel of a fourth. After all these characteristics were enumerated, he added a final quality - whiteness, and he pointed to a sheet and said 'I want that white'. The mill manager had assured Tyler that he could make whatever he wanted, but at this point said that this 'white' was not possible. When Tyler asked why, the mill manager answered 'This is February paper'. This story makes several interesting points about commissioned paper. The water to make the paper comes from a local stream and in spite of an elaborate filtration system, an amount of silt remains in the water. The colour of the whiteness is affected by the silt. The month of February in the Vosges mountains is the coldest of the year and therefore the less silt than at any other time and consequently the whitest paper is made. Tyler had a making of 'February paper'.

It is possible for anyone to have a special making and the majority of the mouldmade papermills listed above offer this service. Paper agents occasionally have their own dandy rolls made up with their own watermark in order to offer their own mouldmade range from a particular mill. The requirements for a make usually start at about one tonne but it depends on how close your requirement is to one of the mill's standard ranges. As an example an Imperial size (22x30 in.) heavy paper (250gsm) one tonne makes 10,000 sheets.

MOULDMADE PAPERS

This list contains a wide range of mouldmade papers currently in manufacture or for sale at the time of going to press, listed alphabetically under the manufacturer's name. The larger manufacturers who promote and market their papers widely will be better known than the smaller organisations. You may recognise names like *Arches, Somerset* and *Fabriano* but not perhaps *Lana, Whatman* or *Zerkall*. This list, like the other paper lists in this book, does not distinguish between the papers which dominate the market and those with smaller sales. It has not been compiled as a sales comparison, merely a review of the range of mouldmade papers available to the artist.

Wherever possible the manufacturer's mill-branded names for the mouldmade papers have been used. Many agents throughout Europe and America commission special makings of various papers from the mouldmade manufacturers and call them by different names. It is wise to consult your paper agent to check his own mouldmade lines as well as these papers listed below.

The *specifications* listed here have been compiled from manufacturers' and retailers' recommendations and advice. If you require any further details or explanations, contact your local supplier or retailer in the first instance. The *applications* listed are simply suggestions and the terms (e.g. pastel, pen and ink) are general; this listing is to help those who need an indication of the range of uses of a specific paper. Every job is individual and a paper that will suit one use/user may not suit another. It is always wise to obtain a sample and to test a paper before use. Refer to *Paper in Use* section (p.83 ff) for more details about the requirements of specific media.

Note that these papers are specifically directed at 'hand' usage; the papers listed for printmaking are directed at those processes which are practised autographically. A few papers are suggested for 'Offset Printing'. This term refers to trade printing on fast running machines which are not hand fed and its requirements differ from autographic printing. It is advisable to obtain a sample and test print the paper before running it on any machine.

Note also that in the specifications where 'two deckle edges' are listed, the two other edges will usually be torn.

Moulin du Gué

Fabriano No 5, trimmed

Schoellershammer 10W

Velin Arches

SihlArt Aquarelle, trimmed

Velin de Lana

LanaGravure, trimmed

Hanhemühle Aquarelle

Hanhemühle Mediaeval Laid

Somerset White Satin

Zerkall 7625

MOULDMADE PAPERS LIST

• ATLANTIS GIANT DRAWING & WATERCOLOUR PAPER

According to Atlantis, this is the largest sheet of drawing and watercolour paper available in the world and a very popular paper in Britain, having two deckles and a Not surface.

Specifications
Mouldmade
High Alpha Cellulose wood fibre
Two deckle edges
Gelatine tub sized
Not surface
Acid free
One weight 400gsm
One size 1524x1219cm
Natural white
Applications
All types of drawing
Watercolour

ARJOMARI PAPERS

The Arjomari company today is responsible for some of the world's best known brand names in fine papers for artists, notably the Arches and Rives ranges. Papers in these series include *Rivoli, Opale de Rives, Arches Aquarelle, Arches 88, Arches Lavis Fidelis (En Tout Cas), Velin Arches, Arches Textwove, Moulin de Gué (Rives de Lin), Velin Pur Fil Johanno, Velin BFK Rives.*

• ARCHES AQUARELLE (or ARCHES PERRIGOT)

This is currently one of the most popular watercolour papers, made by Arjomari at the French mill in the town of Arches. It is gelatine sized, air dried and hand inspected as part of the mill's stringent quality control. It has a neutral pH. Many watercolourists like this wove sheet because it combines the qualities needed for non-absorption of colour, some scrubbing, scratching and erasing yet still maintains a certain softness. The Not surface is suitable for offset litho and the Hot Pressed quality is suitable for platinum printing.

Specifications
Mouldmade
100% cotton fibre
Gelatine tub sized
Air dried
Two natural deckles
Grain fin (Not), *Grain satiné* (Called also Fin or H.P.) or *Grain torchon* (Rough) surfaces
Available in 5 weights from 185-850gsm
Range of sizes 560x760 - 1016x1524mm
Available in sheets, rolls and blocks
White only
Applications
All waterbased media
Watercolour/Gouache
Pen/brush and ink
Calligraphy
Acrylics
Crayon/Pastel
Drawing
Letterpress
Printmaking / Platinum printing

• ARCHES 88

This is a major paper in the printmaking and publishing range of Arjomari papers. It is unsized (waterleaf) and therefore absorbs ink freely. It is available in white only with a H.P. surface (Satiné). *Arches 88* is also known as *Arches Silkscreen* in the USA and is recommended highly for screenprinting and, if slightly moistened, for intaglio processes.

Specifications
Mouldmade paper
100% cotton fibre
Neutral pH
Calcium carbonate buffered

Unsized (waterleaf)
Watermarked
Two natural deckle edges
H.P. surface
Standard weight 300gsm
Imperial, double Imperial and rolls
Fine, clear white only
Applications
Screenprinting
Printmaking

• ARCHES LAVIS FIDELIS (EN TOUT CAS)

This paper is 25% cotton fibre and made on a cylinder-mould machine. Also called *'En Tout Cas'* which means for general use. This is an economical paper suited to student's use. It can be used on both sides, one side being being slightly rough (Not), the other having a smooth, satin finish (H.P.). No deckles.

Specifications
Mouldmade
25% cotton, 75% Woodfree
Gelatine tub sized
Watermarked
4 trimmed edges
Two surfaces, Not and H.P.
No deckles
Sheet sizes 50x64, 54x75, 75x108cm plus rolls
White only
Applications
All drawing techniques
Watercolour

• ARCHES INGRES MBM

Deveopled by the famous painter, Ingres, at Arches , this is a white, laid paper with a toothy surface suitable for pencil, pastel and charcoal. It is cid free with an alkaline reserve.

Specifications
Mouldmade
75% cotton linter

Laid paper
Acid free
Watermarked
Gelatine tub sized
Various weights 85-130gsm
Several sheets sizes
Warm white
Applications
Drawing
Pencil
Pastel/Crayon
Charcoal

• ARCHES TEXT WOVE

A mouldmade paper with 100% rag content. Main uses are drawing, calligraphy and printmaking.

Specifications
Mouldmade
100% cotton linters
Neutral pH
Laid and wove surfaces
Two natural deckles
White and cream
Applications
Intaglio
Lithography
Screenprinting
Letterpress
Drawing
Calligraphy

• MOULIN DU GUÉ (RIVES DE LIN)

Another well-known paper from Arjomari, produced especially for intaglio and copper-plate printing. This is a paper with an open surface described by the makers as having a 'cloudy look-through appeal'. It is highly consistent to cope with intaglio and copperplate printing methods from fine drypoint to heavy solids, with an even-textured surface. It has no optical dyes so the the paper will not fade. It has long fluffy deckle

edges and a small linen content in the fibres indentified by the three flowers of flax symbol in the watermark; it also includes the infinity symbol which indicates that the paper is acid free and alkaline buffered to assure its conservation. The long watermark contains the words *Moulin du Gué*, the three flowers, 'FRANCE' plus the infinity symbol.

Specifications
Mouldmade
85% cotton, 15% linen
Acid free
Internally soft sized
Wove paper
Watermarked
Two natural deckle edges
Not surface (with wet strength)
Weight 270gsm only
Two sizes 56x76 and 50x65cm
White only
Applictaions
Intaglio techniques
Embossing
Relief printing
Letterpress
Screenprinting

• VELIN ARCHES (ARCHES COVER)

This fine quality, well-known, cylinder-mouldmade paper is one of the most widely used papers throughout the world. Made specifically for printmaking and publishing, it features a pronounced grain. Since the introduction of neutral pH sizing, this paper has been marked with the infinity symbol along with the *Velin Arches* watermark. Note the large sheets.

Specifications
Mouldmade
100% cotton fibre
Neutral pH
Buffered with calcium carbonate

Internally sized
One surface - Not
Two natural deckle edges
Two watermarks (Infinity and 'Velin Arches')
Wide range of sizes 55x65 - 120x160 cm
White (*Blanc*), cream (*Crème*) and black (*Noir*)
Applications
Printmaking
All forms of lithography including offset litho
Screenprinting
Intaglio
Embossing
Relief printing
Typography
Selected drawing techniques

• VELIN BFK RIVES

Another popular, well-known and well-used paper from the French company Arjomari. Smooth, with an absorbent surface, it is suitable for all forms of printmaking. It is soft-sized (less sizing than *Velin Arches*) with a neutral pH. Whiter than *Velin Arches*.

Specifications
Mouldmade
100% cotton
Neutral pH
Soft sized
Watermarked
Two natural deckle edges
Antique finish
Smooth and extra rough surfaces
Range of sizes from 50x65-76x112cm
Wide range of weights
Available in sheets and rolls
White, cream, grey and tan
Applications
Lithography
Intaglio
Screenprinting

Relief printing
Linocut
Collotype
Drawing

• VELIN PUR FIL JOHANNOT

Another well-known paper made by the Arjomari
Group, this French paper was originally made from
100% linen pulp hence its name 'Pur Fil' and an old
wrapping packet may specify that this is the case.
Today, it is a mouldmade paper with 75% cotton and
25% esparto mix (called alfa). It is lightly textured with
two natural and two torn edges and is excellent for
wood engraving, linocut, letterpress and typography.

Specifications
Mouldmade
75% cotton, 25% esparto
Acid free
Calcium carbonate buffered
Watermarked
Two natural deckle edges
Lightly textured surface
Weights 125 and 240gsm
Imperial and Royal sizes
White
Applications
Relief printing
Engraving
Linocut
Letterpress
Printmaking

R.K. BURT & CO. LTD.

R.K.Burt & Company is a London-based paper
company with a wide range of fine papers in their lists.
They have commissioned makings of a variety of
mouldmade papers from several European mills
including the papers listed below.

• RKB LANA PRINTMAKING

A printmaking paper made for R.K.Burt and Company
Ltd. at the Lana mill in France especially for
autographic litho, although it can be used for many
other printmaking processes. It has a smooth, very
slightly textured surface but is not as smooth as, for
instance, the RKB Arches.

Specifications
Mouldmade
100% cotton
Watermarked
Acid free
Surface sized
Two natural deckle edges
Fine textured surface
Appications
Offset litho
Printmaking

• RKB LANAQUARELLE

A watercolour paper made for R.K. Burt and Company
Ltd., at the Lana mill. This special making is slightly
whiter than the Lana mill range and represents a fine,
strong watercolour paper with a certain softness.

Specifications
Mouldmade
100% cotton
Internally and tub sized
Watermarked
Two natural deckles
Not (fin), H.P.(Satinée) and Rough (Torchon)
surfaces
Sheet size 56x76cm
Applications
Watercolour
Drawing

• RKB ARCHES

This paper was made for R.K. Burt by the Arches mill
to a special size for lithography; it has an allowance for
the gripper edge of the litho press allowing the sheet to
be torn down to a full Imperial size after printing.

Specifications
Mouldmade
100% cotton
Internal sizing
Acid free
Watermarked RKB Arches
2 deckle edges
Smooth and textured surfaces
One size - 58x78.5cm
White
Applications
Printmaking

• CURWEN MOULDMADE

This paper was initially made for the Curwen Studio by
R.K.Burt in collaboration with masterprinter Stanley
Jones. It was made at St Cuthbert's mill especially for
flat bed hand lithography. It has only one deckle to
allow the other edges to be used for registration.

Specifications
Mouldmade
100% cotton
Surface sized
2 deckle edges
Acid free
No watermark
Size 56x76cm
White
Applications
Printmaking
Lithography

ST. CUTHBERTS MILL PAPERS

One of the two mills in England with a mouldmade production, St Cuthberts papers are widely known and used around the world. They include the Bockingford, Somerset and Saunders Waterford series.

• BOCKINGFORD DRAWING & WATERCOLOUR PAPERS

A well-known British name, *Bockingford* is a renowned economical paper particularly suitable for students in watercolour and drawing. Made at St Cuthberts Mill, from high quality woodpulps which combined with the rural waters of England's West Country gives a paper free from contaminants. It has archival permanence being buffered with calcium carbonate and is a strong paper being internally sized. It is made on a cylinder-mould machine producing a stable non-directional sheet to resist cockling and distortion when heavy washes are applied and comes in natural white colour, free from optical brightening agents. *Bockingford* is colour stable, having a blue wool scale reading of 5. It has a distinctive Not textured surface imparted by the woollen blankets of the cylinder-mould machine. In use it performs well and is one of the good papers at the cheaper end of the range.

Specifications
Mouldmade
High Alpha Celulose woodfibre
Buffered with calcium carbonate
Internally engine sized
Colour stable
Acid free
Trimmed on four edges
Not surface only
Five weights from 150-535gsm
Available in Imperial, plus rolls.
White only
Applications
Watercolour

Drawing
Gouache
Charcoal
Pen and ink
Calligraphy
Airbrush
Pastel
Acrylics

• TUB SIZED BOCKINGFORD

The most important feature of this sheet is that it is mill designed for offset litho printing. This makes it ideally suited to the more commercial printing of limited editions or design work when a high quality is desired. *Tub Sized Bockingford* was produced in response to a demand from printers for a character paper that would allow the use of printing inks; hence the surface of the *Tub Sized Bockingford* is gelatine sized so as to have a high pick resistance for the use with machine litho printing.

Specifications
As above
4 weights from 190-425gsm
Available in Imperial sheets
White and cream
Applications
Offset lithography
Blind embossing
Foil blocking
Screenprinting
Autographic Lithography,
Relief printing
Letterpress
Calligraphy
Drawing/Charcoal
Gouache/Watercolour

• SAUNDERS WATERFORD

The Saunders Waterford series is the premium quality watercolour paper produced by St Cuthberts Mill. The range has succeeded in combining all the favoured features of its renowned predecessor TH Saunders with an even stronger surface. It is available in a variety of weights and sizes. It is cylinder-mouldmade giving stability and resistance to cockling. It is a strong sheet being both internally and gelatine tub sized, making the surface resistant to lift when removing masking materials, lines will not feather when pen and ink are used and it will stand multiple erasures when using pencil or charcoal. The surface is also particularly receptive to multiple watercolour washes - washes can be lifted off with water and a new wash laid quite evenly. It is unique amongst watercolour papers in carrying the Royal Watercolour Society's seal of approval. It is also suitable for many printmaking processes as well as for offset litho reproduction.

Specifications
Mouldmade
100% long cotton fibre
Internally and gelatine tub sized
Watermarked, embossed
Two natural deckle edges
Acid free
Buffered with calcium carbonate
H.P., Not and Rough surfaces
Four weights from 190-638gsm
Range of sheet sizes and rolls
White
Applications
Watercolour
Drawing
Charcoal
Pastel
Calligraphy/Pen and ink
Airbrush

Acrylics/Gouache
Printmaking
Embossing
Foil blocking
Screenprinting
Lithography
Offset Litho

• SOMERSET

Somerset is a carefully made, British paper of great character. It was developed in response to demands from printmakers worldwide for a versatile high quality paper in the mid 1970's by Inveresk Ltd with Atlantis (UK) and Crestwood (USA) Paper Companies at the St Cuthberts Mill in Somerset. It is an all-round paper, made from 100% cotton, has a neutral pH and is free from optical brightening agents resulting in a clean, consistent and stable paper which will not discolour with age and will allow good registration when printing. The durability and life of the paper are unaffected by atmospheric acidity. The paper is colour stable having a wool scale reading of 5 and will not change colour when exposed to light. It is suitable for all printmaking processes from deep embossing to extremely sensitive colour washes and is popular with many artists and print studios. It is available in Satin finish in white and Textured finish in white and soft white; whereas *Somerset Waterleaf* (unsized) white, *Somerset Cream* and *Sand* are not stock lines but can be produced for a special 1 tonne making.

Specifications
Mouldmade
100% cotton fibre
Buffered with calcium carbonate
Acid free
pH 8.5
Watermarked
Two deckle edges
Two weights - 250 and 300gsm

Two finishes - Satin and Textured
Range of sheets sizes and rolls
White and soft white
Applications
Intaglio
Lithography
Typography
Screenprinting
Relief printing
Embossing
Pastel, Gouache, etc

DALER ROWNEY PAPERS

This company, an amalgamation of The Daler Board Company and Rowney, manufactures and supplies a wide range of artists' materials and the range of papers in their catalogue is a selected choice of many of the quality mouldmade watercolour papers including *Saunders Waterford, Whatman Watercolour Paper, Bockingford* and *Bloxworth. Some* of the papers are made into pads and blocks and are also available as sheets.

• BLOXWORTH

A mouldmade paper made for Daler Rowney. Acid free with a 'rag 'content. The Rough surface has a distinctive appearance which reflects the uniform weave of the felt on which it is made.

Specifications
Mouldmade
'Rag' content
Acid free
Two surfaces, Not and Rough
One size - 775x533mm
One weight 300gsm
White
Applications
All drawing media

FABRIANO PAPERS

The Fabriano mill dates back to the year 1268. It is one of the oldest known mills in Europe and produces papers of world renown. Mouldmade production dates back to the nineteenth century and the cylinder-mould machines at Fabriano are responsible for producing a wide range of very highly regarded mouldmade drawing, watercolour and printmaking papers containing many intricate watermarks. The introduction of watermarking in Europe is credited to the Italian papermakers at Fabriano.

• FABRIANO ARTISTICO

A cylinder-mouldmade paper which is surface sized, with a watermark (100/100) running along the long sides of the sheet. Less white than No. 5, it is suitable for a variety of graphic media, especially all forms watercolour, plus the printmaking processes. *Grana Grossa, Grana Fina* and *Satinato* surfaces.

Specifications
Mouldmade
100% cotton fibre
Surface sized
Neutral pH
Watermarked
Three weights - 200, 300, 600gsm
H.P., Not and Rough surfaces
One size only 56x76cm
White only
Applications
Watercolour
Pencil
Pastel/Crayon/Chalk
Inks
Charcoal
Tempera/ Acrylics
Oils
Graphic techniques
Printmaking

• FABRIANO NO 5

A mouldmade, 50% cotton sheet watermarked 'FABRIANO 50/100 COTTON'. A cool white colour, recommended by the makers for a very wide range of uses. Acid free with two deckle edges.

Specifications
Mouldmade
50% cotton fibre
Acid free
Two deckle edges
H.P.(*Satinato*) and Not (*Fina*) and Rough (*Grossa*) surfaces
Weights -130,160,210,300,350gsm
Several sizes
White only

Applications
All drawing media
Watercolour
Tempera
Charcoal
Pencil
Crayon/Pastel
Felt tip
Printing
Offset litho

• FABRIANO MURILLO

Fabriano Murillo is a mouldmade paper with 25% cotton, 75% woodfree fibre content. It is one of the Fabriano coloured ranges with twenty one colours available. It has a characterful, heavy, rough-textured surface, suitable for printmaking practices where embossing, etching, etc. are practised.

Specifications
Mouldmade
25% cotton, 75 purified wood fibre (woodfree)
Trimmed 4 edges
Rough, heavily textured surfacee
Range of 21 colours including white, ivory, cream, etc.

Applications
Printmaking
All drawing techniques
Design work

• FABRIANO ROSASPINA

Fabriano Rosaspina is a mouldmade paper with 40% cotton and 60% woodfree fibre. It is an internally sized paper with a neutral pH. It has two deckle edges with the watermark running parallel to the longest side of the paper and is especially suited to printmaking. The two whites are quite distinct.

Specifications
Mouldmade
40% cotton fibre, 60% purified wood fibre (woodfree)
Surface sized
Neutral pH
Two deckle edges
Watermarked
Two weights - 220, 285gsm
One sheet size 70x100cm
White (*Bianco*) and ivory (*Avorio*)

Applications
Special editions
Intaglio
Hand lithography
Screenprinting
Lino and woodcuts
Pencil
Pastel /Crayon

• FABRIANO TIEPOLO

Available in white only, the smaller sheet carries the Fabriano watermark in the bottom right hand corner and the larger sheet has the watermark running parallel with the longest side.

Specifications
Mouldmade
100% cotton fibre
Internally sized

Neutral pH
2 deckle edges
Watermarked (various with sizes)
Vellum surface
Two sheet sizes
One weight 290gsm
White only

Applications
Special editions
Intaglio
Lithography
Lino and woodcuts
Screenprinting
Drawing - pencil/pastel/crayon

• FABRIANO TIZIANO

A mouldmade paper with 40% cotton and 60% woodfree content made in a variety of characterful lightfast colours, for example - *coffee, raw sienna, custard, dark moss, dust blue, fog grey, lemon, burgundy, pink,* all without deckles. Used widely by graphic designers and commercial artists, they are also suitable for drawing and printing.

Specifications
Mouldmade
40% cotton, 60% woodfree
Neutral pH
Lightfast
Not surface only
No deckles
Two sizes - 70x100 and 50x65cm
One weight 160gsm
Range of colours

Applications
Pastel
Pencil/Design work
Charcoal
Airbrush/Tempera
Printing

GUARRO CASAS PAPERS

Based in Barcelona, Guarro Casas s/a have been producing paper in Spain for nearly three hundred years. Sometimes called Papel Guarro, they have a specialised range of mouldmade artists' drawing and printmaking papers plus a large range of machinemade papers for many applications.

• GUARRO CASAS ACUARELA

This is a reasonably-priced, mouldmade paper for watercolour. It is a bright white colour and has a good absorption degree. The *Professional* range of *Acuarela* has a different surface finish on each side of the paper.

Specifications
Mouldmade
Cotton and High Alpha Cellulose wood fibre mix
Two natural deckle edges
Acid free
Internal and tub sized
Two main sheet sizes
Two main weights
Bright white
Applications
Pen and ink
All types of watercolour
Gouache
Tempera
Possible for enamel paints
Plastic and acrylic paints

• GUARRO CASAS BIBLOS

A clean-looking, white Spanish paper which feels soft to the touch; with a Not surface which is decribed as 'Rough' by the makers. It is available in smaller, lighter weight sheets plus larger heavier sheets and is suitable for printing and engraving.

Specifications
Mouldmade
Two natural deckles
Sized

Acid free
Internally sized
Not surface
Weight 160 gsm / 56x76cm
250 gsm / 76x112cm
Applications
Printmaking
Engraving

• GUARRO CASAS CREYSSE

This is an ivory white paper with a gentle, textured (satin) surface suitable for printmaking and engraving.

Specifications
Mouldmade
Acid free
Watermarked
Internal sizing
Satin(Not) surface
One weight 250gsm
Several sizes from 50x65 - 80x120cm
Ivory white
Applications
Printmaking
Printing
Engraving

• GUARRO CASAS SUPER ALFA

This is an ivory shade, creamier than Biblos with a more textured surface; another paper suitable for printmaking.

Specifications
Mouldmade
Acid free
Watermarked
Internal sizing
Textured surface
One weight 250gsm
One size 76x112cm
Ivory white

Applications
Printmaking
Printing
Engraving

HAHNEMÜHLE PAPERS

A German manufacturer specialising in the production of mouldmade papers with a fine artists' range including drawing, etching, litho and lino papers. Paper agents in different countries choose different of papers to stock and if you are interested in this range, ask to see the complete set of Hahnemühle papers.

• HAHNEMÜHLE AQUARELL

A fine quality, bright white watercolour paper (a soft cream is available in Rough) with its own special textures of Not, Rough and extra Rough surfaces. A characteristic not found in an other mouldmade paper is the extra Rough surface which has a 'coarse canvas' type texture to its surface.

Specifications
Mouldmade
High Alpha Cellulose wood fibre
Acid free
Not, Rough and Extra Rough surfaces
White and cream
Applications
Watercolour
Drawing
Crayon
Pen and ink

• HAHNEMÜHLE BOOK

A mouldmade paper in laid (white and cream) and wove (white and natural) made by this mill specifically for certificate and document paper.

Specification
Mouldmade
Alpha Cellulose pulp

Internally sized
Applications
Special Edition Book Printing

• HAHNEMÜHLE BUGRA BUTTEN

A good range of mouldmade coloured sheets available in fifteen colours, one size only and one weight.

Specifications
Mouldmade
Neutral pH
One weight 130gsm
One size 84x104cm
Fifteen colours including black
plus Antique white
Applications
Pastel
Oil pastel
Charcoal
Drawing
End papers

• HAHNEMÜHLE ETCHING

'German Etching' is a name that has been given to several mouldmade papers coming from different German mills. To avoid any confusion, we have used the mill's name preceding any other name and so call this paper *Hahnemühle Etching*. Like the paper above, it is made from high quality, woodfree pulp in a range of white and 'natural' (creamish-white) colours.

Specifications
Mouldmade
High Alpha Cellulose woodpulp
Two natural deckle edges
Acid free
Texured finish
Watermarked and unwatermarked
Variety of weights and sizes
Available in white and natural white

Applications
All forms of intaglio
Printmaking

• HAHNEMÜHLE LAID

Also called *Mediaeval Laid* and *Gutenberg Laid*, this is an 'antique' laid paper made to replicate mediaeval documents. It is a coloured, mouldmade paper with 100% High Alpha Cellulose purified woofibre content, particularily suited to printmaking processes.

Specifications
Mouldmade
High Alpha Cellulose wood pulp fibre
Neutral pH
Laid surface
Two natural deckles
Light tan colour speckled with brown
Applications
Printmaking
Bookmaking

JOHN PURCELL PAPER

John Purcell Paper, a London-based, specialist paper company offers several of his own papers for artists' use including *JPP Mouldmade*, special sizes and weights of standard papers (e.g. 120x160cm 300 gsm *Velin Arches Blanc*), *JPP Bread and Butter* (machinemade) and a JPP heavy weight, acid free blotting paper (machinemade).

• JPP MOULDMADE

A versatile, stable and reasonably priced mouldmade paper specifically made for John Purcell Paper at St. Cuthberts Mill in Somerset. A paper with a range of uses, especially for printmaking where a strong paper is needed. It has a smooth finish, two deckles and is unwatermarked.

Specifications
Mouldmade
100% cotton

Calcium carbonate buffered
Surface and internally gelatine sized
Acid free
Unwatermarked
Two natural deckle edges
One weight only - 285gsm
Two sizes - 56x76 and 76x102cm
White
Applications
All forms of printmaking
Especially for etching and 2/3 plate colour work

LANA PAPERS

In the Vosges region of France, the Lana mill representsof four centuries of continuous papermaking. Today, this mill offers a well-planned and copmprehensive range of artists' mouldmade papers primarily for printmaking, bookmaking and watercolour. The whole range of these papers is not always available in every country and the brand names change, so consult your paper dealer for samples.

• LANAQUARELLE

A natural white paper for wtaercolour available in three surfaces and three weights. It is internally and externally sized (with gelatine), buffered with calcium carbonate and available in pads,blocks, sheets and rolls. Described as 'an extremely forgiving paper, ideal for wet on wet work, dry brush techniques and allows corrections to be made easily.' Note the heavier weight is not available in the Satin finish.

Specifications
Mouldmade
100% cotton
Internally and surface sized
Watermark LANAQUARELLE
Two natural deckles
Not (Fin), H.P.(Satinée) and Rough (Torchon)

surfaces
185, 300 and 640gsm
Pads, blocks, sheets size 56x76cm, and rolls
Natural white
Applications
Watercolour
Drawing
Offset litho

• LANAGRAVURE (LANA 1590 EDITION)

A general printmaking paper in natural white and cream colour. Marked with a 'belier' watermark, this sheet has a textured surface. Buffered with calcium carbonate.

Specifications
Mouldmade
100% cotton
Watermarked 1590 and ram's head
Two natural deckle edges
Surface sized with starch
Acid free
Cold pressed (Not) surface
Weights 200, 250 and 300gsm
Sizes 51x66, 56x76cm
Natural white and cream
Applications
Printmaking
Lithography
Offset litho
Embossing

• LANAROYAL (LANA ROYAL CROWN)

Another fine quality printmaking paper, white plus creamy shade and with a slightly grainier surface. Also called *Lana Royal Crown*. Calcium carbonate buffered. Used for letterpress, litho and all single colour works - monoprints etc.,

Specifications
Mouldmade

100% cotton
Watermarked with a crown
Two deckle edges, two cut
Acid free
Surface and internally sized
Watermarked with a 'Coronne'
Not surface only (Satinée)
Sizes 51x66, 56x76cm
Weights 125, 160, 250, 300gsm
Natural white and cream
Applications
Offset litho
Printmaking
Gold leaf
Embossing
Intaglio

• LANA VERGÉ ANTIQUE

Sometimes called *Lana Superior Laid*, this is an old style paper with 'vergé' laid marks plus Croix de Lorraine watermark.

Specifications
Mouldmade
100% cotton
Acid free
Watermarked
2 deckle edges
Sheet size 51x66cm
White and cream
Applications
Printmaking
Letterpress
Bookmaking
Calligraphy

• VELIN DE LANA

A fine quality mouldmade paper with a pronounced grain particularily suitable for printmaking processes. White and cream available.

Specifications
Mouldmade
100% cotton
Acid free
Buffered with calcium carbonate
Sized with starch
2 deckle edges
Weights 160, 200, 250 and 300gsm
Sheet size 56x76cm
White and cream
Applications
Engraving
Lithography
Etching
Intaglio
Screenprinting
Gold leaf
Fine book printing

CARTIERE ENRICO MAGNANI PAPERS

Papermaking in the Magnani family dates back to the fifteenth century and today the family still fabricate handmade papers of fine quality for limited editions and writing papers, mainly as special makings. They produce a number of mouldmade papers at their mill both as stock lines for drawing and printing and as special orders. Little known in Britain, the papers are named after Italian painters, e.g. *Leonardo* - drawing and painting, and *Giotto* - lithography.

SCHOELLERSHAMMER PAPERS

Schoellershammer, well-known in Germany, manufactures a range of papers for artists, the majority of which are machinemade. They are well respected in Europe but not widely known to the artists' market in Britain. The papers are acid free and listed by number - e.g. the range 10 represents the mouldmade watercolour series. Many of the papers are embossed with Schoellershammer circular stamp. Many of the papers have a 'rag' content but the 'pure rag' paper is machinemade not mouldmade.

• SCHOELLERSHAMMER AQUARELLPAPIERE

This is a fairly light weight paper, made in one surface only. 10 represents the watercolour series, 10W - white, 10G - grey and 10A - Antique. It is available in three sizes and an evenly-textured, Not sheet. It is not surface sized and therefore care must be taken if this paper is soaked for stretching. Suitable also for airbrush techniques. No watermark.

Specifications
Mouldmade
Mixture of 'rag' and Alpha Cellulose pulp
Internally sized
2 deckles
Not surface
Three sizes 44.8x58, 51x72, 62x83cm
Weight 200gsm
White only
Applications
Watercolour
Graphic techniques
Air brushing

SCHUT PAPERS

This large paper group, Papierfabrik Schut, produces a range of fine papers in the Netherlands now generally available in England. These papers are not true mouldmade but made on a unique machine.

The well known *Van Gelder Old Dutch* grades of paper have now been superceded by a wide range of artists' papers, many in block and pad form named after various parts of Holland. A wide range of drawing, several watercolour, oil painting, calligraphic blocks of paper are available which contain a variety of rag and/ or mixed fibres of high quality. Pads and blocks can be found under the name of *Dutch Masters*.

• SCHUT DE KEMPEN

This is the top quality of the Schut range; a watercolour paper made from 100% cotton fibres. It is gelatine sized giving good painting qualities to the sheet. Available in Mat and Rough surfaces.

Specifications
Special machinemade
100% cotton
2 deckle egdes
Acid free
Gelatine sized
Not and Rough surfaces
Sheetsizes 56x76 and 62x98cm
Weights 200 and 355gsm
Natural white
Applications
Watercolour

• SCHUT TERSHELLING

An acid free, white watercolour paper made from woodfree cellulose.

Specifications
Special machinemade
High alpha cellulose wood fibre
2 deckles
Acid free
pH neutral
Gelatine sized
2 sheet sizes 56x76mm and 62x98cm
Main weights 166 and 300gsm
White
Applications
Watercolour

• SCHUT VELUWEZOOM

A mat, off-white watercolour sheet made from 50% rag, 50% woodfree cellulose, in Matt and Rough surfaces.

Specifications
Special machinemade

50% cotton, 50% woodfree
2 deckel edges
Acid free
Gelatine sized
Not and Rough surfaces
Sheet size 56x76, 62x98cm
Main weight 250gsm
Off white
Applications
Watercolour

• OLD DUTCH AQUARELPAPER

Old Dutch Aquarelpaper consists of a range of mouldmade papers for watercolour. They are available in two shades of white - *Designers* which is a clean, sharp white and a softer, *Artists* creamy white. The surface are varied - H.P., Not (called Cold Pressed) and Extra Rough - a characterful sheet which looks like it has fibre conglomerations all over the surface. The surfaces on the sheets are one-sided, the bottom surface in each case being smooth.

Specifications
Mouldmade
Acid free
H.P., Not, Extra Rough
Range of weights from 166 - 355gsm
Sheet size 56x76cm
Two shades of white
Applications
Watercolour

SIHL PAPERS

Sihl paper manufacture dates back to 1471. On the small island of Werd on the River Limmat in the middle of Zurich, an old sawing mill was converted into a paper mill which gave its origins to the present-day Sihl company. Handmade paper manufacture lasted for four hundred years until the mid nineteenth century. Today most of the papers made at Sihl are made from cotton very carefully prepared for paper production with the purest water taken from the Swiss Alps. This company is well known for having a constant dialogue with practising artists and producing papers to meet the specific needs of the end users.

• SIHLART AQUARELLE

This is the only mouldmade paper in a wide range of artists' papers from the Sihl mill. The mill has a rigorous quality control assurance system so that care is taken at every stage in the making including invidual visual checking of sheets. Sihlart Aquarelle 693 is a paper produced from 100% cotton fibres; acid free and buffered with calcium carbonate, this sheet is a natural but strong white without optical brighteners or other colour additives. It is a strong paper with high stability made in a range of weights from 190-550 gsm. The three surfaces (H.P. , Not and Rough) are gently distinct from each other and have been developed for better control of colour and to avoid bleeding. This firm sheet is both internally and surface-sized and the surface consistency is very even. The undersurface of many of the weights has a criss cross-type texture distinguishing it from the top surface. Sihl recommend first dipping the paper in water and letting it dry (on a frame) before use.

Specifications
Mouldmade
100% cotton fibre
Internally and surface sized
Buffered with calcium carbonate
Acid free - pH 7
Two deckles, two cut egdes
Surfaces of H.P., Not, Rough
Standard weights 250, 300, 550gsm
Sheet sizes 56x76cm
Natural white
Applications
Watercolour

Pastel
Gouache
Offset litho
Lithography
Screenprinting

WHATMAN PAPERS

1990 marked the 250th anniversary of Whatman papermaking which begun as a hand operation and now part of the large Whatman plc. Although production of mouldmade papers ceased in 1963, they began production of two ranges again twenty years later - a printmaking and watercolour paper both identified by the Whatman watermark.

• WHATMAN PRINTMAKING

A fine quality paper made by Whatman Mill, lightly sized to facilitate absorption of printing inks, but suitable for all techniques.

Specifications
Mouldmade
100% cotton
Acid free
Neutral pH
Engine sized
Two natural deckle edges
Watermarked
Imperial and double elephant sizes
Matt and fine surface finishes
Natural white only
Applications
Intaglio
Single and multi colour lithography
Screenprinting
Relief printing
Typographic printing
Selected graphic techniques

• WHATMAN WATERCOLOUR

This is a a strong, hard-sized, robust paper which has been achieved without the aid of gelatine sizing resulting in a very pure and quality paper capable of taking all techniques of watercolour. Due to the fact that the paper is not gelatine sized, it maintains its whiteness adding to the luminosity of colour when applied in washes.

Specifications
100% cotton
Mouldmade
Acid free
Neutral pH
Engine sized
Two natural deckles
Three weights 90lb, 140lb, 200lb
H.P., Not and Rough surfaces
Sheet size 56x76cm
Natural white only
Applications
All forms of watercolour techniques
Drawing
Tempera
Charcoal

WINSOR & NEWTON ARTISTS' PAPERS

Winsor and Newton have been selling artists papers since 1830's. Today, in its catalogue alongside its fine art and graphic materials, it lists a range of papers suitable to all tastes.

• WINSOR & NEWTON ARTISTS' WATERCOLOUR

Their new range, *The Artists' Watercolour Range*, is a series of high quality mouldmade papers, enticing in appearance, strong enough to withstand repeated sponging, scratching and rubbing plus a degree of absorbency. It is a white paper, whiter than most 100% cotton sheets; acid free and of archival quality and suitable for a wide range of water-based media including watercolours, inks, gouache and acrylics.

Specifications
Mouldmade
100% cotton rag
H.P., Not and Rough surfaces
Heavier weights in Not and Rough only
Acid free
Neutral pH
Watermarked
Internally and surface sized
Two deckle edges, two torn
H.P., Not, Rough surfaces (no H.P. in the heaviest weight)
Three weights - 190, 300, 555gsm
One sheet size 76x56cm
White
Applications
All forms of watercolour
Pen and ink

ZERKALL PAPERS

This old and established German mill dates back to the sixteenth century and produces a very large range - some of the finest quality mouldmade papers in Europe. The Zerkall mill is especially well known for its specialised printing papers which are frequently used by many private presses. The mill lists its papers by reference numbers only not by brand names and retailers give the papers names such as *Zerkall Copperplate, Zerkall Frankfurt, Zerkall Nideggen*. The furnish of the majority of papers is a percentage of cotton plus High Alpha Cellulose varying with the grades - 25% cotton on light weights, 75% cotton on heavier weights. All papers are acid free, calcium carbonate buffered, lightfast with two deckles. Zerkall also makes a special range of stationery. This mill is also well known for its special makings, again especially

popular with private presses. A good example of this is a recent publication of a limited edition book printed from the original woodblocks commissioned by Lewis Carroll for the first edition of *Alice in Wonderland*. The paper used was the standard 7625 specifications made extra smooth and in a special shade.

• ZERKALL 7624/5/6

In the smooth finish, these arguably some of the best of the European mouldmade papers for fine wood engraving. These papers are used extensively for book work having good printing, handling and folding characteristics.

Specifications
Mouldmade
25% cotton, 75% Alpha Cellulose
Acid free
Internally sized
Smooth and Rough
2 deckles
53x76cm short grain
Off white, white and cream
Applications
All forms of printing
Letterpress
Woodblock
Linocut
Calligraphy

• ZERKALL 7315/6/7/8

Two waterleaf and two sized papers manufactured specifically for intaglio techniques. The waterleaf sheets provide an economical alternative to Japanese papers when printing direct from wood blocks or lino by hand burnishing. The heavier weights are particularly good for deeply etched plates and carborundum printing.

Specifications
Mouldmade

25% cotton, 75% Alpha Cellulose
Wove
Acid free
2 deckles
Textured
7315/6 Waterleaf
7317/8 Internally sized
Weights 7315-250, 7316-150, 7317-350, 7318-450gsm
Size 76x106.5cm
White
Applications
Etching
All forms of intaglio
Embossing
Releif printing

• ZERKALL 602612/622/662

This is a unique range of heavy weight, laid papers, available in soft colours, suitable for printing especially lithography.

Specifications
Mouldmade
25% cotton, 75% High Alpha
Acid free
Internally sized
Laid
Smooth and Rough
2 deckles, 2 torn
225 gsm
48x64cm
White, pale grey, rose, blue
Applications
Printmaking
Lithography
Screenprinting

MACHINEMADE PAPERS

Machinemade papers represent the cheaper end of the paper market and are manufactured in quantity mostly for industrial and commercial uses. Their properties, processing and ingredients vary according to the use to which they are to be put. This section looks at some of the machine grades which are made for practice, for availability and for student work plus some of the better quality machinemade grades that are produced for artists and designers. For a comparison of the qualities of mouldmade and machinemade papers see p.49.

WOOD AS A PAPERMAKING FIBRE

Wood is by far the most common source of fibre for machinemade papermaking, constituting about 92 per cent worldwide and about 98 per cent in the UK and North America.

Wood fibre falls into two categories as far as papermaking is concerned :

Hardwood

This comes from deciduous trees e.g. beech, birch, eucalyptus, maple, oak. The main characteristics of hardwood pulps are short fibres, good bulk, opacity and surface smoothness.

Softwood

This comes from coniferous trees e.g. pine and spruce. The main characteristics of softwood pulps are long fibres and improved strength. Softwood

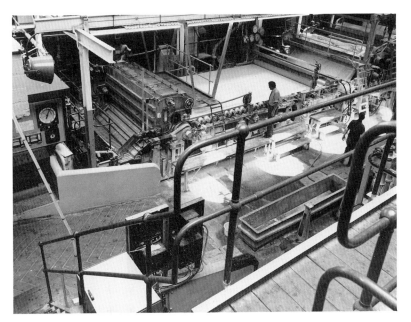

36 A Fourdrinier papermaking machine

yields less pulp than hardwood; on average 5 cubic metres of timber are required to produce one tonne of softwood pulp whereas 3.8 cubic metres of hardwood timber will yield the same amount of pulp. Even so, softwood pulp is better suited to most papers and boards and is the timber source most commonly used.

MACHINEMADE PAPER MILLS

Pulp mills, like paper mills, are usually sited near forests and they vary in size and scope. At one end of the scale are pulp mills which only debark and extract the fibre by mechanical grinding; at the other end of the scale are the integrated pulp and paper mills where the whole process is carried out on one site. Non-integrated pulp mills produce sheets of pulp which are then dried and sold in bales to outside papermills; integrated mills combine pulping with papermaking and cut out the intermediate 'dry pulp' stage.

Fibre is extracted from wood by three basic methods: mechanical, chemical and semi-chemical :

MECHANICAL PULP

Mechanical pulp is produced from coniferous woods. After felling, the trees are selected, cut into suitable lengths and put into an open-ended drum where they are debarked. As they tumble against one another they are saturated with water and the loose bark drops through slots in the sides (in some mills it is used as fuel). The debarked logs pass by conveyor belt to the grinder and any oversized logs will be cut up by power saws. The logs are guided downwards into the grinder through a hopper. At the bottom of the hopper is a large grindstone and the timber is crushed against it by the weight of the logs above. At this point the pulp can be used for low-grade paper or packaging materials. If, however, the pulp is meant for superior papers is may be cleaned or bleached to improve colour. Peroxide, sodium hydroxide and binders are used. Without any bleaching, newsprint has a brightness of about 60 on the International Standards Organisation scale. After bleaching, mechanical pulp can achieve a brightness of 70. (Standard white trade printing paper made from chemically produced pulps have an ISO of 90.) At an integrated unit, the pulp (or 'stuff' as it is known) is stored in chests before it is refined and cleaned ready for papermaking.

Depending on variations during the grinding process, longer or shorter fibres may be produced. Mechanical extraction gives a high yield of fibre (approximately 90 per cent) but as a result much of the non-fibrous matter from the tree is mixed into the pulp. This contains lignin and other impurities which produce paper of a poor colour, which yellows quickly in bright light and is not very strong.

CHEMICAL PULP OR 'WOODFREE'

Chemically treated wood pulp process starts mechanically with debarking. The tree lengths are then cut into chips approximately two cm thick along the wood grain. Rotating hammers pound these chips into fragments which are passed through screens similar to those described in the mechanical process. These chips are stored before being treated with chemicals and they are then processed by one of two methods - *sulphite* (or acid process) and *sulphate* (or alkaline process). Both are used with softwood and hardwood. In the chemically treated process, the fibres remain longer, stronger and much more free of lignin and other woody matter than is the case with mechanically pulped papers - hence the term 'woodfree' meaning 'free from mechanical wood'. This still means, however, that the paper is made from wood and has the characteristics of that fibre. In Britain, in a 'woodfree' paper, papermakers are permitted to include up to 10 per cent mechanical pulp and 1 per cent lignin.

MACHINEMADE 'PERMANENT' PAPER

Papers sold as 'acid free' are very popular with many artists. (See p.15) A move to make certain grades of machinemade papers, (mostly artists' and book papers) acid free has come about partly due to pressure put on manufacturers by librarians particularly in the USA. The principal technique by which this condition is brought about in the machinemade grades of paper is by removing all the acid from the paper. The ANSI Z39 (USA) Permanent Paper Standard lays down that permanent machinemade paper should have :

- a neutral pH (7.5. or greater)
- it should contain alkaline reserves such as calcium carbonate

- it should have a furnish of entirely chemical woodpulp or ideally 'rag' fibres
- plus several other characteristics including tear and fold resistance.

This means that many of the artists' machinemade papers manufactured today are termed 'acid free', indicating that they should last for several hundred years at least without significant deterioration under 'normal storage conditions'.

PAPER USED IN THIS BOOK

The paper that this book is printed on is an acid free, woodfree, blade coated paper called *Fineblade Smooth*, 115 gsm. It is made at the British mill Townsend Hook, in Snodland, Kent, where where the highest possible standards of technological and quality production are maintained and where care for the environment both globally and locally is of prime importance. The paper is made from virgin fibre (from well-managed forests or plantations where the rate of seedlings planted are well in excess of the number of trees harvested, and none of which comes from the rain forests), mill broke (their own waste produced at various stages in the process), china clay and calcium carbonate. The coating of the paper is predominantly calcium carbonate with the result that the surface pH is in excess of 7.5.

TYPES OF MACHINEMADE PAPERS

The range of machinemade papers is very extensive and papers from every manufacturer compete with one another. For every one sheet of cartridge that an artist uses, a commercial printer will use five hundred, the range of offset papers for commercial litho work is huge and thus forms the bulk of the market in this area.

Types of machinemade papers include :

Cartridge papers Any standard, uncoated, white paper; a term originally derived from 'drawing cartridge', better known now in the printing trade as 'offset cartridge' and used mostly for fast-running printing machines, particularly offset litho; within the weight range of 90-220gsm and normally uncoated but surface-sized. A coated version is called *blade cartridge*.

Coated papers Papers can be coated with almost anything - china clay, coloured ink, metallic coatings, fine sand, and are often polished either to a matt or high sheen surface. *Art paper* - heavily coated with a high gloss surface; *matt art paper* is made in a similar way but with a different coating that gives a matt finish; *cast coated* is either one or two sided and produced by a special drying process to achieve an extremely glossy surface.

Twin-wire Paper produced on a purpose-built machine in which separate wires place two sheets together before they dry. This results in the under-sides bonding together so that the paper has two uniform topsides resulting in a higher-grade paper mostly for the trade printing processes.

Bond Paper that has been sized to prevent penetration by writing ink.

Bristol boards A term, more commonly used in the USA, for one of the more durable types of all-purpose machinemade papers. Bristol papers often have a surface that has been very heavily sized and compressed. In their thinnest form, they are a one-ply board and as they increase in weight two-, three, four- and even five-ply are available. Bristol boards can be made from quality fibres, often from 100 per cent cotton cloth trimmings, and as the surface is highly compressed, polished and heavily sized they are multi-purpose, useful for drawing, pen and ink, calligraphy, felt tip, etc.

Visualising and drafting papers These include both transparent and translucent papers. Although these papers do not come within the scope of this book, a small amount of information may be useful. Tracing paper is basically one of two types- rag and non-rag. Non-rag (or sulphite) can be cheap or expensive and the quality can vary. Rag tracing paper is made transparent with oils or resins, the papers are less affected by moisture and do not tear or crack so easily but are not as transparent and not as durable a surface as non-rag.

Stencil papers Although again not strictly within the confines of this book, traditional stencil papers are either oiled or waxed to resist buckling when used with water-based paints. Today, plastic and clear films are made specifically for this purpose.

MACHINEMADE PAPERS

Alphabetically listed by name below is a range of machinemade papers. Most of these are cartridges but the list includes some colour ranges specifically manufactured for the artists' market. The papers in this list have specific names. Many large art manufacturing companies, such as Winsor & Newton, Daler Rowney, etc., produce their own range of cartridge papers in sheet form (and usually in pads and blocks too) and often do not give them a specific name - just 'cartridge paper' or a number ; these are not listed here.

• ALEXIS
An off-white machinemade drawing paper available in the USA from Strathmore.

• ARTEMEDIA ART & PASTEL PAPER
A new range from Winsor & Newton. A high rag content with a surface texture, in a range of thirty five colours plus white and black. All colours are light fast and the paper is acid free. It is a multi-purpose paper suitable for drawing, water-based colours, printmaking as well as mounting and framing. One sheet size and one weight but also available in pads, etc.

• ATLANTIS COLLEGE CARTRIDGE
An economical, good quality drawing paper from refined woodfree fibre and acid free, internally sized with a vellum surface.

• ATLANTIS HERITAGE WOODFREE
is a widely used, versatile, acid free paper and is used extensively by artists, fine printers and conservators. It is made from photographic-quality High Alpha Cellulose chemical pulp from which impurities such as lignin have been removed. The paper is tub sized to resist fibre-picking on machine litho printing, and which also helps to give extra fold and surface strength to the paper. Available in white and bookwhite, in four weights plus range of sheet sizes and rolls.

• BALKIS
A machinemade 'woodfree' range of twenty four coloured papers from the Lana mill. Light fast in 180 and 240gsm, size 71x100cm.

• BASIK DRAWING CARTRIDGE
Made by Guarro Casas in Spain this is a popular, reasonably priced, matt-surfaced drawing paper. It has a neutral white colour and a surface hardness. Rolls are very popular.

• CANFORD COVER PAPER
Made by Daler Rowney, this is an extensive range of fifty five matt-surfaced, coloured papers including black and white, used for display and presentation but also suitable for drawing and pastel work. Supplied as sheets and in pads, the black Canford paper is supplied in a 'Raven' pad

• C'À GRAIN
A white, machinemade paper with an accentuated grain in the Canson range. Gelatine tub sized. Suitable for all waterbased media.

• CANSON MI -TEINTES
Canson Mi-Teintes is a machinemade drawing paper, acid free with a high rag (65%) content that ensures long life without deterioration. Coloured in the pulp stage, the shades are highly light-resistant. The paper is gelatine sized and ideal for pastel, oil pastel, chalk, pencil as well as gouache, watercolour and acrylic, etc. Available in fifty one colours which includes soft tints, mid tones and rich colours plus a range of greys and white. The top side of the paper is 'vellum' which has a texture but the reverse side of the paper is flat offering opportunity for choice. Weight 160gsm.

• CANSON INGRES VIDALON
The sister range to Mi-Teintes, a lighter weight, laid drawing paper with a high rag content, acid free except for the black. Gelatine sized and available in twenty one colours that are light resistant. Again muted tones, rich colours and a range of greys. Suitable for chalk, pastel, crayons, etc.

• COLORPLAN
A range of thirty nine coloured, wove-surfaced papers manufactured by Strathmore; well known to and well used by designers and printers.

• COTMAN
This is a warm white, machinemade paper in the Winsor and Newton range; an inexpensive and versatile alternative to their more expensive mouldmades. Acid free and internally sized.

• COVENTRY RAG
A paper from America's largest art paper manufacturer ANW Crestwood (the amalgamation of two large paper companies Crestwood and Andrews Nelson and Whitehead). Machine made from 100 per cent cotton with neutral pH. Available in smooth and vellum surfaces in three weights. Large sizes available. Recommended for drawing and printmaking especially screenprinting. Also available with a smooth clay-coated surface especially recommended for drawing techniques.

• CROB'ART
A paper in the Canson range, gelatine tub sized, free from optical brighteners and suitable for pastel, conté, pen and ink, felt tip, drawing and watercolour.

• DE KEMPEN RUW
Off-white, acid free, sized watercolour paper made from textile fibres. Made by Papierfabriek Schut.

• ELEPHANT HIDE
A machinemade paper from Schoellershammer which is a smooth, sturdy, pliable and parchment-like in a range of colours. Suitable for calligraphy, design, decorative and display purposes and printing.

• FABRIANO ACCADEMIA

100 per cent pure cellulose, good, soft, white drawing paper with a fine quality matt surface. Available in two sizes and three weights and rolls.

• FABRIANO 2

A general purpose drawing paper, suitable for schools and colleges and all beginners in the graphic arts. Woodfree, watermarked and trimmed on four edges. Smooth is recommended by the makers for pencil, crayon, brush and Indian ink and the Not surface for soft pencil, charcoal, pastel and watercolour.

• FABRIANO NO 3

A deep black paper, entirely lightfast, for students and professionals. It includes some high quality cotton in its furnish. The manufacturers recommend it as ideal for pastels, tempera and white Indian inks.

• FABRIANO NO 4

A bright white, high quality, woodfree paper for drawing. Available in sheets and rolls in smooth and matt surfaces The manufacturers recommend it for the professional graphic artist, architect, draftsman. It has a high degree of sizing and is ideal for most types of application.

• FABRIANO RUSTICUS

A versatile range of soft-coloured papers and boards with a textured surface grain much used for multi - colour offset printing. Made from 100 per cent pure cellulose fibres, free from mechanical woodpulp, they are produced in a range of soft tints and are available in four different weights.

• FOLIO

A machinemade paper from ANW Crestwood. 100 per cent rag, with a neutral pH and a Not surface. Sheets available in a range of soft tones, white and black also in rolls.

• FINEBLADE CARTRIDGE

A woodfree, matt, coated paper manufactured at Townsend Hook, acid free, neutral sized and alkaline coated. Its sister paper, Fineblade Smooth, is a woodfree, demi-matt, coated paper. (See p.69)

• GALLERY 100

A paper manufactured by the Rising Paper Company in USA especially for fine printing and limited editions. Soft, flexible and absorbent but also specially developed to work on modern presses and according to the manufacturers 'never limp or picky and guaranteed not to delaminate'. 100 per cent cotton content, acid free and buffered with calcium carbonate.

• GELER CARTRIDGE

An ivory white paper made by Guarro Casas in Spain. Internal and external sizing makes this a strong paper and it is available with a satin and matt surfaces.

• GEORGIAN WATERCOLOUR PAPER

This is an acid free paper with a Not surface specially made by Daler Rowney to meet the needs of a low-cost alternative to mouldmade papers. Available in two weights and a single Imperial size.

• GUARRO CASAS INGRES

A subtle range of colours in the Ingres range from the Spanish manufacturer. A laid paper with a watermark. Eleven colours including white.

• INVERURIE CARTRIDGE

A Fourdrinier paper, trimmed on four edges. A general paper with a matt surface.

• JPP BEAD AND BUTTER EDITION

A woodfree paper, internally and surface sized, white with a wove surface made for John Purcell Paper in Britain as a low cost alternative to mouldmade paper.

• KENT EDITION

A woodfree, neutral pH, white drawing cartridge, with a matt surface.

• LANA INGRES

A machinemade range with eighteen colours watermarked along the long length. Some rag content. Three weights. One size 65x100cm.

• LENOX

A machinemade paper from ANW Crestwood. 100 per cent rag with a neutral pH, Not surface and buffered. A reasonably priced paper suitable for students for drawing and printmaking.

• MARLY

A relatively new paper in the Canson watercolour range with a gentle surface suitable for crayon, ink, pastel and drawing media. Natural white, free from optical brighteners, acid free and lightly grained.

• MONTVAL

A fine quality, all round paper especially for water-based techniques. Acid free with various weights and sizes. Rolls also available.

• MOULIN DU ROY

Another recent addition to the Canson watercolour range of papers. It is machinemade, acid free, natural white paper which doesn't yellow with age, a paper for all water-based and drawing media.

• MIRAGE

Another American paper manufactured by Rising Paper Company developed by and for artists' screenprinting. It is made from 100 per cent cotton and available in vellum and smooth surfaces in white only. Recommended for printing - screen, litho and collatype and also for drawing and technical illustration.

37 Part of the papermaking plant at Townsend Hook showing four cutters which sheet paper

• **PAROLE**

A machinemade paper with cotton and sulphite content made by the German mill, Schoellershammer. A neutral pH and H.P. surface that has been heavily sized. White only, it is recommended for all types of drawing media and 'wet' processes.

• **PAST TINT**

A range of machinemade coloured drawing papers from Papierfabrik Schut in the Netherlands. One sheet size with a textured matt surface, available in twenty two colours including black and white. Used for pastel and charcoal. Woodfree with a limited rag content.

• **RAGCOTE**

A paper manufactured in USA by ANW Crestwood from 100 per cent cotton with a neutral pH and a smooth clay-coated surface. A two-sided paper - one side mat and the other side gloss. White only and recommended for printing. New in the same range - Ragcote Vellum which has less coating and more tooth.

• **RIVOLI**

A machinemade paper with 25 per cent cotton linter, 75 per cent High Alpha Cellulose. It is calcium carbonate buffered with a pH of 8.5 for good permanence. It is a wove paper with smooth and matt surfaces, which is surface sized. It is made in three weights, two sheet sizes, two shades of white - white and book-white. Especially developed for offset litho giving good printability and ink holdout.

• **ROCKET CARTRIDGE**

A machinemade, book-white, acid free cartridge suitable for letterpress work.

• **SCHOELLERSHAMMER MACHINEMADES**

This mill produces a wide range of quality machinemade papers. Reference 4 designates papers for Graphics and 9 designates fine art papers. 4G is a calendered popular paper, and 9R a general purpose paper with line and wash capabilities. 9HG is a watercolour paper in 300gsm with pure 'rag' content. Schoellershammer produce a bristol board called Laminated Drawing Board in which the sheet sizes do actually double, treble and quadruple, etc. so that from a basic 250 gsm 1 ply board good heavy weights can be obtained.

• **SCHUT INGRES**

A Dutch machinemade range of laid Ingres papers with white and black and a range of nine colours including many subtle buffs and greys. One size only - 51 x 66cm.

• **SIHLART ALBUS**

A soft-white paper made from selected cellulose without optical brighteners; manufactured for drawing and painting by Sihl Paper Company in Zurich. Fine grained on one side to enable optimum results in universal use - pencil, pastel, inks, tempera, watercolour, gouache, etc.

• **SIHLART AQUA**

A machinemade watercolour paper made from cotton and high quality cellulose, buffered with calcium carbonate, acid free and natural white. Specially suitable for all wet techniques plus drawing, charcoal, pastel etc.

• **SIHLART OPUS**

A paper especially popular in the United States, Opus is made from pure cotton, acid free, a good bright white because of material cleaning before production and free from optical brighteners; resistant to ageing and good lightfastness. This paper was developed for multi-colour offset printing and screenprinting in limited editions and so has good dimensional stability and press performance and is used widely for all types of printing plus drawing and painting.

• **SNOWDON CARTRIDGE**

A wood free neutral pH white drawing cartridge available in a large size - 100x140cm.

• **STONEHENGE**

An American paper manufactured by the Rising Paper Company. 100 per cent cotton content, neutral pH and buffered with calcium carbonate. It is a soft, flexible and absorbent paper resembling a mouldmade paper and is available with a Not surface and two deckle edges. Available in sheets and rolls in a range of muted colours including white. Recommended for printmaking, especially intaglio, and also drawing.

• **STRATHMORE**

A range of high quality machinemade papers for artists for watercolour and drawing use, manufactured especially with the student market in mind. *Aquarius II* and *Strathmore Excalibur* especially formulated to lie flat when wet; *Strathmore Charcoal* is manufactured especially for pastel and charcoal work with a laid textured surface and two soft edges in a range of colours.

• **SURREY DRAWING CARTRIDGE**

100 per cent cellulose 'woodfree' fibres, surface sized and trimmed on four edges. A matt. off-white cartridge suitable for most applications.

• **TERSCHELLING**

Acid free white watercolour paper made by Papierfabriek Schut from top quality woodfree cellulose.

• **TUMBA INGRES**

A fine, laid machinemade paper with 50 per cent cotton linter content. Fifteen colours available.

• **TUMBA TRE KRONOR**

A machinemade woodfree laid paper with wide range of nineteen colours.

• VELOUR PASTEL PAPERS

A range of soft, velvety-surfaced machinemade
coloured papers from Swedish manufacturers Tumba.
They provide an excellent surface tooth and are
recommended for pastels.

• WACHEREN

Acid free, white watercolour paper; 100 per cent rag
with good washability from Papierfabriek Schut.

• WROXFORD WATERCOLOUR PAPER

Developed for Goldline (Frisk) in Britain for artists
who require a watercolour paper at reasonable cost.
Acid free 50 per cent rag paper with a Not surface
available in two weights 185 and 300gsm.

PAPER IN PRACTICE

Before the paper reaches the user, it has travelled through many stages - making, drying, packing, shipping, unloading, transporting, distribution, unpacking into retail outlets, selling, wrapping, transporting and unpacking again before it is ready for use. By this time the paper has already had quite a long life. At each point in its 'production' life it has been treated with care to enable the user to buy it in perfect condition. This whole section deals with paper after it has left the mill, offering guidelines and advice about many areas of usage.

HANDLING PAPER

When a sheet of paper reaches its user, it can easily be marked, damaged or harmed quite unintentionally. Robert Lepeltier in his *Restorer's Handbook of Drawings and Prints* remains convinced that the principal enemy of a piece of work on paper is man himself, whether intentionally through vandalism, theft, act of war or indirectly or accidentally by tearing, burning, staining (especially by tea and coffee), folding or knocking. Any type of paper can be bruised, creased, wrinkled, stained or soiled almost too easily and much of this damage is caused by handling, for example, greasy finger marks, creasing or small tears.

Paper bought in single sheets from a local art shop can suffer the most damage, often caused by poor rolling of the sheet after sales. It is worth working out how to buy paper efficiently not only in terms of cost but also

38 Storing Japanese handmade papers

in terms of damage. Handmade and mouldmade papers can be bought in quires or reams and are delivered flat, packed in strong-quality waterproof packing papers.

The following information will help to prevent some damage :

• Limit the handling of paper to a minimum.
• Paper should be touched only with clean hands (or with paper fingers, rubber finger covers or white cotton gloves).
• Paper should always be held using both hands so that it flows in an even, unbroken curve. It should be held carefully between the thumb and fingers at opposite edges or corners in a way that will not cause the paper to buckle. Faulty handling causes a kink in the paper and the creases produced are often irreparable.
• Paper in poor condition should be carried with or on a support, such as a piece of cardboard.
• All works should be stored flat if possible (see below).
• Loose works on paper should never be rolled up for long-term storage. A large-diameter tube should be used if works are to be carried or sent in the post and the contents should be unpacked as soon as possible and allowed to straighten.
• Works on paper should ideally only come in contact with a quality rag mounting board (with neutral pH) or other good quality paper. Low-quality cardboard or chipboard folders, mounts or frames, for example, will stain the paper it has contact with within a short period of time and help make the paper brittle.

TEARING PAPER

It is often best to preserve the natural deckle edge of a sheet of paper whenever possible as it gives an indication of the type and helps identify the paper used; however, trimming paper to a certain size or shape different to the bought size is sometimes unavoidable. Most paper can be torn using a heavy metal straight-edge or a tearing bar. It is advisable to work on a clean, sturdy, flat table and lay the paper face down while tearing because the ruler leaves a visible straight line along the torn edge. Pull the paper to be torn off in an upwards direction and towards the centre of the sheet

while tearing. This method of tearing allows a soft-edge imitation of a deckle to be produced. For convenience, if much tearing is done the table itself can be marked for efficient measurement of a given paper size and guidelines semi-permanently attached.

Another way of trimming paper to retain a deckle-like or soft edge is to make a fold in the paper where the tear is required and burnish the fold lightly with a piece of ivory or other smooth, clean tool. A long knife is inserted into the fold and the blade drawn slowly against the fold making sure that it remains parallel to the paper surface.

If a deckle-like edge is desired on a quantity of machine-cut paper, this can be done working with the paper in quantity. The paper stack should be clamped to or held firmly on a clean table overlapping the edge of the table by about 1cm; a wood rasp drawn along the overlapping edge will consistently roughen or soften these cut edges. It is advisable to practise this technique before attempting a large number of irreplaceable works.

Feathering - drawing the blade of very sharp knife (or razor) over the back edge of a sheet of paper and scraping away part of the paper surface at an angle - will also feign a soft edge.

JAPANESE PAPERS

Japanese papers present a particular problem in trimming. Because they have very long fibres, it is difficult to trim them by means of the tearing techniques above. The paper must first be folded, and the fold burnished with a piece of ivory or a burnisher. Open the paper, turn and refold it, and burnish it again. The fold is then placed along the edge of a table top, overlapping the table by a fraction of an inch. A moist elephant-ear sponge (or a wet cotton bud!) is gently run along the edge of the folded paper. Open the sheet again and separate it along the damp scored line. This technique creates a natural-looking edge with fibres of varying lengths extending from the paper border.

TRIMMING PAPERS

Cutting a straight line with a sharp knife and metal straight edge must always be done on a cutting board at least 2 cm thick. Again, the table being used to cut on should always be sturdy and clean and the knife movement away from the body. When all four edges need trimming, it is most efficient to make a template, preferably of metal, to the desired format. Note that when using a guillotine, it is usual to place protective sheets top and bottom of the stack to be trimmed.

GLUEING PAPERS

Any material which adheres to a support will cause the area of contact to respond differently to moisture changes. This means that two materials stuck together will respond differently, creating different pressures. Artists using collage with acidic materials on an acid free base paper will know that their work will inevitably suffer and the use of adhesive tapes offers an extreme example of staining. Most glues in use today are quickly manufactured for a fast application and instant results. If you require an acid free glue then there are specialist conservation manufacturers whose products are guaranteed acid free. They can normally be found in art shops that are aware of what is in the products they stock. An ideal adhesive should retain bonding or holding properties sufficient for their use and remain acid free and also remain soluble (water-soluble adhesives are most preferred). The traditional wheat- or rice-starch paste, used by many conservationists, is strong, smooth and white, retains is stickiness even when diluted and is safe for any purpose which involves papers.

STARCH PASTE

Wheat- or rice-starch pastes represent the best way to adhere anything onto a sheet of fine paper, whether it is collage or simple mounting by hinges. There are many starch recipes and the following is a common one :

• Measure by volume one part starch to four and a half parts water.
• Mix the starch with about a third of the water in the top of a double boiler.

• Simmer the remaining water and add it to the starch mix.
• Continue stirring to avoid over cooking until the paste thickens and becomes translucent, at which time it is ready for use. This takes about fifteen to twenty minutes. Try to obtain pure startch.
• When using the paste, use blotters and weights if necessary, to allow the glued part to dry.

STRETCHING PAPERS

The main objective in stretching paper onto a board is to help keep the surface even, to prevent any buckling that may occur when applying various watercolour washes and to arrive, at the end of the work, with a painting that remains flat when dry. Heavy papers (200 lbs and over) do not necessarily need to be stretched; most thin to medium weight papers may need it. However, it is not always the weight of the paper that is the criteria for stretching. If the work does not cover more than 50 per cent of the paper area or if you are working in the wet-into-wet technique, stretching may not be necessary at all.

A suitable size, thick (3 or 5 gauge plywood or marine ply), smooth board should be used, approximately 2 in. larger than your piece of paper. Brown gummed tape is best because it will become taut when dry. Self-adhesive tape should not be used because it does not adhere to wet paper. The paper to be stretched is dampened by running under the cold water until it is wet on both sides. If you are stretching very heavy paper, then a ten minute soak in a bath of cold water is recommended. The paper should be blotted lightly with a soft, dry, absorbent tissue or sponge but not over-dried before laying it on the board. Wipe a dry edge all around the sheet and, having presoaked the gummed tape with water, lay it around all four edges of the paper ensuring that at least half an inch of gummed tape overlaps the edge of the paper. Run the palm of your hand over the sheet to dispel any air pockets and leave the board to dry in the air before beginning work. It is possible to use a hairdryer after approximately ten minutes to accelerate the drying process.

STORING PAPERS

A work begins to age almost before it is finished and the environment into which it is placed will accelerate or modify the aging process. The ideal environment for a sheet of paper is air-conditioned and non-urban. Paper likes a temperature of 60-65°F and a relative humidity (water vapour in the air expressed as a percentage) of above 30 per cent but below 70 per cent. Conditions that are too dry and too hot will encourage the paper to become brittle; if conditions are too damp, mould (which feeds on sizing and fibres and can make a feast out of a thumbprint) will have a marvellous time. In warm and damp conditions, all chemical action tends to accelerate, including the ravages of acidity.

Paper, being composed of natural fibres, absorbs and gives off moisture according to its environment and in our changeable climate this means that one tonne of paper can contain anywhere between 9/25 gallons of water. It is this fact which provides the major difficulty in storing paper because when lying in a stack, the paper will give off or reabsorb moisture much more quickly from the exposed sides and top than from the centre of the pile. When the fibres absorb moisture they can swell up to three times their original size and this affects the dimensions (and also the cross grain) and the thickness of the paper. When a paper absorbs moisture in this way, the increased size of the edges compared to the unchanged middle appears as a wavy edge. When the opposite occurs and the paper gives off moisture, the edges of the stack contract and cause 'tight edges'.

Printmakers are often faced with these problems and paper badly stored can effect the registration of colours dramatically. One way to combat this is to handle or hang the paper before using it, so that it achieves the temperature of the studio in which it is being used. Other ways include not unwrapping the paper at all until you need it and only then at the last possible moment. If paper is to be printed on more than once, cover the stacks of prints with waterproof covers between printings.

FLAT SHEET STORAGE

It is obvious that an individual artist is not going to equip himself with a sling psychrometer or take controlled easurements like a museum, but he or she will need to adopt common sense precautions when storing paper ready for and after use.

Paper is best stored flat. Wooden plan chests, solander boxes or other flat storage chests are most convenient. Acid free boards should be placed top and bottom of any plan chest drawer to avoid migration of acids. Metal plan chests can condense moisture inside the chest causing high humidity. Metal is also prone to rust. Wood gives better protection against fire because the heat is transmitted much more slowly through it. Wooden plan chests also assist in stabilising relative humidity.

A solander box is an ideal way to store finished works since, when closed, the box seals out the dust and moisture and allows the work to remain flat; when opened, it lies flat allowing the removal of work with complete freedom.

It is advisable to interleave each piece of work with white acid-free tissue to prevent any offset or discoloration from work stacked together. All paper surfaces are vulnerable to friction and stacking work allows this to occur. It is also advisable not to stack hundreds of finished works on top of one another as the weight of the stack may also force offsetting of some sort. Store unused paper in wrapped packs of 25 (quire) to a maximum of 50 sheets. (See also p.96)

BULK PAPER STORAGE

Storing quires or reams of unused paper or finished work for any length of time (months or even years) presents a more difficult problem. It is best not to store more than 25 sheets in one wrapper, interleaved (if worked on) and wrapped top and bottom with acid free clean papers, preferably with a large oversize board on the outside to prevent damage from constant shifting or relocating. Kraft paper is the normal brown wrapping paper used in such circumstances. It is made from kraft sulphate pulp which contains long strong fibres; cheap kraft papers are likely to contain a high proportion of recycled waste; some varieties are waterproofed on one side to prevent moisture from entering the pack. Atlantis Paper Co. in the UK supply a blue archival 'Kraft' wrapping (See *Papers For Printmaking*, p. 89 ff) which is acid and lignin free and with good strength and fold resistance, perfect for storing works which need wrapping up.

MOUNTING PAPER

Poor mounting (and framing) is one of the major causes of damage to paper. In the past, and even today in many cases, little regard has been paid to the qualities and properties of the materials and methods used for mounting.

Museums traditionally store all works on paper in window mounts made of special archival quality board called Conservation or Museum board. This makes them easier to handle and offers opportunity for less damage to the work. If the mount is made of inferior board (most cardboard comprises two sheets of reasonable paper making a sandwich of often inferior and dangerous woodpulp filling) then this board will infect all the paper it touches because acids migrate from one paper to another, especially when in prolonged close contact. The results of this can be seen when a work on paper that has been permanently framed is removed and found to have discoloured badly. This can be due to contact with the backing board where either an inferior cardboard, hardboard or wooden backing has absorbed atmospheric pollution or has impurities present in it.

Just as the mount must be of good quality for long-term health so all other materials close to the paper need vetting. The sheet should be attached to the mount by hinges on the top edge, never by glueing down on one or all sides. Paper needs to breathe and expand and contract according to the prevailing atmospheric conditions even when mounted.

The traditional way of fixing paper to a mount is by hinges made from long-fibred (and thus strong) Japanese paper plus a glue of rice or wheat starch freshly cooked in a double boiler (see above). Other methods are best avoided. Proprietary tapes should not be placed in direct contact with a work on paper. For example, pressure sensitive tapes, masking tapes and transparent tapes can stain and are difficult to remove, gummed cloth tape is thick and could make an indent in the paper, gummed paper tapes, either brown or clear 'glassine' stamp hinge tape, should not be used because they are acidic, spray adhesives and all synthetic and rubber glues should be avoided at all costs. Most modern glues and adhesives are secondary products produced for speed of execution. Even if it is stated that these products are acid free, in some cases their eventual altered solubilities may make removal difficult.

FRAMING

There are many other do's and don'ts when using a frame to exhibit a work on paper. Additional points to bear in mind include :

• Do not hang the frame on a damp (or outside) wall of a house without attaching corks to the back of the frame to keep it off the wall, thus allowing air movement.

• Avoid positions over radiators, fires or warm air ducts. This is not only because of extremes of temperature but also because upward currents of air can carry dust and dirt and bring these abrasive substances into contact with the surface of your work.

• Spotlights generate heat; when the spotlight is on the picture heats up, shrinks and dries, then when it is switched off the paper cools, absorbs moisture and expands.

• Dust and pollution in the atmosphere (from car exhausts, industrial areas, domestic heating appliances) make the inexpensive sandwich frames in which layers of glass and board are clipped together without a protective edging particularly bad. Linen or paper tapes with animal glue adhesives, or Japanese or European papers and a starch paste should be used to seal the frame (not cellotape, masking or brown paper tapes, etc.).

• Direct contact between the glazing (glass or Perspex) surface and the work is not a good idea either because glass traps condensation against the surface of the picture and an air space between image and the glass is necessary. A spacer is a useful introduction in such cases.

• Non-reflective glass should be avoided if possible because moisture condenses on it easily and mould soon grows on the surface of the work.

• To combat the possibility of migration of acids from the outside air or from a backing board, it is useful to insert a protective sheet either of a specially produced film such as 'Mellinex' or 'Mylar', or a Conservation or Museum board to block any migration. The best protection is to ensure that the glass and backboard are well sealed from incoming air.

Not all framers know about or care about these matters and it is the responsibility of the owner of the work to inform themselves about the care needed. A choice can then be made as to what precautions to take.

DAMAGE TO WORKS ON PAPER

Watercolours, calligraphy, prints and drawings are vulnerable because they can be harmed in many ways. The points below sum up briefly the chief causes of damage to papers :

• Inherent faults in a sheet of paper may occur at the time of making - insects caught in the pulp, hairs, copper or iron particles, drips from the papermaker's hands - can all start a chain of reactions.
• The introduction of various chemicals into the papermaking process, chemical bleaching and even the use of low-quality fibres can cause the paper to be of poor quality from the beginning.
• Pollution is a problem that affects all types of work on paper. Sulphur dioxide, nitrogen oxide and nitrogen dioxide are a particular threat because these gases mix with moisture in the air and are converted to acids that are particularly harmful to exposed surfaces.
• Dust allowed to settle on a work for a prolonged period does not only produces dirty marks but may also abrade or stain the paper.
• Strong light, especially sunlight, has a number of serious effects on works on paper. Few colours are completely immune to strong sunlight and their effect is irreversible. Ultraviolet light (for example in fluorescent lighting) is most dangerous and not only causes colours to fade but also some papers to darken,yellow or lighten and if possible a filter should be used. Besides the damage that the heat of spotlight might cause (see above in Framing, p.79), all tungsten lights cause some fading.
• It is rare that insects such as woodlice, woodworm, silver fish or even cockroaches (which all live on the cellulose of the paper or the glues, sizes and wood used in the framing) are found damaging current work but this sort of damage is possible. All infected pictures should be isolated in dry conditions and a paper conservator should be consulted.

CLEANING PAPERS

If you think that the paper you are using is going to be dirtied by a certain type of handling or usage - for instance, from a gripper edge on a litho bed, a lot of handling whilst racking in printmaking or stretching a paper with brown tape - allow an extra wide margin of paper in your preparations and tear or trim it down to the final size required after use.

• Accidental, light marks on paper can be removed with various kinds of brushes or erasers. It is wise to test an eraser on a sample of paper before attempting to remove dust or dirt.
• A blower brush can remove unattached dust or dirt. A soft sable brush can be used to remove loosely attached particles of dust or dirt. An air spray gun might be used on the back of paper where actually touching the surface may injure it.
• Picking fly specks or small deposits of ink off a paper surface is a delicate task. It can be done by lifting or picking up with a surgical needle or the point of a sharp blade, taking care not to disturb the surface of the paper.
• It is possible to remove light marks with an eraser. However, on very porous paper, erasers can be particularly harmful. Whichever eraser you choose, it should be soft, smooth and free from grit. Anne Clapp in her *Curatorial Care of Works of Art on Paper* states that research has shown that vinyl erasers rather than natural rubber erasers are preferable because the residual traces of natural rubbers left on the paper are more resistant to removal that those of vinyl rubbers. For heavily dirty paper, she suggests a method of crumbling the eraser and advocates massaging the crumbs with a circular motion of flat finger to remove the dirt. Kneadable rubbers contain mineral oil that makes the remains very difficult to remove. However, this type of rubber is useful because it has a picking and sucking action.

CARE OF WORKS ON PAPER

Guidelines have been given in many of the sections above on how to look after your own paper in your own working or living environment. When a work on paper is sold it then becomes the responsibility of the new owner to look after it.

Many of the works of professional artists are bought by museums and collections. The vast proliferation of works on paper collected by museums in the twentieth century has meant that curators and advisers have had to search for methods of preserving works rather more urgently than in the past and the unique properties of paper have led to the introduction of paper specialists in the conservation and restoration fields. A distinction can be made between the 'archival' conservator and the conservator of 'works of art on paper' and they approach their work from differing points of view: The archivist is concerned with strength, legibility and permanence; the conservator of art work is concerned not only with the paper surface but with the effect of the integration of the image and paper that has created the visual effect, a quality that must not be lost if the paper support or even the paint or ink has become damaged.

Working in conjunction with the curators and conservators of museums are the restorers. The art of restoring works on paper is a delicate task requiring considerable professional skill and knowledge. In the first instance of any deleterious effect of a work on paper that you own, it is worth seeking the judgment and advice of a paper restorer or conservator.

To ensure the preservation of prints, drawings and watercolours or indeed any work on paper, it is worth aiming for some if not all of the following conditions to be fulfilled :

• Check your stored work regularly to see that it is not deteriorating.
• Storage areas must be well-ventilated so that air can circulate freely.
• It is useful to make folders and mounts of a standard size out of Museum or Conservation board of 'archival' quality.
• All pictures should be stored carefully taking into account the type of damage that could occur.
• The best possible environment for storage and display is a well-ventilated room with a relative humidity around 60 per cent and a constant temperature at around 60°F (15°C).

MENDING DAMAGED PAPER

Each art work is made up of a number of unique material components constructed in a specific way. With its creation, the work is subjected to various stresses all outlined above - environmental factors, aging, handling, etc. Damage almost always occurs accidentally, often slowly when the owner of the work has no idea what is happening except in the case of emergency such as fire or flood. It is always wise to seek the professional advice of a specialist who will have knowledge and experience of damage to papers. A major museum or quality picture framer could be the starting point for advice if you do not know where to look for a specialist.

For those wishing to undertake small repair jobs themselves, the following points might be useful :

• Hasty removal of old mounts is likely to increase tearing or abrasion of the work. If they are well and truly stuck, consult a professional.
• Distortions in paper can be relaxed by spraying or washing with water. Soaking in a bath of water can also disperse concentrated discolouration. Use uncontaminated water if you are going to attempt this. Please note that this method can be disastrous if used without knowledge.
• To reduce grime deposits on borders dust with a soft brush or rub a little with a soft eraser. Care must be taken not to damage the surface fibres.
• In order to reduce foxing or stains the paper may need bleaching. Bleaching exposes the already damaged area to more chemical stress and is not recommended except in extreme cases.
• Creases can be removed by dampening the work lightly and drying the creased area under pressure.
• Small rips and tears can be mended. A starch, rice or wheat flour mixed with water to form a paste (see above) is applied to a small strip of thin Japanese *kozo* paper which is pressed onto the back of the torn area. If the edges of the mending paper are torn they create a soft edge to the mend.
• A paper that is extremely dessicated, or has many tears, may need an overall support. A backing of *kozo* paper over the whole area applied with a thin rice or starch paste will help the work.
• Papers that need deacidification, i.e. an alkaline buffer introduced into the paper, should be handed to a specialist. Calcium and magnesium carbonate are the most likely buffering agents but this work needs to be done by a conservationist with testing equipment.

39 Stack of handmade papers made by Gillian Spires, showing deckle edges

USES FOR PAPERS

Paper is primarily a surface

for recording information.

As such it exists to be obscured.

Steven Kasher

Papers in this book have been classified mainly by the way they are made - either handmade, mouldmade or machinemade, and referred to by the name of the paper. However, a different way to look at paper is in terms of usage. This section is devoted looking at papers for particular artistic purposes and a list of serviceable papers is included at the end of each section. It is important to note that these lists do not represent the total number of papers that are available, nor are they a recommendation of what to use; they simply indicate a range of papers available from which a personal selection can be made.

The type of paper that each individual artist will select is personal but it will have an essential role to play in the success of the work both from the technical and aesthetic point of view. Take a small sample from a supplier for a test before buying ; take time to think about the paper and its appropriateness. Although price is something that has to be considered, it is never worth turning the right quality down for a cheaper alternative.

Paper comes in sheets, pads, blocks, books, rolls and mounted on boards or other bases. When buying a paper mounted on a board, remember that the acid in the board's filling (substrate) can permeate through to the paper surface. Select a board with alkaline buffering or one which has an acid free filling and has been constructed with an acid free adhesive (e.g. Museum or Conservation boards).

PAPERS FOR WATERCOLOUR

Almost every manufacturer of fine papers produces a watercolour grade. Watercolour paper is available in loose sheets; much can be found in the form of pads either spiral-bound or with glued edges, or laminated onto boards, the majority of which are acid free. Sizing is particularly important in watercolour papers as it allows the colour to stay on the surface as the water sinks in, often accounting for the 'brilliance' of the colour (see below). Unsized paper or 'Waterleaf' is not especially recommended for watercolour due to the extremely absorbent nature of the paper. However it may suit some artists who want their colour to spread.

A Rough surface of a sheet which will allow the pattern of roughness in the finished work is popular with many watercolourists. Interesting and unusual effects can be achieved on this surface due to the occasional unpredictable and varied way the surface can catch the light. Some times in the case of a wash, small isolated patches of white paper will show through giving a sparkle to the work. The Not surface is possibly the most popular of the three surfaces, although the Not (and the Rough) surfaces vary from manufacturerto manufacturer. A Not surface is neither too flat nor too rough for varied techniques. The H.P. surface is probably the least popular surface because it can feel 'slippery'; it can be difficult to obtain flat, even washes and they may appear dull and lifeless. However, for very fine detail, this quality may be appropriate.

Many papers are right-sided and the side in which the watermark reads the right way round is usually the correct side which the manufacturer intended for use.

Richard Dixon-Wright of St Cuthberts Mill (a part of Inveresk Ltd.) explains the differences in the manufacturing process that affect the properties of good watercolour papers :

PROPERTIES OF GOOD WATERCOLOUR PAPERS

A work of art takes considerable time and talent to produce. Once completed it often sells for a large sum of money to a collector who hopes that his purchase will last for years. It would, therefore, seem to be false economy to buy anything less than the best quality paper. How do we define good quality paper?

The main requirement for a good watercolour paper is that it will accept a watercolour wash in an even, reproducible manner. It is the degree of sizing which controls the amount of water absorption into the paper. Sizing is the method of treating the paper to limit the absorption of a liquid. There are two main types of sizing - internal sizing and surface sizing. With internal sizing, the sizing material is added to the papermaking fibre in its wet state prior to the formation of the sheet; the most common material used for this method is rosin which is obtained from gums occurring mostly in pine trees. Rosin needs to be attached to the papermaking fibre using the acidic material known as alum. For this method to be effective, the acidity or pH of the slurry of papermaking fibre has to be in the region of 4.5 to 5.0. Rosin itself yellows with age and is unsuitable for use in artist's paper. However, there are modern synthetic sizing materials which provide a neutral pH and these types of sizing materials are used in Bockingford and Saunders Waterford which we make at St Cuthberts Mill.

Surface sizing (or tub sizing) is a separate process whereby the dry sheet is immersed in a bath of hot gelatine which forms a skin over the surface. This produces a paper that is capable of being worked on to a greater degree than an internally sized paper. It is usual for the papermaker to harden this gelatine so that when the paper is soaked by the artist, it is not easily washed off. Many chemicals used to harden the gelatine are acidic but at St Cuthberts Mill we use a hardener that shows a neutral pH when tested by the extract method and the indicator method, thus indicating that both the bulk of the paper and the surface film are neutral.

During recent years, there has been a trend towards whiter papers. This increased whiteness is often achieved by the use of chemicals known as Optical Bleaching Agents. Whilst these chemicals do produce a white sheet, they have a major drawback - they yellow with age. If you are looking for a paper which will maintain its colour over the years, do not use a bright white paper as it is likely to contain Optical Brightening agents. Both Saunders Waterford and Bockingford are entirely free of these chemicals and can be used with confidence.

Both these papers are made on a cylinder-mould machine, a very slow process which produces an extremely stable sheet, having minimal directional variation. The result of this slow making process produces a sheet which exhibits minimal cockling on the application of a heavy wash, and also a sheet with a random grain pattern which is even on both sides. There is no reason why artists should not paint on both sides of these papers. It is for the artist to choose which of the surfaces which will only differ minimally he or she prefers as each side will take a watercolour wash in an identical manner.

Many artists ask the question 'What should a good watercolour paper be made from?' The highest quality watercolour papers are made from 100 per cent cotton which is the purest form of cellulose and produces a paper of extremely long life and high strength. Because the cotton is such a pure form of cellulose, a relatively mild chemical treatment is necessary to give a nice white fibre for papermaking. There are a large number of papers on the market made from wood pulp. It is, however, too much of a generalisation just to say 'made from wood pulp' as there is a wide range of pulps available from mechanical wood used in newsprint, to the highest-quality chemical wood pulp used in photographic papers. St Cuthberts uses a range of thirty different wood pulps. For Bockingford the highest quality chemical wood pulp is used, giving a life expectancy only marginally less than that of pure cotton-based papers.

WATERCOLOUR PAPERS

ATLANTIS GIANT DRAWING AND WATERCOLOUR (Machinemade)
AQUARIUS (Machinemade)
ARCHES AQUARELLE (Mouldmade)
ARCHES LAVIS FIDELIS (EN TOUT CAS) (Mouldmade)
BARCHAM GREEN RWS (Old paper)
BOCKINGFORD (Mouldmade)
FABRIANO ARTISTICO (mouldmade)
FABRIANO ESPORTAZIONE (handmade)
FABRIANO MURILLO (Mouldmade)
FABRIANO ROMA (Handmade)
FABRIANO NO 5 (Machinemade)
GELER (Machinemade)
J.B.GREEN (Old paper)
JPP MOULDMADE (Mouldmade)
GUARRO CASAS AQUARELA (Mouldmade)
HAHNEMÜHLE AQUARELL (Mouldmade)
INDIAN PAPERS (Handmade)
LANAQUARELLE (Mouldmade)
LESSEBO AQUARELLE (Handmade)
MEIRAT VELAZQUEZ (Handmade)
MOULIN DU FLEURAC AQUARELLE (Handmade)
MOULIN DU VERGER AQUARELLE (Handmade)
MONTVAL (Mouldmade)

RICHARD DE BAS AQUARELLE (Handmade)
RKB LANAQUARELLE (Mouldmade)
SAUNDERS WATERFORD (Mouldmade)
SCHOELLERSHAMMER (Mouldmade)
SCHUT DE KEMPEN (Mouldmade)
SHEEPSTOR (Handmade)
SIHLART AQUARELLE (Mouldmade)
STRATHMORE ELCALIBUR (Machinemade)
TWINROCKER GELATINE SIZED (Handmade)
TWO RIVERS WATERCOLOUR (Handmade)
WHATMAN WATERCOLOUR (Mouldmade)
WINSOR & NEWTON WATERCOLOUR (Mouldmade)
WROXFORD (Machinemade)
ZERKALL WATERCOLOUR (Mouldmade)

PAPERS FOR DRAWING

The most popular colour for artists' drawing papers is white. The most popular papers often have a slightly 'toothed' surface (Not) and are of a light to medium weight. Internally sized papers can be used quite well but a harder, surface-sized paper is necessary if a lot of rubbing out and reworking is necessary. With these specifications, the choice is very wide.

Lead pencils are manufactured in a range of grades from very hard to very soft to produce a range of tones from soft grey to thick black; charcoal and carbon pencils make strong black lines and there is a wide variety of coloured pencils available, some of which when mixed with water provide a 'wash' effect. For this range of drawing materials, a large range of white drawing papers is available and mostly termed 'cartridge'. Cartridge derives its name from its original use - to hold a small charge of gunpowder in a firearm. Most cartridges produced today are machinemade and the most persistent factor which effects the choice is the cost. Good quality, fine machinemade cartridges are produced at a lower price than mould- or handmade drawing papers. Every manufacturer of artists' papers has a drawing paper range. Once again, it really is the purse of the artist which dictates the choice of paper.

CARTRIDGE PAPERS
ARTISTS' DRAWING & BRISTOL VELLUM (Machinemade)
ATELIER DRAWING (Machinemade)
ATLANTIS COLLEGE CARTRIDGE (Machinemade)
BASIK DRAWING (Machinemade)
BRISTOL PAPER (Machinemade)
FABRIANO NO 2 (Machinemade)
FABRIANO NO 4 (Machinemade)
FINEBLADE CARTRIDGE (Machinemade)
FIVE SEASON RECYCLED DRAWING (Machinemade)
GELER (Machinemade)
JPP BREAD AND BUTTER (Machinemade)
HERITAGE WOODFREE (Machinemade)
INVERURIE DRAWING (Machinemade)
LENOX (Machinemade)
PAROLE (Machinemade)
SURREY DRAWING (Machinemade)

PAPERS FOR PASTEL AND CHARCOAL

To accept charcoal or pastel the paper must have a 'tooth' to retain the grains of colour and there are a large number of papers with a wide variety of 'tooths'. A finer or medium tooth is normally accepted as most useful and 'laid' papers are very popular. The 'tooth' describes the surface characteristic and a variety of Not (medium texture) and Rough (very textured) surfaces are available. Each individual paper manufacturer produces a slightly different surface character even when they are described in a similar manner so it is important to ask for sample pieces and to experiment to find the surface you like the best. A few papers are available as 'Rugged' (this surface could well be described as mountainous!) and it would need a daring approach in use. Occasionally papers are sand-coated to grab the pastel or charcoal; some retailers actually sell fine grades of sandpaper as a drawing paper. Many artists using pastel have traditionally used the soft colour tints of Ingres papers and other gentle-coloured papers which give perfect expression to subtle, harmonious tones, while the darker tones of a coloured paper - rusts and browns - require a more vigorous contrast in colour and a firmer drawing technique. Several black papers are perfect for the artist who wishes to force dramatic contrasts. (See p.105)

Charcoal has a strong tendency to reflect the grain of the paper and, as with pastel, it is a often a good ideas to utilise this characteristic. A paper most suitable for charcoal will be able to stand up to erasures and rubbing and will not loose its 'bite'. The strength of the charcoal black works well on coloured papers as well as on white grades, and for the compressed charcoal stick or pencil, a smoother surface may offer a different opportunity.

The effect of oil pastels is different altogether from pure pastel and they relate more to oil painting, perhaps used as preparatory sketching tool. Oil pastels can be combined with a turpentine wash, spreading the colour with a brush and consequently a sized paper is more useful.

PAPERS FOR PASTEL AND CHARCOAL
ARCHES MBM INGRES (Mouldmade)
ARTEMEDIA ART & PASTEL PAPER (Machinemade)
CANFORD COVER PAPER (Machinemade)
CANSON MI -TEINTES (machinemade)
CANSON INGRES (Machinemade)
CROB'ART (Machinemade)
FABRIANO INGRES (Mouldmade)
FABRIANO ARTISTICO (Mouldmade)
FABRIANO ESPORTATZIONE (Handmade)
FABRIANO MURILLO (Machinemade)
FABRIANO ROSASPINA (Mouldmade)
FABRIANO ROMA (Handmade)
FABRIANO TIEPOLO (Mouldmade)
FABRIANO UMBRIA (Handmade)
GUARRO CASAS INGRES (Machinemade)
HAHNEMÜHLE BUGRA BUTTEN (Mouldnmade)
HAHNEMÜHLE INGRES (Mouldmade)
MEIRAT VELASQUEZ (Handmade)
MOULIN DU VERGER STRAW (Handmade)
SCHUT INGRES (Old Dutch Ingres) (Mouldmade)
SOMERSET TEXTURED (Mouldmade)
STRATHMORE CHARCOAL (Machinemade)
TUMBA INGRES (Machinemade)
ZERKALL INGRES (Mouldmade)

PAPERS FOR PEN AND INK

Drawing inks made for artists are normally waterproof and dry to a slightly glossy, hard film which enables other colour to be laid on top; they vary from the very black Indian ink to a wide range of colours. The paper choice is important and a suitable surface must be chosen with the right weight. The surface needs to be smooth to allow the pen to move over it and a soft paper with a tendency to fluff should be avoided as it will catch the nib or tip of the pen, especially when a quick stroke is made. A paper both internally and surface-sized is often preferred; this will allow washes, stippling, scratching, hatching, special effects and also removal of mistakes by glass fibre erasure or a very sharp blade. Occasionally, a paper with a small amount of absorption can be beneficial for certain effects. Lighter weight

PAPERS FOR CALLIGRAPHY

The essential components of calligraphy are the writing tool, the medium and the surface. Anyone with a bottle of ink, a pen and a sheet of paper can start to practise this craft without acquiring a specialist set of materials immediately. However, there is a large variety of traditional tools, surfaces and techniques that a calligrapher can use; quills and reed pens, metal pens and fountain pens, fel-tip pens, pencils and brushes are just a few of the tools used for calligraphy. Modern scribes have a number of high-quality brand name inks to choose from and a basic rule is to choose non-waterproof inks - waterproof inks are often thick and fibrous and tend to clog the pen; the resultant ink shine is a desirable calligraphic characteristic.

  Any paper that will not bleed, feather, scratch or wrinkle when used with a pen and ink is suitable. Vellum (prepared from calfskins and goatskins) is the writing surface traditionally preferred by scribes for many centuries; it has a velvet nap and a spring to the surface and calligraphers can choose from various types or grades according to the nature of the job in hand. Parchment is made from the inner layer of a sheepskin by a process similar to vellum preparation but it is different in character to vellum; an alternative not a substitute - the parchment is oilier and tougher than vellum (see p.46). Today many paper imitations of these skins are available, with an especially wide range from the machinemade manufacturers. Handmade papers are preferred for important pieces of work, whereas for

practice a draughtsman's layout pad is an inexpensive base. Calligraphers should not feel limited to a paper labelled 'calligraphy' but could try anything from a H.P. surface, white handmade to an Ingres mouldmade paper. Very fine-surfaced (H.P. or calendered) papers will allow a pen or brush to move evenly and cause a minimum of broken texture in the strokes; coarse-grained (Rough) papers will give a broken effect to the pen stroke and a more ragged edge. Japanese calligraphy particularly exploits the qualities of different paper textures. A surface with a strong colour will increase the weight of the written page.

PAPER FOR ORIENTAL CALLIGRAPHY

Oriental calligraphy inks are made primarily from oils and their exact shade is often regulated by additions of various plant matter as well as the source of the glue (shin or bones of whatever animal). *Gasen (Gasenshi)* is one of the oldest types of paper preferred for calligraphy, it is thin, highly sized, with a very smooth, calendered surface and is remarkably strong.

Dr. Ian Scott and his wife, Jennifer, became involved in traditional Chinese painting in the mid 1960s while living in the Far East and now import the full range of materials for brush painting selected during their annual visits to China. Below Dr Scott describes Chinese papers :

CHINESE PAPERS FOR PAINTING AND CALLIGRAPHY

As the true source of paper, i.e. matted felts of vegetable fibres, China has the longest continuous tradition of papermaking by hand. Almost without exception, the papers currently used in China for painting and calligraphy are handmade at a small number of sites. The most famous is in Anhui Province and these papers are called Xuan. The fame of this site is such that most handmade papers from China carry this name although they could be made elsewhere.

  Chinese papers are made predominantly from bark fibres but other fibres, such as rice, bamboo and kapok, are frequently included to confer particular properties or to provide greater output. Papers which give interesting textures are those described as 'linen' and 'hemp'.

  Chinese papers are made in a range of thicknesses to cater for the demands of the artists and in one, two or three ply. This latter variation is accomplished because the Oriental papermaker does not separate the sheets on the stack where they are pressed. They can therefore be peeled off as required before being spread on the drying boards.

Sheets generally come in two sizes - the 'six foot' sheet measuring 72x38in, the 'four foot' measuring 54x27in. Other sizes are available, such as longer sheets for the painting of hand scrolls. Chinese papers are generally white, but papers which are coloured to represent antique paper are available.

The vast majority of Chinese papers for artists are unsized. This enables the pigment to be carried into the paper where it becomes firmly attached to the fibres. The pigments used in Chinese painting are finely ground solids suspended in water with a small quantity of glue. The most used pigment is ink, made from the soot prepared by the partial combustion of fats and oils. The capability of the paper to absorb the water medium permits a wide range of effects which are the basis of the traditional Chinese painting technique. Silk, which is also used for painting, is sized and this permits a meticulous form of painting as opposed to the 'free' form which uses the unsized papers. Sized papers are also available for this meticulous form of painting.

The quality of Chinese papers can be judged mainly by appearance. Extraneous matter such as woodchips, small stone material, clumps of fibres, etc. can easily be seen by looking through the thin sheets, as also can the evenness of the distribution of fibres. The paper should have a clean fresh white appearance although it will not be as white as a chemically bleached paper. When a sheet is shaken, it should not make a harsh crackling sound, but a rather soft sound. One side of a Chinese paper will be smoother than the other, being the one against the board when being dried. This smoother side is the one most commonly used.

Some machinemade papers are sold for brush painting. As far as we know, these come from Japan and Taiwan and are called 'Moon Palace' papers. They are sold in continuous rolls of approx. 72ft and in various widths from 12-24in. The rolls of Chinese papers which are handmade, are prepared from a number of separate sheets rolled together, or as is sometimes the case, glued to make a continuous strip. A very inexpensive paper available in sheets called 'grass paper', with a distinctive yellowish colour, is used for practice work.

PAPERS FOR PEN AND INK AND CALLIGRAPHY
ARCHES AQUARELLE H.P. (Mouldmade)
BODLEIAN REPAIRING (Old paper)
BRISTOL PAPERS (Machinemade)
CHINESE PAPERS (Handmade)
COVENTRY SMOOTH (Machinemade)
DIEU DONNÉ LINEN (Handmade)
ELEPHANTHIDE (Machinemade)
FABRIANO ARTISTICO Mouldmade)
FABRIANO ESPORTAZIONE (Handmade)

40 Chinese papermakers laying wet paper on walls to dry in the sunshine

FABRIANO MURILLO (Mouldmade)
FABRIANO ROMA (Handmade)
FABRIANO UMBRIA(Handmade)
GAMPI TORINOKO (Handmade)
GRIFFEN STUDIO (Handmade)
GUARRO SATINADO (Machinemade)
HAHNEMÉUHLE INGRES (Machinemade)
JAPANESE CALLIGRAPHY PAPERS (Handmade)
INDIAN PAPERS (Handmade)
LANA VERGÉ ANTIQUE (Mouldmade)
PARCHMENT (Genuine and imitation)
PAROLE (Machinemade)
RICHARD DE BAS CANTON LAID (Handmade)
VELLUM (Genuine and imitation)
WOOKEY HOLE (Handmade)
WHATMAN VINTAGE (Old paper)
HOT PRESSED WATERCOLOUR PAPERS

PAPERS FOR PRINTMAKING

As with any other media, there are a wide range of papers specifically made for the printmaking processes. The most popular papers in a medium which allows many identical impressions to be taken are those which are evenly made, stable and consistent so that the printing does not need to take account of the variables in a paper. Understanding the paper and how it behaves is an important aspect in successful printing and experience will encourage the best choice of paper to be made; each section below contains information about paper and its reactions and it may be worth glancing at each different printing section because much of the information is relevant to the other printing processes.

Note again that these papers are simply a general indication of what is available; the lists are not comprehensive and the papers are not recommended. What is recommended is a test printing before bulk buying.

Not all printmakers' paper troubles are due to the short comings of the paper. Even though the workshop may choose a suitable paper, receive it in good condition, variable atmospheric conditions or improper handling can make the paper curl, wrinkle or fail to print in register. Improper adjustment of ink to paper can cause such troubles as picking, offsetting, failure to dry, smudging or scuffing. Improper press conditions can cause misregister, paper splitting, stretching, scumming, streaks and slurring even on the very best of papers.

WHY PAPER WON'T STAY PUT

Humidity is the amount of moisture vapour present in a given amount of air. Britain has a damp, insular climate and there is often a high degree of humidity present in its atmosphere. When the air can hold no more moisture, humidity becomes visible, in the form of rain or mist.

Paper is very sensitive to humidity. If the air is damp, paper absorbs moisture from it and expands. When the air becomes drier, it in turn absorbs humidity from the paper which contracts. The expansion and contraction is not even - it varies with the width and the length of the paper. Paper that is made on a cylinder mould or Fourdrinier machine has a 'grain', i.e. most of its fibres lie lengthwise in the direction in which the papermaking

machine was running. The fibres expand proportionately far more in width than in length and the sheets of paper do likewise.

When stacked, paper absorbs and loses moisture through its edges. Tight edged paper results when piles of paper are exposed to a very dry atmosphere and the edges dry out; wavy edges paper results when piles of dry paper are exposed to a humid atmosphere and the edges absorb moisture. Moisture absorption is quicker than moisture loss. This reaction of paper to the humidity in the air is a problem for all who have to work with it.

A CURE FOR WAVY-EDGED PAPER ?

The traditional way of getting over these undesirable effects of humidity was to hang the paper up or lay it out in the studio before printing. It is advantageous, to store paper at approximately the temperature of the print room since cold paper brought suddenly in to a much warmer atmosphere, either moister or dryer, will react more rapidly. So, if it is impossible to hang it, store it in its wrappers in the printing room for as long as possible before printing.

The following are some suggestions which may help :

• Use 'mature' papers.
• Keep the original packing on the paper until you are ready to print.
• Move the packages well in advance of use and still in their wrappers to a position where they can achieve the temperature of the printing room.
• If extremely accurate registration is needed, run sheets of paper through the press before printing.
• If the sheets of paper are to go through the press more than once, cover the partially printed stacks with waterproof covers between printings.
• Print onto the paper with the grain direction lying across the printing machine, i.e. use the so-called 'long grain' cut paper. Since paper stretches much less in the grain direction, the cross direction should be the smaller dimension.
• In litho printing, keep the amount of damping water to a minimum since cases are known when even the amount of water absorbed in processing has caused distortion and mis-registration.

PAPERS FOR PROOFING

Before an edition is printed, a certain amount of testing, called proofing, takes place. During proofing, ink mixing is adjusted, inking patterns determined, pressure of the presses are adjusted and minor corrections are made to the image. A certain number of impressions, all of which will be imperfect in one respect or another, will be printed before the work is agreed to be just as the artist wants it to look. Termed 'trial proofs', these are usual before the beginning of any job and are usually destroyed after the edition is completed. In order to minimise paper costs, the printer relies on inexpensive papers for proofing rather than risk expensive sheets of fine paper which will be discarded.

To economise further, the proofing process is separated into several stages with appropriate paper types for each stage :

ROUGH PROOFING

Newsprint is the best paper for certain types of rough proofing, mostly in screenprinting and lithography, occasionally in relief printing. Usually from three to six impressions must be taken before various alignments such as weight of stroke, printing press pressure, etc. are made and the image reasonably stabilised so as to print satisfactorily. Newsprint is also used in quantity for 'slip' sheets, to interleave between freshly printed impressions as a guard against offsetting during the test printing. Newsprint is used in lithography as tympan backing sheets and set-off paper, in screenprinting and relief printing for cleaning up, etc. making newsprint one of the most useful and necessary papers in the printing studio. It is possibly most useful in the 30x40in size, from which smaller sizes can easily be cut. Quantities from 500 to 1000 sheet packs are a necessity for workshops engaged in steady activity. The newsprint should be of medium weight and medium surface finish in order to suit the various activities.

CRITICAL PROOFING

Following rough proofing, a more critical type of proofing is usually done in which the colour mixture and ink consistency are viewed, minor corrections in the image are made, accurate paper positioning marked and the quality of the printed impression assessed. The paper for critical proofing should be closer in colour, weight and surface to that of the final edition paper. Workshops in which many different types of editioning paper are used often have a general paper - a semi-smooth, white, proofing paper - in use. Occasionally machinemade cartridges are used, although more preferable are the cheaper mouldmades such as Bockingford. For really critical proofing, to produce the BAT, the same stock as the edition is to be printed on is essential for final approval.

PAPERS FOR INTAGLIO

The paper for intaglio printing must be of a quality that will allow it to be dampened and it must be capable of picking up the finest detail on the printing plate. Papers for intaglio should be heavy enough to withstand the stretch and pull of the varied surfaces of the plate. When the built-up area of the plate is shallow, printing can be done with little or no change from the usual procedures. As the relief of the plate increases (and for extremely deep plates), it will be necessary to provide greater cushioning effect with the blankets in order to push the paper sufficiently into the recessed surfaces to contact the ink.

DAMPENING PAPER

For all intaglio work the paper must be dampened to soften the fibres and allow it to be pressed into the plate to pick up the ink. There are many ways of doing this. Some papers can be dampened and printed on almost immediately; others - such as heavy, well-sized papers - need to be soaked for several hours. Paper can be dampened with a sponge or soaked in a bath of clean water and dried between blotters under weights to absorb excess moisture. The method chosen depends on how readily the paper which is being used accepts water. The amount of water is controlled by the amount of time the paper is left in the soaking tray as well as by the temperature. Waterleaf papers, for example absorb water like blotting paper because they contain no sizing and they cannot be dipped into a tray or bath without disastrous results. Spraying or sponging on every second or third sheet could give the required amount of softness to allow stretch when printing.

Each paper will be found to have its optimum dampening time and it is necessary to build up your own experience with each paper in use. The perfect condition for paper for printing is soft and pliable with a mat surface and no glistening water spots. Papers can be dampened overnight if required but those left dampened for too long will allow a mildew growth which will stain the paper. The cause of paper wrinkling as the plate is printed is often attributed to uneven dampening although deposits of size on the blankets can also help this to happen. A stainless steel, pump-action spray-diffuser (originally used in Japan for laundry) has been imported into Britain by Atlantis for dampening paper; used mostly by conservationists, this sprayer maintains pressure for long periods of time and gives a (variable) fine water vapour spray without dribbling.

DRYING PRINTS

Drying intaglio prints should follow the same procedure as with heavily embossed prints. The prints are placed between absorbent blotting papers (with frequent changes of blotters), interspaced at intervals with boards (such as Sundaler Boards) until they are almost dry, in a room where a reasonable temperature can be maintained. The final stage is to leave the prints between clean, dry blotters and boards until they are quite dry. Dried slowly like this, problems such as later cockling and distortion in the sheets should not occur. Prints that have been dried too quickly may be prone to change when mounted or framed.

EMBOSSED PRINTS

Embossed prints are inkless prints often with a deep relief surface. They are simply prints in which a raised image is forced into the paper under pressure. As no ink is used, the image is represented by the paper relief on the surface, rather than by line or colour. The choice of paper for embossing is most important. Usually very heavy-weight papers are chosen; the heavier the paper the more embossment it will retain and the more evenly will it dry. Thin papers tear easily as they stretched to accommodate great depths in a plate. Embossed prints are often printed with dampened paper on an intaglio press with the addition of a special soft blanket in addition to the other press blankets.

Inkless intaglios can present a special problem in drying. Heavy pressure

on the prints when drying between boards can squash the embossment. Each print could simply be pressed between two or three blotters after printing; the weight of the blotters alone may help keep the print flat. A cover of plastic may help to prevent the edges from drying sooner than the centre of the sheet. As the prints dry, a little more weight can be placed on top thus increasing the flattening pressure without losing the embossment.

CHINE COLLÉ

Chine Collé is another method of obtaining colour in the intaglio process through the use of coloured paper collage. In this process, differently coloured papers are adhered to the printing paper allowing the artist the use of flat colour areas without two colour printing. Coloured paper is torn or cut into shapes as part of the image and when run together with the plate through the etching press, the coloured paper and etching paper are laminated together. Coloured papers that might be used include *Moriki, Mingei, Tsujuko* and *Toyogami* from Japan, plus papers that do not fade in the light - for instance, *Fabriano Text*. Coloured tissue papers that at first glance seem attractive rapidly fade and have almost no permanence.

PAPERS FOR INTAGLIO
COVENTRY (Machinemade)
DIEU DONNÉ (Handmade) ✓
DUCHENE (Handmade) ✓
FABRIANO MURILLO (Mouldmade)
FABRIANO ROSASPINA (Mouldmade)
FABRIANO TIEPOLO (Mouldmade)
HAHNEMÜHLE ETCHING (Mouldmade)
HMP (Handmade)
JPP MOULDMADE (Mouldmade)
LANA GRAVURE (Mouldmade)
LANA ROYALE (Mouldmade)
LENOX (Machinemade)
MEIRAT VELASQUEZ (Handmade)
MOULIN DU GUÉ (Mouldmade)
MOULIN DU VERGER (Handmade) ✓
RKB ARCHES (Mouldmade)
RKB LANA PRINTMAKING (Mouldmade) ✓

BFK RIVES (Mouldmade) ✓
SOMERSET (Mouldmade)
ST. ARMAND (Handmade)
STRATHMORE ETCHING (Machinemade)
VELIN ARCHES (Mouldmade)
WHATMAN PRINTMAKING (Mouldmade)
VELIN PUR FIL JOHANNOT (Mouldmade) ✓
ZERKALL COPPERPLATE (Mouldmade)

PAPERS FOR EMBOSSING
Heavy weights in the above papers, plus
TUB SIZED BOCKINGFORD (Mouldmade)
FABRIANO MURILLO (Mouldmade)
MEIRAT GOYA (Handmade)
RICHARD DE BAS AQUARELLE (Handmade)
SAUNDERS WATERFORD (Mouldmade)

PAPERS FOR HAND LITHOGRAPHY

Up until the time of Senefelder, the inventor of lithography, all paper was handmade. Generally speaking, all printing processes were originally designed to print on the papers then available and attempts to develop particular papers suitable for certain printing processes came afterwards. Lithographic paper can be defined as any paper suitable for lithographic printing but in the context of this book, lithography is referred to as an autographic process either on a direct or indirect, usually flatbed, press; a process in which the artist draws directly on a metal plate or stone which is then hand processed, usually hand inked and a limited number of impressions taken.

The responsibility for perfect production and good quality printing is divided between the papermaker and the lithographer and it is important therefore that the papermaker knows exactly how the paper functions in the lithographic process and how to make paper to meet its requirements. It is equally important for the lithographer to know and understand the nature of paper and to handle and print it in such a way as not to impair its printing qualities.

REQUIREMENTS OF PAPER FOR LITHOGRAPHY

• Flatness
• Good dimensional stability
• Proper relative humidity
• Accurate trimming (where relevant)
• Minimum curling tendency (where relevant/long grain sheets)
• Resistance to picking
• Freedom from chemicals
• Good ink drying qualities
• Freedom from lint and dust

The irregularity of the deckle of a handmade sheet makes the placing of a printed image difficult. This can be overcome, as in screenprinting, by the trimming of two edges or part of the edges which fit into the lays. Note that R.K. Burt in London has had two papers of special sizes made especially for lithography - one that is a larger size which will fit into the grippers and when torn down reduces to full Imperial size and the other with only one deckle edge, the other sides trimmed for registration (see p.). Hand- and mouldmade papers when used for printing lithographs are usually free from what are often termed 'active chemicals' - any water-soluble material that contaminate the dampening water and cause damage to the printing plate or the water-ink balance during printing.

Picking (individual fibres) or, more especially, linting can be a problem, caused by surface fibres that are only partly bonded to the sheet being picked up during printing. Sometimes, in the third or fourth colour of a print, when the surface size which has held the fibres in place has become softened by the moisture, the fibres are picked up by the tacky ink.

Japanese papers are suitable for lithography, although the lighter types can only be printed by direct press work as the sheets will tear in the grippers. The lighter papers are also only suitable for single colour images.

PRINTING WITH DRY OR DAMPENED PAPER

If a paper makes good contact with all the minute traces of ink on an image, it will pick up more ink, and therefore the print will be more faithful to the original. The quality of the contact depends on the amount of pressure used, the basic texture and softness of the paper itself and whether the paper is dry or damp. A good paper can be printed either dry or damp within certain limitations.

There are definite advantages and disadvantages to using paper in either state. Dry paper has one slight disadvantage - it requires very heavy pressure in order to push the fibres of the paper into close contact with the inked image. Dry paper also produces slightly harder-looking and more contrasting tones, although perhaps not all the nuances of the plate or stone. For colour printing, however, dry paper has definite advantages. Registration is much simpler and more accurate, due to the fact that there is less paper stretch. The problems of maintaining a constant and equal balance of moisture in each sheet throughout the entire edition and printing are avoided. Dry paper is also easier to handle and no drying or pressing is necessary once the printing of the edition has been completed. Waterleaf papers must be used dry.

All papers, however, are made softer and more sensitive once they have been dampened. The basic disadvantage of a dampened paper is its tendency either to expand or to contract when wet, with the result that it becomes extremely difficult to produce good colour registration. A dampened paper requires less pressure (making longer editions easier on the printer), picks up more detail from both stone and metal, and requires less ink to produce a fully intense image. For printing subtle crayon or tonal washes, dampened paper is far superior to dry paper, because of its ability to extract every small detail the stone or plate is capable of producing. Since less ink is needed, as well as less pressure, there is less chance of the ink spreading and filling in the image. Many rough, heavily textured or fully sized papers can be used to advantage if dampened, greatly increasing the list of good, edition-quality papers available for lithographic prints.

DAMPENING THE PAPER

Dampen the paper with a clean sponge, using distilled water to avoid discoloration. If it is to be printed damp, the paper should be dampened until it is just limp and not wet. Sponge evenly and quickly over the entire surface without neglecting the edges. Heavy papers may have to be turned over and dampened on the other side also. The dampened sheets can be placed on top of the other. If they begin to buckle as the lower sheets expand slowly, reorder the sheets. Once they have been dampened, the sheets should be

kept wrapped in plastic. Use paper fingers for handling any dampened sheets because the papers pick up dirt more easily.

Paper should not be kept wrapped in polythene for very long, a maximum of four to five days. Formaldehyde can be added to the bath before soaking to prevent mildew but this is not a particularly good practice; and carbolic acid although it can prevent the formation of mould should not be used at it can upset the acid/alkaline balance of the paper.

PAPER STRETCH

Paper stretch must be taken into consideration with all kinds of printing papers, although it is less of a problem with dry papers than with damp ones. Most of the stretch occurs the first time a paper is run through the press under pressure and is reduced each subsequent time. Whenever critical registration is needed, a dry paper is recommended. Each sheet should be run through the press once or twice before any printing actually takes place to stretch the paper (and smooth out some of the Rough surface of a paper) allowing for more consistent printing results. Take note of the grain direction of the paper if this is relevant as paper stretches more when it is run through the press against the grain.

PAPERS FOR LITHOGRAPHY
ATLANTIS HERITAGE (Machinemade)
BASINGWERK(Machinemade)
CURWEN MOULDMADE (Mouldmade)
FABRIANO ARTISTICO (Mouldmade)
FABRIANO ESPORTAZIONE (Handmade)
FABRIANO ROMA (Handmade) ✓
FABRIANO ROSASPINA(Mouldmade)
FABRIANO TIEPOLO (Mouldmade)
FABRIANO UMBRIA (Mouldmade)
GALLERY 100 (Machinemade) ✓
JPP MOULMADE (Mouldmade)
LANA GRAVURE (1590 EDITION) (Mouldmade)
LANA ROYALE (ROYAL CROWN) (Mouldmade) ✓
LENOX (Machinemade)
RKB ARCHES (Mouldmade)
RKB LANA PRINTMAKING (Mouldmade) ✓

BFK RIVES (Mouldmade)✓
SAUNDERS WATERFORD (Mouldmade)
SIHLART OPUS (Machinemade)
SOMERSET (Mouldmade)
TUB SIZED BOCKINGFORD (Mouldmade)
VELIN ARCHES (Mouldmade)
WHATMAN PRINTMAKING (Mouldmade)
ZERKALL (Mouldmade)✓

PAPERS FOR SCREENPRINTING

The choice of paper is extremely important for the success of a printing project. The right paper brings out the full effect of good printing and increases the intrinsic value of the work.

41 The screen shop at Curwen Chilford printingmaking studios with paper stacked ready for use

A great variety of papers produce excellent results and screenprinting is less dependent on the choice of paper than almost any other process because of the versatility of the medium. Waterleaf paper will allow inks to sink in and and internally sized papers yield excellent luminosity in transparent overlays of colour; sized papers will allow a build up of layers of ink; very smooth (H.P. and calendered) papers will allow a very crisp image to be printed, reproducing the finest detail, although textured (and even heavily textured) sheets can be successfully used for many projects. Both heavy and lightweight papers are equally usable and papers for etching, lithography, many handmades plus Japanese and Indian papers, etc. all are suitable depending on the final requirements.

PAPERS FOR SCREENPRINTING
ARCHES 88 (Mouldmade)
ARCHES LAVIS FIDELIS (Mouldmade)
ATLANTIS HERITAGE (Machinemade)
BOCKINGFORD (Mouldmade)
COVENTRY (Machinemade)
FABRIANO ROSASPINO (Mouldmade)
GALLERY 100 (Machinemade)
JPP MOULDMADE (Mouldmade)
LANA ROYALE (ROYALE CROWN) (Mouldmade)
LENOX (Machinemade)
MIRAGE (Machinemade)
MOULIN DU GUÉ (Mouldmade)
RKB ARCHES (Mouldmade)
BFK RIVES (Mouldmade)
SIHLART OPUS (Machinemade)
SOMERSET (Mouldmade)
VELIN ARCHES (Mouldmade)
VELIN DE LANA (Mouldmade)
WHATMAN PRINTMAKING (Mouldmade)
ZERKALL (Mouldmade)

PAPERS FOR RELIEF PROCESSES

Relief printing is the most direct of the four printmaking techniques and encompasses any image that is taken from the relief surface of a block or plate. This includes lino cutting, wood engraving, found-object printing, wood cutting, collograph, letterpress, stamp prints, plaster relief prints, reduction prints, cardboard relief prints, stencilling, pochoir, etc. Many of the papers used in relief printing have a smooth surface because of the intrinsic needs of the process to reproduce surface detail although if presses are being utilised it is possible to pull hard on type, etc. and print onto textured and even 'wavy' papers. Both hard-surfaced and soft-surfaced papers can be used although a hard-surfaced paper may produce better results in some cases if dampened slightly. Watercolour papers give a nice crisp print but need heavy pressure but are not very suitable for book work.

Smooth, thin papers are usually associated with wood engraving because they produce sharp crisp images. A wide range of Japanese, Indian, Thai and other Eastern papers are available for this use and only by experiment can a personal choice be made. Mouldmade and handmade papers will print beautifully if slightly dampened (not waterleaf) before use. Oil-based inks can be printed dry on Oriental papers and the traditional Japanese papers such as *moriki, sekishu, hosho* and mulberry papers take oil-based inks well, either in colour or black and white. Some will argue that no European paper is a match for the best quality Japanese papers in terms of sheer whiteness and luminosity combined with a highly porous nature and a silky softness.

The classic Japanese Ukiyo-e woodcut technique is a highly skilled and specialised process and for best results all the traditional tools, blocks and papers should be used; *hosho* paper is used for the key drawing (very thin) and a *minogami* (lightly sized) paper for key impressions; for the main printing hundreds of Japanese papers are available but perhaps well-suited to the Ukiyo-e technique is *hosho* in a heavier weight with the deckles trimmed off to facilitate registration. *Hosho* paper is usually unsized but if printing takes place with water-based (or rice-paste) inks, then the paper should be lightly sized in order for it to remain flat and maintain good registration. Dampening the paper for printing is also a specialised task and the dampness must be kept as uniform as possible on this lightly sized paper. The Japanese arrange their paper after printing in two traditional methods - *otosu* where the papers are stacked individually overlapping each other from left to right or *hawasu* where the sheets are arranged in a staggered fashion from left going to right.

PAPERS FOR RELIEF TECHNIQUES
ARCHES 88 (Mouldmade)
BOCKINGFORD (Mouldmade)
FABRIANO ARTISTICO Mouldmade)
FABRIANO ESPORTAZIONE (Handmade)
FABRIANO MURILLO (Mouldmade)
FABRIANO UMBRIA (Handmade)
FABRIANO ROSASPINA (Mouldmade)
FABRIANO TIEPOLO (Mouldmade)
GUARRO CASAS BIBLOS (Mouldmade)
JPP MOULDMADE (Mouldmade)
JAPANESE PAPERS (Handmade)
INDIAN PAPERS (Handmade)
LANA GRAVURE (1590 EDITION) (Mouldmade)
LANA ROYALE (ROYAL CROWN) (Mouldmade) ✓
MOULIN DU GUÉ (Mouldmade)
RKB ARCHES (Mouldmade)
BFK RIVES (Mouldmade) ✓
THAI PAPERS (Handmade)
VELIN ARCHES (Mouldmade)
WHATMAN PRINTMAKING (Mouldmade)

PLATINUM / PALLADIUM PRINTING

It is not easy to recommend a paper for this process but various papers have been used successfully, for example BFK Rives, Fabriano no 5, Stonehenge, etc. Several paper studios have made papers especially for this process using a bast fibre base and this also has worked well.

PAPERS FOR PLATINUM PRINTING
ARCHES AQUARELLE (Mouldmade)
ANW OPALINE (Machinemade)
CANSON OPALUX (Machinemade)

FBARIANO NO 5 (Mouldmade)
RIVES DE LIN (Mouldmade)
BFK RIVES (Mouldmade)
SAUNDERS WATERFORD (Mouldmade)
STONEHENGE (Machinemade)
STRATHMORE BRISTOL (I ply board, Machinemade)

BLOTTING PAPERS

Many print workshops employ blotting paper especially in the intaglio process where it is used interleaved with dampened prints during the slow drying process. Again it is important to have a white stock which is acid free, a good weight (around 280 gsm), a high wet strength able to withstand a lot of handling. A wet strength agent added to the pulp may not allow the blotting to be acid free although it will help it to hold together if the blotting is used a lot e.g. Barcham Green's Multisorb. Most blotters come in sheet and it is important when buying to work out the best size for your studio. Large sizes are available. Blotting paper also comes in rolls. Archivart in the USA produce a very heavy weight, large size, acid free blotting that is 100pt (2000 micron, approx. 1/8in) thick, exported into many countries. Blotting paper can be made to order - One British print studio has had a mouldmade blotting paper special making, screenprinted with lay marks which has withstood very heavy use and the ravages of time and also allowed continuous accurate placing of prints.

INTERLEAVING SHEETS

Interleaving, or separating sheets, are most commonly found in printmaking practices and where prints are stacked they are interleaved to prevent any ink offsetting. Interleaving sheets can also be used to wrap work up, to protect paper surfaces from handling and for storage of any kind. Interleaving sheets come generally in the form of thin tissue paper which must be white or the natural colour of the fibre - a coloured tissue interleaving may bleed its colour onto the surface above or below if damp or moist conditions arise. Tissues need not necessarily be of quality cotton fibres but the type of interleaving chosen must be acid free, neutral pH and non-abrasive. Thin tissues used for conservation can supply a good interleaving source

and although obviously more expensive, they do provide a stronger and purer source of interleaving and wrapping; tissues such *tengujo* or *gampi*. are very suitable. A thin, transparent film is also available for this purpose, often supplied to museums by archival/conservation paper merchants. Glassine, a more traditional interleaving, is a glossy, transparent coated paper (particularly popular among photographers) and often used to protect negatives and photographs, although this may not be acid free in which case it will stain the paper.

GLASSINE (Machinemade)
MYLAR (Machinemade)
ORIENTAL TISSUES
SRATHMORE SLIP SHEET (Machinemade)
WHITE ACID-FREE TISSUE (Machinemade)

WRAPPING PAPERS

Most paper comes wrapped in strong, waxed or waterproofed brown paper. It is possible to buy an acid free, lignin free, strong paper with a good fold strength to wrap prints in. This is a good idea particularly if you are wrapping prints for long-term torage. (See p. 78) Consult a conservation/archivist paper supplier for details.

42 Simon Green standing with packed paper in Hayle Mill

PAPER FOR ARTISTS' BOOKS

Matthew Tyson, founder and owner of Imprints, artists' book dealer and artist bookmaker, outlines some of his personal preferences in terms of fine paper for artists' bookmaking.

THE BASIC ELEMENT OF THE SPIRITUAL INSTRUMENT [1]

Paper is, of course, the true medium of the livre d'artiste, its very structure. Usually the artists and/or publishers involved require a high standard of acid free paper. The question: Why use good quality papers? is easily answered by an example; some years ago, we organised a touring exhibition of livres d'artiste in which the visitors were invited to handle the exhibited books whilst wearing cotton gloves. All the books were made from high quality mouldmade or handmade papers. Three venues later and handling by thousands of people only one of the forty books on display showed any real wear and that was on unsized paper which is by its nature softer.

When making a livre d'artiste it is important to have a paper which is durable as it is forced to work continually. However, the paper must be right for the job, the wrong paper can ruin the feel of a book. I often use in addition to Arches, Zerkall, a German paper and Somerset, from Inveresk whilst lamenting the demise of Barcham Green papers, an old favourite of British book artists. It is interesting to have a look at some livres d'artiste which illustrate the combination of good paper and its absolute suitability for that particular publication -

Patrick Caulfield's book 'Some Poems of Jules Laforgue' published by Petersburg Press employs a synthetic paper called Neobond which provides a base that brings up all the flatness and colour of Caulfield's screenprints. Bruce McLean and Mel Gooding's collaboration 'A Potato Against a Black Background' is entirely screen and potato printed on a selection of Japanese papers with handmade lace-paper interleaving.

My father's (Ian Tyson) book 'Hybrid Shoji' has images made entirely with paper collaged together to show a contrast between the dark blue Colorplan (G.F.Smith & Son) and the creamy Tonasawa papers. In France Daniel Buren's book 'Theatre' published by Collectif Generation had the paper specially made in the Auvergne by Richard de Bas, the watermarked images allow light to shine through them and the text as the viewer turns the page.

Sometimes the books demand a lower quality paper and this is certainly true of the Oblivion Boys publications which employ such unreliables as newsprint and cartridge paper already yellowing at the edges.

It is not always the right thing to use a fancy paper and it is easy to get caught with a beautiful paper which is just not right.

1 S. Mallarmé Concerning the Book

PAPERS FOR LETTERPRESS

See Papers for relief printing, plus
ARCHES INGRES MBM (Mouldmade)
DIEU DONNÉ (Handmade)
DUCHENE (Handmade)
ELEPHANT HIDE (Machinemade)
FABRIANO ROMA (Handmade)
FABRIANO TIZIANO Mouldmade)
GALLERY 100 (Machinemade)
HAHNEMÜHLE BOOK (Mouldmade)
HAHNEMÜHLE LAID (Mouldmade)
LANA ROYALE (ROYAL CROWN) (Mouldmade)
LANA VERGÉ ANTIQUE (Mouldmade)
LANA SUPERIOR (Mouldmade)
LARROQUE DUCHENE (Handmade)
MOULIN DU VERGER (Handmade)
MOULIN DU POMBIE (Handmade)
PLANT PAPERS (Handmade)
RKB LANA PRINTMAKING (Mouldmade)
RICHARD DE BAS (Handmade)
TWO RIVERS (Handmade)
BFK RIVES (Mouldmade)
TWINROCKER (Handmade)
WOOKEY HOLE (Handmade)
VELIN PUR FIL JOHANNOT (Mouldmade)
ZERKALL (Mouldmade)

PAPERS AND THE PHOTOCOPIER

In theory any uncoated paper of a suitable weight (usually around 80gsm) can be used on plain paper copiers. Copier machines are, however, becoming more sophisticated and make greater demands on the paper. Most copying machines generate considerable heat when working which can cause the paper to curl, and some machines use a liquid toner that requires an especially smooth paper. The machines can jam because the wrong sort or weight of paper is used which results in a high waste rate.

Many manufacturers of specialist copier papers install special machinery at their plant to improve the sheet formation and give control of moisture content. However, working at Falkiner Fine Papers in London has allowed Chris Hough to come in contact with many customers requiring papers for many needs, including an increased demand for special papers for the photocopier. He has discovered that once again the traditional roles of certain papers, produced originally for fine artists, are being redefined :

Following the vogue for colour photography, where illustrators and graphic designers flock to the copy services to test and manipulate the reproduction qualities of the images they have created, the logical step was to find more interesting papers than those readily available to copy on to.

Lightweight Japanese tissues, are sometimes selected for their fibrous or translucent qualities; lightweight flecked papers and papers from India and Nepal containing curious plant fibres and grasses have been used so that their surface quality might interact with the printed image, although it is not guaranteed they will be suitable for a copier. Paper on which the designer can work in ink or water-based paint, after the copy has been printed, has been in constant demand, particularly by architectural visualisers. They often photocopy a plan or line image onto a large, lightweight paper (preferably with a cotton content and well sized) and thereafter hand-colour the image to create the appearance of an individually produced visualisation. Frequently a cream- or buff-coloured paper with an 'antique' feel is sought for representing old buildings and the modern photocopy printing is disguised by hand colouring. No paper has been found specifically made for this purpose and current fill-ins range from large end papers for bookbinding to archival storage papers for plan chest. The application of a surface sizing to the paper after the copy has been made, can greatly enhance the application of water-based paints.

As long as photocopy is considered a viable and exciting reproduction medium, Chris Hough believes that the papermills, traditionally producing fine quality artists' papers, may have reason to consider a sheet where photocopy image and traditional drawing and paint media might effectively combine.

43 A selection of Indian papers

PAPERS FOR NEW TECHNOLOGY

Simon Lewandowski, artist, printmaker, writer and lecturer uses 'new technology' in much of his own work. He outlines his experiences below :

Increasing number of painters, printmakers and designers use photocopiers and computers in the production of their work. Sometimes, images produced worked and altered by a machine, will finally be resolved by more traditional media, other artists want to exhibit actual copies or computer prints as finished work.

Most people using a copier tend to accept whatever is in the paper tray at the time but with 'plain paper' copiers (most of them nowadays) there is potential for variation. The factors artists take into account when choosing paper for any other kind of process (colour, texture, conservation value, etc.) apply equally to copier prints. The choice of papers is perhaps not so wide, but there is some choice.

Manufacturers recommend particular types of paper for their machines. Their choice is based on factors of porosity, moisture content, electrical resistance, roughness and friction coefficient. Photocopiers can be damaged by by a gradual build-up of dust or moisture, so even though a particular paper stock is producing good copies, it may be slowly ruining the machine - unfortunately this is a particular problem with recycled papers. From the point of view of the user, experimentation, where possible, is the key but there are some useful guidelines to follow :

• Mass-produced paper for copiers and laser printers is a chlorine-bleached and acid-packed bond paper of around 75-90gsm. Anything of a similar weight will work just as well (for instance Fabriano Ingres 90gsm, Arches Ingres 90gsm are both pretty good and will go through a colour laser copier).

• Generally, copiers have a hand feed that will take individual sheets and this is the best way to use non-standard papers. Most machines will take thin card (around the equivalent of a postcard weight) and watercolour papers up to 120-140gsm.

• Non-standard size papers (not A3 or A4) need to be cut down accurately - the leading edge that feeds into the machine particularly. Most commercial printers will guillotine batches of paper down to standard sizes quite cheaply.

• Handmade papers can be particularly bulky in relation to their weight - these may not feed at all - and, of course , the more textured the surface of the paper the less likely it is for the image to reproduce clearly. Because the image on the paper is 'fixed' or fused by heat, the image may be transferred onto heavier papers but not fully fused; a normal fixative should solve this.

• Very thin papers such as Japanese tissues, will take a copy reasonably well but are too lightweight and usually too soft to feed through without snarling up inside. They need to be pasted, just along the leading edge, to a thicker stock of the same size and fed through by hand. Tracing paper generally copies very well and can be used as a positive for making photo-etchings or screenprints.

• If a copier or computer printer won't make an image directly onto the surface you want, there is a way of getting round the problem; copies sprayed with a solvent can be transferred directly to the paper by putting them both through an etching press. Solvent- transferred copies also produce an excellent image on a litho plate. There are various types of transfer papers (usually silicon-based) which can be copied onto and will release their image onto another surface when ironed on the back : Letraset make a product that works with a copy like their dry-transfer lettering but the backing sheets of some brand of sticky labels work just as well for a fraction of the cost.

Experimentation is the key. Electronic-image technology is still new and most of its vast creative potential remains unexplored. Because it is so new there are few precedents - the users can shape and direct the medium as they go along, guided by their own needs. What you thought was impossible yesterday might be there for the asking tomorrow. It will, no doubt, soon become possible to transfer electronically-synthesised images to virtually any surface or material as fluently as we paint or draw now. The lasting value of the work created with new technology, however, still depends on the same qualities as that which was made with the old - qualities which are not found in a machine but are put there by us, the users.

STOCK OPTIONS FOR DESIGNERS

What is the single most important product in the world of graphic design? The answer is paper. In the past, it was necessary for graphic designers to be acquainted the types of papers that printers used so they could accurately specify and show and a visualisation to their clients. Recently designers have become more adventurous and aware of the range of fine quality papers that can be applied to certain special jobs.

The beginning of the 1990s has seen a new market for fine and decorative papers and Chris Hough, an artist who also works at Falkiner Fine Papers in London, gives a personal view of the new trends :

Recent trends in design have signified a wider and more adventurous use of paper and particularly a consciousness of the role of paper in visual communication. Unusual and fine quality papers have taken on far greater importance in areas such as graphic design, illustration, design for corporate identity, packaging and studio photography for advertising. Designers are personally specifying paper to be used for a job, rather than leaving the choice entirely in the hands of their printers. Paper merchants are setting up advisory teams to work closely with design companies in order to cater for the increasing complexity and breadth of paper specification. In addition to the grades for commercial printing, fine-quality papers, traditionally used by artists and craftsmen, have found their way into design usage. The trend towards 'pastiche' in design of the late 1980s, led to the rediscovery of papers as diverse as papyrus and antique-looking, handprinted end papers. Fine paper suppliers have unexpectedly had to find unusual papers to fit design concepts, often bearing little relationship to the traditional purpose of the sheet. The designer may use its visual qualities, its texture or its performance when worked on in diverse media to achieve an effective result.

REPRODUCTION OF DECORATIVE PAPERS

The availability of swift methods of high quality reproduction have made it possible to take a sheet of decorative paper, 'scan' it and thereafter use the image as an integral part of a design. Graphic designers may then, with computer-based technology, overlay further images or type, manipulating the image to their needs, and the final art work will often be reproduced by laser printing methods. I will not attempt to explain the technology, but to discuss the implications for the decorative papermaker. First, there

has been a great increase in interest in decorative papers, from hand marbled and block printed papers to patterned Japanese and oriental papers. Enter High Street shops and you will find these papers reproduced on book jackets, cosmetic packaging, food packets, brochures, etc. Recently, papers which create a 'period feel' or reflect a nostalgic style have been in seemingly endless demand. However, the issue of copyright and permission to reproduce has become an increasingly difficult area. Many decorative papermakers regard their individual creations as 'original art work' and some will copyright the design. Others, particularly those who form the sheet by hand from a pulp rather than print an image on the surface, have found their work reproduced in prestigious design contexts and have been unable to take issue with the Company involved as their work may be regarded as a 'sheet of paper' and not an' original work of art'. Recent computer-aided design and printing technology have made it possible to transform the decorative sheet into a printed image, bearing little resemblance to the original, particularly when used as a subliminal part of the overall design. Thus papermakers may find it virtually impossible positively to identify their original work and current copyright laws are hard to interpret in the context of an image transformed in such a way. The desire to reproduce and thereby avoid prohibitive costs of using multiple original sheets is a useful source of income to some decorative papermakers and a source of endless concern to others.

FINE PAPERS AND COMMERCIAL PRINTING

Readers of the advertising and design press may have been puzzled by a leading paper merchant offering to provide samples of 'watercolour paper for print'. There is technically no reason why this should not be acceptable, as long fibred, cotton linter papers, which many watercolour sheets are, can be a positive advantage in some offset litho printing jobs. But is this paper the best for the job considering the relatively high cost per sheet ? Clearly the 1980s design boom has encouraged companies to spend large sums of money in promoting their image and the money put forward for corporate identity projects has enabled designers to consider fine artists' papers in their search for a sheet which conveys the required 'message' through its physical qualities. Just as a marketing director may choose a recycled paper to give an ecologically caring feel to the company literature, he or she may also specify an artist's quality paper to convey the feeling of a high-quality limited edition to a prestigious company brochure. The subtlety of a handmade paper compared to the hard, plain feel of some machine made papers has not escaped the designers' attention and often they have tried to find a paper which is uneven and seemingly primitively formed to stress an 'anti-technological feel' and to provide a radical contrast to other printed matter. Craft book-binding has also contributed to recent, small-edition, designed booklets. Simple unsophisticated binding styles such as 'Japanese binding' with a limp cover have been used to enhance the individuality of an edition.

So image-conscious has paper specification for print become amongst leading design groups, that bizarre and impossible requests such as 'paper like the Romans used' are not unknown. It is the paperseller's job to be helpful, however, and the traditional fine quality papers for artists/printmakers, watercolourists, bookbinders, etc., may yet benefit from design and print usage as high sales of these papers will help to keep the specialist paper mills and smaller papermaking outfits in business. The lack of mutual understanding between the fast-moving world of design for commercial print and the more leisurely, small-scale realm of suppliers of paper to fine artists will soon, I feel, be ironed out, particularly if the supplier wishes to remain competitive. I feel also that the innovative uses of these papers by designers, will give back inspiration to the fine arts and the radical combination of traditional papers and new printing technology may save certain papers from being consigned to obscurity.

44 A selection of decorative papers which include (from top to bottom) :
indigo, stencil-dyed *kata-zome paper*, wrinkled *danshi* paper, a yellow-coloured *unryu-shi* paper with red and green added fibres, Japanese 'lace' paper - *Ohgoshi*, brown paper made from flax, *papyrus*, thin Japanese paper, *Inclusions Florales* from Richard de Bas mill, Japanese *shibori-zome* (tie and dye) paper, Indian paper, Japanese *itajime-zome* (fold and die technique).

RECYCLED PAPER

An important source of fibre which is becoming increasingly popular is recycled paper and board. The White Paper on the Environment published by the British government in 1990 proposed the recycling of 50% of appropriate household waste by the year 2000. According to the British Paper and Board Industry Federation, using one tonne of recycled paper can save seventeen trees. For obvious economic reasons paper mills have always used their own waste whether this is trimmings from cutters or rejected paper (known as 'broke'). However as costs of raw materials have risen so has the used of paper products and there is now a much greater supply of waste paper and board than ever before. The industry has developed techniques such as deinking newsprint so that the recycled materials can be processed and mixed with stronger virgin fibres.

However the use of waste pulp has its limitations; the quality of waste paper varies and it is only used for lower grades. It cannot be used if high standards are required, for example, in durability, burst strength or brightness, and supplies cannot be guaranteed to the same extent as for virgin fibres. Though ecologists applaud the increasing popularity of recycled waste paper, this does not affect the responsibility of the major forest product companies to replant more trees than they harvest in order to maintain the supply of high quality timber.

The information about recycled papers is scattered and users must not imagine that all recycled papers are ecologically sound - the term is on a par with 'natural foods' and can mean any number of things. All recycled papers are machinemade and as such have the qualities of that processing. Perhaps not so attractive to the artist who is looking for a fine quality archival-type paper, recycled paper may be of more interest to designers who need to search out accurate information before recommending for print.

Lesley Jones of Paperback UK Ltd., a paper supplier specialising in recycled paper, sets out below her ideas on recycled stock.

RECYCLED PAPER - ITS RISE AND RISE

Over the past two or three decades, public reaction has turned against the throw-away trend of modern society. In the realm of recycled paper and board, the reaction has come late but very swiftly.

Recycled paper has been used for many years in newsprint, packaging and tissue manufacture. Over the past ten years, technology and consumer demand have made it possible to produce high quality printing and writing papers. Availability has improved as paper merchants have realised that selling recycled paper is a commercial proposition. Companies like Greenpeace, Friends of the Earth, and the Bodyshop in the UK have led the way for others to use recycled paper, not only for the photocopier but for high profile promotional material such as catalogues and company reports. Specifying recycled paper is a good way of showing that an environmental policy is being implemented.

Contrary to what most people believe, it is not all about saving trees - recycled papers saves resources. Making trees into paper takes twice the energy and three times as much water as making it from recycled paper. Producing paper from recycled waste means greatly reduced use of (and pollution from) chemicals for pulping and bleaching. Recycled paper reduces the dumping resources as waste - half of all domestic waste is paper and we are rapidly running out of holes in the ground to dump it in. Recycled paper also saves trees; most paper is produced from trees grown as a 'crop', but it makes no sense to increase the environmental pressures caused by such plantations when paper can be recycled.

Although for the most part, recycled paper and board is still strictly utilitarian, it is now perceived to have a beauty of its own in terms of colour feel and texture that is worth revealing and many of the off-white and coloured papers offer lots of exciting options for the designer.

New environmental pressures on business mean that more companies will specify recycled paper; paper specifiers - designers and artists - will need to be aware of the quality, price, potential uses and environmental benefits of recycled paper. With a keen consumer demanding more recycled paper, more knowledgeable paper merchants and printers and committed manufacturers, recycled grades will face and exciting and challenging future in the 1990's.

FANCY PAPERS

Papers that are decorative, marbled, patterned or just plain 'fancy' are capable of provoking an immediate creative response occasionally even more so than the plain sheet chosen for a specific media. Choosing a paper that is different often requires more thought relating to its use but can present a very effective background even to quiet, unassuming work. Many manufacturers, especially the handmade mills, produce delightful and often awe-inspiring papers alongside their standard and serious paper ranges, where the individuality of the paper is a most important factor.

Some of the most astonishing 'fancy' papers are handmade in Japan where tradition has allowed these techniques to become an art and the papers to be recognised worldwide. Special effects include additions of long and/or coloured fibres, pieces of bark, silver and gold flecks, couching in different ways, folding and crumpling papers when wet, spraying of waterjets through a pattern to effect holes in the paper (lace paper), laminating papers with leaves and butterflies sandwiched between the layers. Swirled papers, coarse-fibred papers, etc. (See p.38.) Indian papers, too, can contain exciting ingredients which imbue the papers with a different character to those of the Japanese - more to do with the fibre quality itself , the fibre colour and mixing than specific inclusions (see p. 41).

Marbled and hand-decorated papers are increasingly in demand by stylists and photographers as backgrounds as well as for their traditional use in bookbinding. Styles of marbling vary widely from the intricately combed designs traditionally used for endpapers in bookbinding to the more open and freeform patterns achieved with a variety of inks and techniques. Marbling is delicate and skilled work and machinemade copies of the hand -produced sheets are available at lower cost but often without the lustre and beauty of the original sheet. American hand papermakers in particular are extremely creative in their approach; New York Central Paper Supplies holds an impressive list of handworked (and copyrighted) papers.

Of the handmade European papers, several include indigenous leaves, petals and grasses. Many are made from special plant bases that give the paper a specific colour and quality which differs from the normal cotton linter or linen paper. Several papermakers specialise in shaped papers; note especially Twinrocker in USA who hold stocks of paper of intriguingly interesting shapes and sizes. Many handmade makers produce gentle tints intrinsically characteristic of the makers and, of course, the large sizes and the very heavy weights of some of the handmades make the papers quite outstanding in appearance.

FANCY PAPERS
ABBEY MILLS LAID (Machinemade)
AMATE (Bark cloth)
ARCHES INGRES MBM (Mouldmade)
ARTLAID (Machinemade)
COLOURED GLASSINES (Machinemade)
COLORPLAN (Machinemade)
ELEPHANT HIDE (Machinemade)
HAND MARBLED PAPERS
HAHNEMÜHLE INGRES (Mouldmade)
INDIAN PAPERS (Handmade)
INGRES PAPERS (See p.105)
JAPANESE DECORATIVE (often Handmade)
KHADI DECORATIVE PAPERS (Handmade)
LARROQUE FLEURS (Handmdade)
PAPYRUS (Handmade or Imitation)
PATTERNED TRACING PAPER (Machinemade)
PLANT PAPERS MILL (Handmade)
RICHARD DE BAS INCLUSIONS FLORALES (Handmade)
SPECIAL MAKES (Hand- or Mouldmade)
TAPA (Bark cloth)
THAI PAPERS (Hand- or Machinemade)
TWINROCKER (Handmade)
VENEER PAPERS

COLOURED PAPERS

'Beirut reds' and 'Belgian light pinks' were terms used in the papermaking trade in Europe in the Middle Ages to describe the colours of papers made from rags collected from as far afield as the Middle East. Early manufacturers of coloured papers also used a host of naturally found substances such as berries, herbs, barks, minerals, soot, madder, saffron, woad, indigo, etc. and to make the colour-fast, substances such as salt, rusty nails and vinegar were all used mostly with disastrous effects!

Historically, various methods exist to colour a sheet of handmade paper - dipping it into a bath of colour, rubbing or brushing on dye. Today, however much investigation has gone into the quality of colouring with permanence and lightfastness in mind. Two basic methods exist to add colour to a paper and both are applied to the fibres in their wet state :

• Pigments. These are inert particles suspended in water and are harder to attach themselves to the fibres
• Dyes. These are chemical substances either natural or synthetic.

The range of coloured papers available for sale is vast. Coloured handmades are probably the most individual. Several mills have a large range of coloureds (note especially Twinrocker and Fabriano ranges) and many have coloured tints that have specially developed to suit their practices or traditions. Only the largest mouldmade producers have a standard range of coloureds and occasionally this includes an interesting range of Ingres papers too. By far the largest manufacture of coloured papers is machine-made papers of which there are enormous varieties and choice is often dependent on what your stockist holds (see also 'Ingres Papers' p.105).

COLOURED PAPERS
ARTEMEDIA ART & PASTEL PAPER (Machinemade)
CANFORD COVER PAPER (Machinemade)
CANSON MI -TEINTES (Machinemade)
COLORPLAN (Machinemade)
DIEU DONNÉ (Handmade)
DUCHENE PAPERS (Handmade)
FABRIANO MURILLO (Mouldmade)
FABRIANO ROMA (Handmade)
FABRIANO RUSTICUS (Machinemade)
FABRIANO TIZIANO (Mouldmade)
HAHNEMÜHLE BUGRA BUTTEN (Mouldmade)
JAPANESE PAPERS (Hand and machinemade)
LARROQUE DUCHENE (Handmade)
MOULIN DU POMBIE (Handmade)
RICHARD DE BAS (Handmade)
ST ARMAND (Handmade)
STONEHENGE (Machinemade)
STRATHMORE 50 (Machinemade)
THAI PAPERS (Hand and machinemade)
TWINROCKER (Handmade)
TWO RIVERS (Handmade)
TUMBA TRE KRONOR (Machinemade)
VELOUR PASTEL (Machinemade)

MOULDMADE INGRES PAPERS

This coloured paper is named after the French artist, Jean August Dominique Ingres (1780-1867). It is suitable for many processes - drawing, pastel, crayon, charcoal or conté - plus many printing techniques and is also widely used by bookbinders. The quality of its fibre structure, often incorporating small pieces of cut wool, lends a certain distinction to the sheets and most grades have a Not or Rough surface. Ingres papers are generally laid papers and incorporate the personal watermarks of the manufacturers :

• ARCHES MBM INGRES
Mouldmade 75 per cent rag, with a neutral pH and laid surface. Two deckles and available in white only. Made by the original Michallet papermakers.
• FABRIANO INGRES
This series is vailable in two weights - 90gsm with sixteen colours, 160gsm with nineteen colours which reflect the subtle beauty of the Italian Fabriano range of makings.
• HAHNEMÜHLE INGRES
Mouldmade range made from sulphite pulp, neutral pH with an antique white, Not and slightly textured, laid surface. Often referred to as Dresden Ingres. Available in range of colours including black and white.
• ZERKALL INGRES
A very subtle and sophisticated range of Ingres papers made on a cylinder mould machine with two finishes. Two watermarks- the word 'Ingres' and a small lion - are in the paper. Chemical wood furnish with a neutral pH, and available with a smooth or rough surface in a range of fifteen colours.

There are many other machinemade Ingres ranges, all differing slightly in colour and tone. Not all suppliers stock the full colours of these ranges, often only the most popular.
Examples are :
CANSON INGRES VIDALON (Machinemade)
GUARRO CASAS INGRES (Machinemade)
LANA INGRES (Machinemade)
SCHUT INGRES (Old Dutch Ingres) (Machinemade)
TUMBA INGRES (Machinemade)

BLACK PAPERS

Black papers were traditionally made for white chalk and pastel drawing so that a heightened effect of chiaroscura could be obtained. Today they are not only used for white drawings but also white printing, pen and ink, and wax crayon too plus colourd pastels and chalks.

BLACK PAPERS
BLACK BACK-DROP PAPER (very large rolls)
COLORPLAN (Machinemade)
CANSON MI-TEINTES (Machinemade)
HAHNEMÜLE CHARCOAL Machinemade)
HAHNEMÜLE BUGRA BUTTEN (Mouldmade)
DUCHENE (Handmade)
ELEPHANT HIDE (Machinemade)
FABRIANO NO 3 (Machinemade)
FABRIANO INGRES (Mouldmade)
FABRIANO TIZIANO (Mouldmade)
FABRIANO MURILLO (Mouldmade)
JAPANESE CREPE (Handmade)
MEIRAT VELASQUEZ (Handmade)
STRATHMORE CHARCOAL (Machinemade)
VELIN ARCHES (Mouldmade)

SPECIAL SIZES AND SURFACES

If there is a demand, paper manufacturers will often accommodate special requests. In the 1990s, artists appear to want to work in a large size and consequently more manufacturers are producing mouldmade paper in rolls than ever before; variety and individuality are keynotes as far as choice is concerned and the range of surfaces and weights of fine quality papers available is greater than ever before. It is unlikely that you will find one stockist that holds all these rolls.

FINE PAPER ON ROLLS

ANW DRAWING (Machinemade)

ARCHES AQUARELLE (Mouldmade)

ARCHES 88 (Mouldmade)

ARCHES LAVID FIDELIS (EN TOUT CAS) (Mouldmade)

BOCKINGFORD (Mouldmade)

CANSON 'C À GRAIN (Machinemade)

CANSON MI TEINTES (Machinemade)

COVENTRY RAG (Machinemade)

FABRIANO NO 4 (Machinemade)

FABRIANO ACCADEMIA (Machinemade)

GUARRO CASAS AQUARELLE (Mouldmade)

GUARRO DRAWING CARTRIDGE (Machinemade)

JAPANESE MACHINEMADE (Various - e.g. *Chiri, Sumi, Kinwashi, Kozo, Natsume, Unryu*)

JPP BREAD AND BUTTER (Machinemade)

LANAQUARELLE (Mouldmade)

LENOX (Machinemade)

MOULIN DU ROY (Machinemademade)

MONTVAL (Machinemademade)

BFK RIVES (Mouldmade)

SAUNDERS WATERFORD (Mouldmade)

SOMERSET (Mouldmade)

STONEHENGE (Machinemade)

STRATHMORE ALEXIS (Machinemade)

VELIN ARCHES BLANC (Mouldmade)

VELIN ARCHES NOIR (Mouldmade)

THE LARGEST HANDMADE SHEET IN THE WORLD

In Japan, at the 1983 Kyoto paper conference, the papermakers from the Ueyama Papermill, Eichizen, succeeded in making the biggest sheet of paper in the world. The nature of the traditional process of forming a sheet of paper has been limited by human scale. The largest paper size an individual can form using the Nagashizuki method is 180x90 cm. The demonstration at the conference consisted of a sheet 5.5 x 5.5 metres being formed by hand, employing the assistance of twelve craftsmen.

45 Twelve Japanese craftspeople hand forming the largest sheet of handmade paper in the world in Kyoto, Japan

LARGE SIZED PAPERS

Rolls of paper plus
ATLANTIS DRAWING PAPER (Machinemade)
ATLANTIS HERITAGE (Machinemade)
ARCHES AQUARELLE (Mouldmade)
JPP BREAD & BUTTER (Machinemade)
KOZO FUSUMA (Handmade)
LENOX (Machinemade)
MEIRAT PAPERS (Handmade)
PAPEL DI AMATE (Handmade)
BFK RIVES (Mouldmade)
SAUNDERS WATERFORD (Mouldmade)
SOMERSET (Mouldmade)
SNOWDON CARTRIDGE (Machinemade)
STONEHENGE (Machinemade)
TWINROCKER (Handmade)
VELIN ARCHES BLANC (Machinemade)

SMALL SIZED PAPERS

CAPELLADES (Handmade)
DIEU DONNÉ (Handmade)
DUCHENE FOLIOS (Handmade)
HMP PAPERS (Handmade)
JAPANESE PAPERS (Handmade)
INDIAN PAPERS (Handmade)
LESSEBO (Handmade)
MEIRAT (Handmade)
MOULIN DU VERGER (Handmade)
PLANT PAPERS MILL (Handmade)
RICHARD DE BAS CANTON LAID (Handmade)
TERVAKOSKI (Handmade)
TWINROCKER(Handmade)
WOOKEY HOLE MILL (Handmade)
Note also the stationery ranges of many of the small handmade mills and
ZERKALL, ARCHES, FABRIANO, RICHARD DE BAS, TWINROCKER, etc.

EXTRA ROUGH SURFACE PAPERS

ARCHES AQUARELLE ROUGH (Mouldmade)
DUCHENE COLOMBE (Handmade)
FABRIANO ARTISTICO (Mouldmade)
FABRIANO ESPORTAZIONE (Mouldmade)
J.B.GREEN PASTELESS BOARD (Old handmade)
MEIRAT (Handmade)
MOULIN DU VERGER (Handmade)
MOULIN DU FLEURAC (Handmade)
RICHARD DE BAS (Handmade)
SAUNDERS WATERFORD ROUGH (Mouldmade)

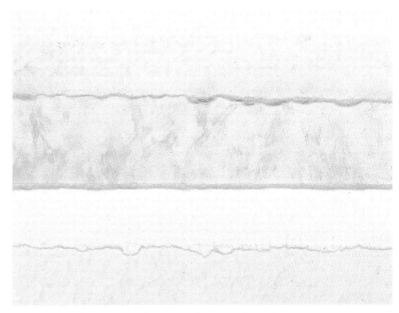

46   A selection of extra rough surface papers (from top to bottom):
Fabriano Esportazione, Old Dutch Aquarelpaper, Meirat board weight, Moulin du Verger pur cotton

OLD PAPERS

Handmade papers can age beautifully. Much can be discerned by looking at an old sheet of paper and Peter Bower, papermaker and paper historian, has recently completed the first part of a study of the papers used by JMW Turner and held in the Turner Bequest at the Tate Gallery, London, culminating in an exhibition and book *Turner's Papers: A Study of the Manufacture. Selection and Use of his Drawing Papers 1787-1820* , published by Tate Gallery Publications. He describes below some of what can be gleaned from old papers.

Perhaps millions of makings of handmade papers survive as books, letters, documents, prints, drawings and watercolours and, perhaps surprisingly, as unused and often usable blank paper, prized by many for its rich warm tones, its great internal and surface strengths and for its stability and durability. Old papers are also collected both for their watermarks and for the information contained within them. Every sheet of paper contains a history of its making - a surprising amount of information as to the origin, purpose and manufacture of a sheet can be deduced from a careful examination of any sheet of old handmade paper. Whilst many of the finer details can only be revealed under a microscope or through destructive testing, much can be learnt without resorting to sophisticated techniques.

Paper is usually examined closely in terms of its function, its date and where and who made it, either with a view to its use or when already worked on, for dating, for attribution or in order to understand more clearly a particular artist or craftsman's working methods and approach to his or her materials. But all such examinations are subject to certain limitations. It is not always possible to determine the original designed use of the paper or particular artists' original intentions because time and the hand of man have conspired to blur the distinctions, have hidden the original information. The trimming of edges, some conservation treatments and sometimes the artist's own preparation of the paper prior to working, have changed the nature and appearance of the sheet. It must be remembered also that many of the behavioral characteristics of particular papers will only become apparent while a sheet is actually being worked on.

Any artist's choice of a particular paper for a particular work is of necessity subjective and relates directly to their actual methods of working and vision of the work in hand. It is often the highly specific and sometimes idiosyncratic choices of paper that individual artists make that contribute so much to their work.

The examination of old paper, whether it has been worked on or not, involves the consideration of a very wide range of details. To determine the original function of a particular sheet the size, weight, colour, tone, bulk, opacity and texture of the sheet, the depth and degree of sizing, the fibre used, the presence of dyes or loadings, and sometimes the design or position of the watermark (if one is lucky enough to find one present)in the sheet all need to be examined. Some of these details are relatively simple to determine and need no real equipment other than a lens, a trained eye and an understanding of the various ways in which paper can be worked - watercolour, engraving, lithography, calligraphy, letterpress, etc. But many of the finer details of the manufacture structure and capabilities of the particular paper only become apparent under a microscope or via destructive testing.

Watermarks are always of interest but in themselves are not always to be trusted; both names and dates can be misleading. Marks were copied by other mills, moulds changed hands, dates were sometimes only changed irregularly. The design of watermarks exhibit many differences, dependent on the country of origin and the changing fashions of the time. Lettering styles and pictorial images change and evolve, the position of watermarks in the sheet shift. Even faced with only a part of a watermark in a torn or trimmed sheet, it is sometimes possible to match or recognise the style of a particular papermaker. The actual wire profile, not just of the watermark, but of the forming surface itself can often give some guide to the date, origin and type of paper. Moulds changed as wire technology developed and the changes can be read in the sheet, in the traces of different gauges and configurations of wire. Such impressions are more or less visible depending on the choice and beating of the fibre and the weight and the finishing and opacity of the sheet.

The vast range of papers made throughout Europe over the past centuries are gradually giving up their secrets. Much can be learnt from their study, not as an end in itself, but as an aid to the present design of papers and to increase our understanding of the work of so many artists.

DEALING IN OLD PAPERS

Occasionally, artists, having bought up a stock of paper and kept it for a long time, decide they no longer want to use it. They sell it back to a dealer or agent from whom it finds its way onto the market to be sold again Mills close and remaining stocks are sold to agents who find suitable customers. John van Oosterom of JvO Papers describes below some of the reasons why he likes specifically to trade in old papers :

"This, my boy, is the Chateau Lafite of paper."

"Well, Sir ... it may be ... and if so, then I shall be delighted to buy it from you and put it on my list along with many others such as the Tub Sized Fourdrinier made 102gsm Cream Wove Cartridge which you by the same token would probably describe as Plonk."

"And there you could be so wrong, for that plonk might just have a perfect surface finish for the fine woodblock printers whereas your lovely old 1916 Hot Pressed Whatman Watercolour paper could be useless for watercolour if it has crazed sizing."

"Crazed sizing! One man's corked wine is another man's vinegar - quick, ring up a printmaker..."

Old papers have their quirks. Why then deal in them? J v O Papers does, as a special interest which informs our main activity supplying the many hand and mouldmades, European and Oriental, in production at the moment. Naturally enough, knowledge of old makings is helpful when specifying a new one, quite apart from the pleasure of selling old papers in their own right.

Anyone involved in the production of a good printmaking sheet might do well to study the eggshell-like character of the old J Green Mouldmade (perhaps without the paint flakes which fell from the mill ceiling into the pulp of one of the makings); those makers of some of the rather soft offerings which are said to be hard watercolour paper, should try painting on a truly hardened gelatine sized sheet before making their claims; as for printings and writings, the wonderful pearly translucency in an all-rag gelatine sized sheet which has been pressed between hot plates or rollers, seems to be a thing of the past. Its equivalent is to be found only rarely in present day papers - mouldmades such as the lightweight smooth Zerkall printings, or more nearly, in the handmade Chatham Vellum H.P. made until recently by Barcham Green - yet even

these have not the look of a rolled T. Edmonds mouldmade or some the old hot pressed handmade ledger papers.

All is not lost. Despite the changes in economic and practical factors affecting papermaking, it is cheering that there are new mills setting out to make handmade paper in this country, which may once more have the ability to produce sheets that are in the more compressed English manner, as well as the rather softer, bulkier sheets in the French tradition which seem to result from the everyday use of a cotton linter pulp and Aquapel sizing. Such a choice is important for those seeking something different from the run of mouldmades such as Arches and Rives printmakings, which though excellent sheets in their own right have come to seem 'run of the mill', because of their sales success. There are many good mouldmades available now, but there are always buyers for old sheets, which suggests that their qualities are, if not better, at least different from papers currently in production. It would be wonderful to see some of those qualities reappear in new makings.

So what is characteristic of old paper as opposed to new? Take, for example, a modern sheet of watercolour paper made from cotton linter which has been sized with Aquapel only and lay a wash on it. So far so good, providing the wash does not sink into the surface, thus losing the luminosity which results from light striking the paper surface and returning through the paint film. Assuming that does not happen, try lifting the wash off again in order to make some adjustment. You may be partially successful, though any rubbing may have disturbed the fibres. Had you used an old linen paper with a gelatine sizing of sufficient depth upon the surface (tub sizing), the wash could have been lifted off clearly, taking a little of the gelatine with it but leaving enough to repaint without loss of luminosity and without impairing the paper surface. This is not to say that you cannot buy gelatine sized sheets today, but gelatine size hardens over time (sometimes to the point where crazing, i.e. cracking, destroys its effectiveness) and it is in part this which toughens it against very rough treatment. By comparison, sheets made from cotton are more vulnerable to abrasion than those made from linen, and if sized only with Aquapel, which is mixed in with the pulp, are the same through the whole thickness of the sheet and therefore lack the concentration of size on the surface which is where watercolourists may need it most.

In old papers, also, there are many interesting dimensions for specific purposes, with glorious names like 'Double Nicanee', 'Extra Large Lump' and 'Double Double Small Hand'. There are interesting watermarks, wiremarks, fibres, blanket or felt marks, fine surface finishes and a tremendous colour range within the term 'azure' alone, with papermakers using all manner of dyes as and when they became available. Smalt, one of the earliest, is a finely ground cobalt blue glass, which is inclined to sink to the back of the sheet during formation, thus tinting the sheet more on one face than the other. Over time it may turn a greener hue. Prussian blue, indigo and synthetic ultramarine all make their appearance in sheets through the nineteenth century and on, and with age take on a subtlety which is rarely present in the colouring of a modern sheet.

Of course, it would be absurd to insist that just because papers are old, they are good. Not all are well made and many one comes across have a substance below 150gsm which anyway limits what they may be used for. It is a fact that uniformity is essential for many present users of paper, but for the individual wanting something special, character is of the essence. Old paper has that in abundance.

ARCHIVAL AND CONSERVATION PAPERS

In their catalogue, the archival suppliers Atlantis define 'archival' papers as not only acid free but also lignin and sulphur free. To conservators and curators, the importance of a paper's archival pedigree is defined by the need for longevity - of the paper itself and the other materials it will be in contact with. Lignin, the fibre bonding material found in wood, is an undesirable impurity in wood pulp paper.

A number of paper agents specialise in archival qualities and often have special 'conservation' makings to bookbinders' and paper conservators' specifications. Moulin du Verger, a mill founded in 1539 and located near Angoulême, makes two standard shades of handmade restoration papers exclusively for conservation, using mixed cotton, linen and manilla fibres on eighteenth century style moulds. The conservation value of such paper is its visual and functional similarity to the historic documents it is used to repair and compliment.

Some conservation applications require papers deliberately specified to breach the general rule of conservation papers - that they should be biased towards alkalinity on the pH scale. The highly sensitive emulsions of acid-stabilised, silver-image photographs, for instance, are damaged by free

alkalinity, sulphur or chlorates that may be present in some cheaper, alkaline-buffered papers.

Other archival papers are specified to provide strong and safe storage for archive materials and museum artifacts. Allied to this range is often an archival boxboard, designed as a safe boxmaking material for archives and libraries.

There is a long tradition in the Far East of papermaking using the inner fibre of mulberry and other local tree species to produce extraordinarily light and translucent papers of exceptional purity and great individual character, some of the fibres have a natural smell that is repellent to insects. Japanese tissues (and some of the machinemade paper rolls with weights as low as 4.5gsm) are used by paper and painting conservators in repair and lamination, where their unobtrusive, translucent quality, porosity, high strength-to-weight ratio and chemical purity are not matched by any other papers.

THE AVAILABILITY OF FINE PAPERS FOR ARTISTS HAS NEVER BEEN SO GOOD....

Paper suppliers often have a great knowledge and experience of papers. If you give your paper supplier an exact description of what you are looking for, whilst this book may recommend, for example, twenty watercolour papers, he or she may well suggest only three or four papers that would perfectly suit your especial requirements.

John Purcell, the well-known British paper supplier, describes his views of the fine artists' paper trade circa 1991.

I was reading an article published during the thirties which stated "The best permanent paper is most carefully made from linen rags (a small percentage of cotton is permissible)." If this were to be taken as gospel, then we would have to retitle this piece to say that the availability of fine papers has never been so bad. Times have changed and it is no longer possible to manufacture paper from linen rags, as it is not possible to collect these in their pure form - they are contaminated with synthetics in our everyday clothes. We now subscribe to the view that papers made from cotton (either waste cotton after spinning or cotton linters from the cotton plant, is an excellent raw material) are the best papers for any medium. Alternative raw materials are used, for instance flax in the Meirat hand papers, lokta in the Nepalese hand made papers and many different fibres are used in the manufacture of Japanese papers.

In the intervening years however, a great deal has been learned about properties of paper and how they are affected by the presence or lack of ingredients other than the actual raw material that is the source of cellulose fibre that is the basic ingredient of paper. For instance we know the damage caused by acidic compounds in paper and by acid migration into paper from surrounds and contact with other materials. Therefore today's good quality papers which are for instance alum free (alum is an acidic compound widely used in papermaking), buffered with calcium carbonate, sized with neutral (i.e. non-acidic) chemicals are, in terms of their long life properties, superior to papers made before this knowledge was widely available to paper suppliers and more importantly, paper users.

The supply chain for good papers for use by artists starts with the manufacturing plant - The Paper Mill. Paper is made all over the world in anything from a one person cottage industry mill to an enormous plant where one papermaking machine can occupy several acres of buildings and one mill can employ many hundreds of people. In both cases, the manufacturer has to bring the product to market. This bringing to market can be achieved in many different ways. The smaller handmade mill might well prefer personal contact and recommendation and encourage visitors who might buy. This method of marketing cannot work on a large scale and the larger mills (and many smaller mills) have a distribution policy with specialist contributors to reach their end users.

Quite often in news matters, the explosion in communication technology gives rise to the expression 'Global Village' to give an idea of how the whole world is more readily accessible to all. The concept of the Global Village is quite naturally applicable to the supply of fine papers for artists.

Paper distributors are able to communicate quickly and effectively with mills all over the world by telephone and fax. Paper made in one part of the world can be sent by air and be 5,000 miles away being used in a matter or two or three days. Therefore with the effective combination of mill and distributor, it matters not in what country an artist is working; the right paper could and should be available without too much difficulty.

Within this whole industry to make papers readily available there is a lot of specialist knowledge available to the artist. At the other end of a telephone call are answers to questions such as "I want to do a large linocut on waterleaf paper without a join - what can I use?" or "I'm producing a large watercolour for a commission, what is the best paper for this?"

By far the vast majority of artists' paper requirements are supplied from existing stock held for immediate delivery or collection from warehouses or shops. There is however a significant amount of paper supplied that is specially made for a particular paper project. This could either be handmade, mouldmade or machinemade. Typically, it is possible to have a special making of handmade paper for as little as 1000 sheets, or even less. For a mouldmade paper, this would need to be the equivalent of about 8000 sheets of Imperial 140lb paper (approximately one tonne), for a machine made paper, anything from two to five tonnes depending on specifications needed.

With respect to the papers supplied from stock, if you are in any doubt about the paper suitability, talk to your supplier. Any good supplier will welcome enthusiastic interest and intelligent enquiry. At this stage it also appears appropriate to encourage experimentation. It is a source of continuing surprise to me, the myriad of uses to which paper is put. However there is one caution. If you use a paper in the way that is recommended by the supplier, then you have a come-back on that supplier in the rare event of a paper being faulty or substandard. You may not have a come-back if you use a paper in a non-standard way.

47 John Purcell, David Dodsworth and Ian Mortimer making a 2x2 metre sheet of paper at Meirat handmade paper mill in Madrid in Spain.

If whatever you are producing, for instance a commission or publication, requires enough paper then a special making could be the best way to proceed. Some examples of special makings from recent times are shown here as a guide to what is achievable -
• Standard specification of paper wither in a special size, colour or weight
• Standard specification with or without special size, colour or weight with a

customised watermark
• Change of surface characteristic, smoother or rougher
• Addition or withdrawal of additives, for instance addition of sizing to make a paper harder or removal of sizing to make a paper absorbent.

Elsewhere in this book you will find lists of the manufacturers. Some of them are smaller handmade mills, some larger hand- or mouldmade mills. The papers from handmade mills are not always readily available ex-stock in depth for a quick delivery. Knowledge of the mill's limitations in terms of level of stock holding, delivery times if stock is not carried and stocking and distribution policy will help in making the correct decision in terms of which paper to use. Some of the mills who do work with distributors can either be large companies, or individual shops in the High Street.

Whatever the size of the paper mill or paper distributor and whatever your paper requirements, there is a hard-working professional person somewhere waiting to supply your needs and be able to demonstrate that the availability of fine papers for artists has never been so good.

APPENDICES

Often when I am in in front of a sheet of paper...

I cannot avoid thinking how unpretentious this

inanimate material is, a material which since its

invention, has given new possibilities of

recording, from the greatest to the most

modest expression of artistic creativity

Marc Balakjian Artist

A SHORT HISTORY OF PAPERMAKING

Paper is thought to have been invented in China some 200 years B.C. and certainly examples of paper discovered along with wooden tablets carrying that date exist. The earliest examples of paper were made of silk floss or flax but were of poor quality for writing on and were mainly used for wrapping.

The invention of paper is usually accredited to Ts'ai Lun in A.D. 105, who was at the time chief eunuch to the Chinese Emperor, and head of the Imperial Supply Department. Ts'ai Lun was the first to organise the production of paper on a large scale and managed to award himself the patents for doing so. China at this time was already a bureaucratic society and as such required documents and written records in abundance. Therefore, a material lighter in weight and easier to store and transport than existing wooden tablets and silk cloth had to be developed.

The important role that Chinese written characters or ideographs played in this unification should be noted here owing to its ability to be understood by peoples speaking different languages throughout China as well as in countries like Korea and Japan, whose cultures were influenced by China. It was about this time that paper began to be used for written records and methods of papermaking using *kozo* and *mulberry* bark began to appear. These plant fibres were already in use for the manufacture of clothes.

A development in the 9th century China was the use of *bamboo* as a fibre anticipating the development of wood pulp in 18th century European papermaking. By the 10th century, watermarking and the use of paper for money and printing were all in operation. The manufacture of paper spread from China to Korea. In 610, the priest Ramjing from Koryo in Korea went to Japan to provide instruction in the making of brushes, ink and paper. This was the begining of serious paper production in Japan.

Paper came to the West via the old silk routes as they crossed Turkestan, Persia and Syria and, by the end of the 5th century, paper was in use all over Central Asia. Following a raid on Chinese territory, papermaking moved westward via Samarkand. Chinese papermakers were forced to disclose the secrets of the craft of papermaking in exchange for their freedom or their lives. Production was established at Samarkand in A.D. 751 using the abundant local flax and hemp to produce paper of soft, fibrous appearance. In A.D. 795, a second factory was started in Baghdad using Chinese papermakers. From then on the craft spread throughout North Africa. The Arabs were to introduce several innovations including standard sizes and colours, a method of antiquing papers plus the introduction of wire in making a mould.

Not until more than a thousand years had passed and Spain was captured by the Moors did papermaking reach Europe. The Arabs wasted no time in establishing local mills for the production of paper. The first mill was founded at Cordoba in 1036, followed by another in 1144 at the town of Xativa (or Jativa) on the Iberian Peninsula. One of the earliest examples of paper made in Spain can be found in the monastry of Santo Domingo of Silos near Burgos, included in a 10th century manuscrips, most of its pages are made of vellum, the remainder is of paper made from long-fibred linen and sized with starch similar to classic Arabian paper. Spain at this time was the main centre of classical learning, medicine and mathematics in Europe, a role in which paper played no small part.

Papermaking is next found in Italy and thought to have come via Spain or Sicily with the Crusaders. The first reference to paper production in Italy is 1275-1276 in the town of Fabriano still famous for its fine handmade, cylinder-mould and machine-made papers. Other mills were soon in production throughout Italy. Fabriano is important to the development of paper for its introduction of rag paper, sized with an animal gelatine glue. This technique was much favoured by scribes and led to a greater acceptance of paper as a substitute for parchment, allowing the sharp quill pens of the day to flow freely without scratching up the surface of the paper and the ink bleeding into the fibres. The technique of writing with a pen, predominant in Europe, as against calligraphic writing with a brush used in Asia, was to define the characteristically different feel of European paper from this period onward to that of China or Japan.

By the 14th century, Italy has surpassed both Spain and Damascus in the production of paper. An early contribution of European papermaking was the invention of the stamping mill made from heavy timbers driven in a vertical pounding action by a waterwheel to beat and defibre pulp in water and was in used by the late 13th century.

This machine produced very good, heavily hydrated fibres, superior to those produced on the later Hollander beater. However, because some of the stampers were shod with iron and iron contamination of the paper occurred from this time which is now thought to be responsible for some foxing in paper.

Production was slow to move northwards to the rest of Europe, but by the middle of 14th century there were mills near Languedoc and Angoulême which is still functioning in the form of Papeteries Moulin du Verger de Puymoyen, famous for its foolscap watermark, first used in 1539.

By the end of the century, papermaking centres were established throughout France. Evidence suggests that papermills existed in Augsburg, Cologne and Mainz by 1320. In 1390, using artisans from Lombardy, Ulman Stromer equipped a mill near Nuremberg and is probably the first papermill to be featured in a published book and illustrated by the Swiss artist, Jost Amman. The illustration is one of the 139 trades and professions shown in the book. Papermaking had become established in the Netherlands by 1586 with the Lunipart and van Aelst mill near Dordrecht although a mill at Gennep existed as early as 1428. Following the Eighty Years War, (1568-1648), Holland became a major producer of paper when Amsterdam became a haven for refugees and tradesmen from all over Europe. By 1579, following the invention of the printing press, distinctions were being drawn between printing and writing papers.

The first paper made in England was produced around 1490 at the mill of John Tate near Stevenage in Hertfordshire. The second mill in England was established some fifty yeares later at Fen Ditton by Thomas Thirlby who was late to become Bishop of Ely. The best known of England's early mills was started in 1558 at Dartford, Kent by the German born John Spilman who held an exclusive patent from Queen Elizabeth to collect rags and make paper. In 1610, a mill was founded at Wookey Hole where paper is still being made today. During the 18th and 19th centuries, England established itself as a major producer of high quality papers with mills such as Hodgkinsons at Wookey Hole and the famous Whatman mill at Maidstone in Kent.

Papermaking was first introduced into the Americas by the Spanish near Mexico City around 1580. Paper-like substances were in use by the Mayas and Aztecs before the arrival of the Spanish. Similar to Hawaiian *tapa* they were made from the beaten bark of fig or mulberry trees which was then smoothed into sheets. This technique is still used by the Indians off Southern Mexico. However, in pure terms, these substances are not classified as paper.

The first papermill in North America was established in Pennsylvania on the Wissahickon Creek near Germantown by William Rittenhause. Other mills were soon established. The Ivy Mill, owned by Thomas Willcox was a training ground for other papermakers and was distinguished by producing paper for Benjamin Franklin's printing and publishing activities.

Late 18th and 19th century developments in the technology of printing along with increased population and literacy, stimulated papermakers to look for ways of mechanising the production of paper. The first papermaking machine was invented by the Frenchman, Nicholas Louis Robert, an employee of the Didot mill in France. Robert's brother-in-law, John Gamble, took out a British patent in 1801 which was developed and financed in England by Henry and Seale Fourdrinier with the aid of a young machinist named Brian Donkin who erected a self-acting machine at Hertfordshire in 1803, the effectiveness of which created a sensation.

The basic principle of the Fourdrinier machine is for paper pulp suspended in water to be poured onto a moving hoorizontal length of web which vibrates from side to side causing the fibres to interlock with each other. It then travels under what is known as a Dandy roll which presses out the majority of water at the same time as impressing the watermarks or laid-lines onto the paper pulp. It is then transferred to heated drying cylinders and finally reeled into a large roll at the end of the process, perfectly dry. Paper made on Fourdrinier style machines is now responsible for the majority of the world's paper production.

Another kind of papermaking machine to appear at this time was the cylinder-mould machine. Being a slower moving process it is capable of producing paper similar in appearance and feel to handmade paper. Although a number of individual were working independently on a machine of this type, it was John Dickenson in England who produced the first commercially viable machine in 1809.

By the end of the 19th century, the history of papermaking had gone full circle when paper machines were introduced to the semi-colonial China and Japan after 1853. The American fleet demanded (at the point of a gunboat), the opening of diplomatic and commercial relations between the USA and Japan followed by the opening of diplomatic relations with England, Prussian and France. Much interest at that time was expressed in the use of vegetable fibres in Japanese papermaking and because rag was not used in Japanese paper, an English trader at the time hit upon the idea of importing rags to Europe for papermaking and by the end of 1861 had shipped 1300 tonnes of rags to England although the removing of the colours did not prove to be an easy task. The first papermaking machine in Japan was a Fourdrinier machine, seventy eight inches wide, imported from England by an American firm, The Walsh and Hall Company, for the Ogi Paper Mill near Tokyo in 1875. Construction of the Ogi Paper Mill was directed by a young English engineer, Frank Cheethmen, who for a period of three years with the assistance of an American machine minder, Thomas Bottomley, ran production at the mill until they had trained their Japanese successors. Japan now produces 10% of the world's paper and pulp and is second only to the USA.

A CHRONOLOGY OF PAPERMAKING

BC

300	Writing surface made from residual silk floss in China
100	Paper probably produced in China

AD

105	Development by Ts'ai Lun of papermaking methods in China
300	Paper made in cases in Central Asia
500	Paper made in Korea
610	Paper made in Japan
650	Paper made in Nepal
700	Starch rice flour and sizing introduced into Japan
794	Paper made in Baghdad (Iraq)
850	Papermaking spreads from China via Nepal to India
900	Paper made in Cairo, Egypt
1036	Paper made in Cordoba, Spain
1100	Papermaking spreads from Baghdad to Cairo to Fez
1144	Papermaking in Xatvia in Spain
1189	Paper made at Hérault, France
1260	Paper made at Fabriano in Italy
1388	Paper made at Augsburg in Germany
1390	Paper made at Nuremberg in Germany
1400	Paper made at Marly in Switzerland
1411	Paper made in Portugal
1428	Paper made in Gennap in Holland
1443	Paper made at Allenwinden Mill, Basle, Switzerland
1490	Paper made by John Tate in Hertfordshire, England
1491	Paper made in Poland
1499	Paper made in Bohemia
1532	Paper made in Motala, Sweden
1536	Paper made in Bavaria
1540	Paper made in Denmark
1546	Paper made in Rumania
1558	Paper made by John Spilman at Dartford in Kent
1565	Paper made in Russia
1570	Paper made by Sten Bille in Denmark
1590	Paper made at Dalry in Scotland
1610	Paper made at Wookeyhole in England
1620	Romani family establish mill at Capellades in Spain
1690	Paper made in Moscow, Russia
	Paper made by William Rittenhouse in Germanstown, USA
1693	Paper made at Lessebo in Sweden
1698	Paper made at Oslo in Norway
1706	Paper made in Wales
1726	Paper made by William Bradford in New Jersey, USA
1802	Paper made in Quebec in Canada
1818	Tervakoski Paper Mill established in Finland
1900	Paper made in Florida in USA

Oldest known watermark from a document in Bologna date 1282

PAPER SIZES AND CONVERSIONS

IMPERIAL SYSTEM OF PAPER WEIGHTS AND SIZES IN BRITAIN

The Imperial system was the name applied to those weights and measures appointed by statute to be used throughout the United Kingdom in 1836 and today is a term loosely applied to the same traditional sizes and linked weights of the pre-metrication era. These traditional sizes are based on the fifteen listed names from which many other sizes are derived. The weight refers to dry paper, as when wet the post can weight over ten times its dry weight. Based on tradition, the paper when packed into reams (500 sheets) was weighed and the descriptive term for the thickness of the sheet was directly related to the weight of the ream. Thus, five hundred sheets of an Imperial size (30x22in) sheet of paper might weigh approximately 140 lb, and the sheet was therefore termed 'Imperial in 140lb'. The same sheet thickness of a larger size would weigh more, e.g. Double Elephant (27x40in) in 246lb, or less for a smaller sheet, e.g. Royal (20x25in) in 106lb. A certain amount of confusion has arisen in the past because of this difference on the same basis weight for more than one size.

Many manufacturers of handmade papers still remain keen on the long-established system of paper sizes related to weight, which seems to suit hand manufacture rather than the highly mechanised papermaking processes of today.

Variations in sheet size (and weight) are common, however, in hand production, and some mills measure their paper from the outside edge of each deckle, while others measure from the inside of the deckle; this can account for up to a quarter of an inch difference in the size of a sheet.

TRADITIONAL BRITISH IMPERIAL SIZES

	inches	millimetres
ANTIQUARIAN	53 x 311	346 x 787

This is one of the largest paper sizes made by hand in Europe, recorded as being made by the Whatman Mill in Kent in 1930. In making these huge sheets the moulds were hoisted on a lifting device called 'The Contrivance', with six to eight men required in the dipping and couching processes.

ATLAS	34 x 26	864 x 660

Originally a size made for map papers printed from engraved plates and coloured by hand.

COLOMBIER	34.5 x 23.5	876 x 597

This paper was originally watermarked with a dove, the emblem of the Holy Spirit. It was extensively manufactured and used by American papermakers in Pennsylvania.

CROWN	20 x 15	508 x 381
Double Crown	20 x 30	508 x 762
Quad Crown	30 x 40	762 x 1016

This is a standard size of printing paper, watermarked with a crown.

DEMY	22.5 x 17.5	571 x 444
Double Demy	22.5 x 35	571 x 889
Quad Demy	35 x 45	889 x 1143

Derived from the original French 'demi', this paper has occasionally carried the fleur-de-lys watermark.

EAGLE	42 x 28.75	1067 x 730

Standard size of old drawing papers which takes its name from the original watermark of an eagle, known as early as 1300.

ELEPHANT	27 x 20	686 x 508
Double Elephant	27 x 40	686 x 1016

This paper takes its name from the original watermark, in the crude shape of an elephant.

EMPEROR	72 x 48	1829 x 1219

This is the largest paper made by hand in Europe.

FOOLSCAP	13.5 x 17	343 x 432
Double Foolscap	17 x 27	432 x 686
Quad Foolscap	27 x 34	686 x 864

The name for this paper has been taken from the old watermark insignia of a court jester. The size dates from the mid-sixteenth century. It was replaced in the eighteenth century by the Britannia watermark but despite this change the name 'foolscap' survives.

HAND	16 x 22	406 x 559
Royal Hand	20 x 25	508 x 635

The name of this paper is derived from the watermark of a hand, although it no longer denotes any special size. Traditionally a hand or glove, the watermark dates back to the sixteenth century.

IMPERIAL	30x 22	762 x 559
Half Imperial	15 x 22	381 x 559
Double Imperial	30 x 44	762 x 1118

A well-used size, still commonly referred to today.

MEDIUM	18 x 23	457 x 584
Double Medium	23 x 36	584 x 914
Quad Medium	36 x 46	914 x 1168

This paper is occasionally even today watermarked with the 'fleur-de-lys' insignia. It was first made by the Whatman Mill (22 x 17.5) who made two sheets on one mould with a deckle running down the centre of the mould.

POST	19.25 x 15.25	489 x 387
Large Post	16.50 x 21	419 x 533
Double Post	21 x 33	533 x 838

The name of this paper is derived from the emblem of a post horn used first as a watermark in the fourteenth century.

POT	12.5 x 15.5	317 x 394

The earliest insignia of a pot found as a watermark pictures a 'sagraaler' pot or chalice divided into compartments for holding food and drink. The use of this watermark was discontinued in the eighteenth century.

ROYAL	20 x 25	508 x 635
Double Royal	25 x 40	635 x 1016
Super Royal	40 x 50	1016 x 1270

Formerly, this paper was watermarked with an ornamental shield surmounted by a 'fleur-de-lys'. The 'Royal' size is linked to the 'Royal Hand'.

OTHER EUROPEAN TRADITIONAL SIZES

A selection traditional French sizes (*possibly the most widely used until metrication). These sizes have been brought to the nearest centimetre.

*Jésus	56 x 76 cm
*Raisin	50 x 65
*Carré	45 x 56
*Couronne	36 x 45
Colombier	62 x 85
Royal	48 x 63
Tellière	34 x 44
Soleil	58 x 80
Cloche	30 x 40
Grand Aigle	70 x 104
*Pot	32 x 40
Cognille	45 x 56

A selection of traditional German sizes. These sizes were an agreed standardisation for paper sizes in 1884.

Bienenkorb	36 x 45 cm
Bischof	38 x 48
Register	42 x 53
Lexicon	50 x 65
Pro Patria	34 x 43
Kanzlei	33 x 42

A selection of traditional Dutch sizes in use around 1800

Schrijfformat	34 x 42 cm
Olifants	62 x 72
Royaal	52 x 62
Vierkant	41 x 62

JAPANESE TRADITIONAL SIZES

The traditional units of measurement for *washi* are *jo* and *soku* , the *soku* amounting to ten *jo*. The *jo* unit, however, varies according to the type of paper and the locality in which it is produced. For example, in the case of *banshi*, one *jo* equals 20 large sheets (subsequently cut into four) while for *monogami* a *jo* equals 48 sheets. A multiple of the *soku* is the *maru* or *shime* consisting of ten *soku*. Paper is traditionally parcelled up in *maru* units for marketing.

The proportions of the moulds used in making the *washi* are characteristically longer and narrower than their Western counterparts. This proportion suits the more complex process of making by the *nagashi-zuki* method. The resultant sheets are often cut into one or more sections after making so as to reduce them to useable proportions, or alternatively the mould may contain internal divisions enabling several sheets to be produced at each make. An average size for a mould is half a metre by one metre, but it is not unusual for a mould of up to two metres long to be used. Exceptionally large moulds are used, for example, at Otaki where paper for the *fusama* partitions is made.

STANDARDISATION AND THE METRIC SYSTEM

The object of standardisation is to assist in the production of a uniform result thus making it possible to save time, energy and expenditure in manufacture. The Imperial system in Britain, and others that followed in Europe, were efforts to aid the papermaking trade and the buyers of paper so that some judgement could be made concerning the quality of papers. Oriental papermaking does not standardise or stipulate paper sizes and throughout Japan, China and India the dimensions of sheets of paper vary greatly, although in the last few decades due to the expertise of the Japanese papermaker some standardisation has been effected.

The metric system is the most recent system of standardisation and probably 90 per cent of the world's population live in countries that now use or are committed to use it. The British printing industry adopted the metric system in 1970 and now use the two basic units of metric measurement, the metre for measuring length and size, and the kilogramme for measuring weight and mass. Larger or smaller quantities are derived by multiplying or dividing these units by 10, 100, 1000 and so on.

In the paper trade, however, the whole international metric paper-size range (ISO series) is based on economics, in that any smaller sizes in the series can be cut without waste from one large basic sheet. The properties of this sheet are based on the classic golden section $1:\sqrt{2}$. Thus every sheet has the same basic proportions as every other (A,B,C series etc.). It is possible that this system of quoting sizes in figures, not by names, will lead to a definite system of standardisation and avoid the confusion of papers of the same basis weight having different weights in pounds per ream because of the difference in quantities per ream.

Metrication of the basis paper weights has also meant that, to a large extent, the anomalies of the Imperial system have been overcome by referring to the basis weight of a single sheet of paper in grammes per square metre weight, expressed as *gsm* here. The weight of a sheet of paper is now referred to as the 'grammage' which is the weight in grammes of a single sheet of paper one square metre in area.

ISO SERIES: METRIC WEIGHTS

International Standard weights are based on the metric system. The basic size of the 'A' series is one square metre in area, and therefore permits the use of grammes weight per square metre (gsm) as a method of designating the basis weight of a sheet of paper. Though this has not totally replaced the old method of measuring paper in pounds per ream it has the advantage of being less complicated as no laborious calculations are necessary to compare the weights of paper of different sizes.

To convert traditional weights to metric weights, factors are applied as follows:

Wght in lb per ream	x	4.06 for Large Post	= *Metric weight in gsm*
		3.57 for Demy	
		3.40 for Medium	
		2.81 for Royal	
		2.34 for Double Crown	
		2.08 for Imperial	

For example :
a 90 lb weight sheet of Double Crown size paper = (90 x 2.34) = 210 gsm.

To convert substance in gsm into the approximate equivalent in pounds per ream weight:

$$150 - 160 \text{ gsm} \div 2.08 = \text{Imperial 72 lb}$$
$$2.81 = \text{Royal 54 lb}$$
$$180 - 200 \text{ gsm} \div 2.08 = \text{Imperial 90 lb}$$
$$2.81 = \text{Royal 68 lb}$$
$$240 - 250 \text{ gsm} \div 2.08 - \text{Imperial 120 lb}$$
$$2.81 = \text{Royal 90 lb}$$
$$285 - 300 \text{ gsm} \div 2.08 = \text{Imperial 140 lb}$$
$$2.81 = \text{Royal 106 lb}$$
$$410 - 425 \text{ gsm} \div 2.01 = \text{Imperial 200 lb}$$
$$2.81 = \text{Royal 150 lb}$$

Note that one tonne (metric) paper = 1000 kg weight
and that one ton (Imperial) paper = 2240 lb weight

ISO SERIES : METRIC SIZES

Many countries have already decided to adopt the International System of Units - Système International d'Unités - as the only legally acceptable classification of measurement. The system has been adopted by the General Conference of Weights and Measures (CGPM) and endorsed by the International Organisation for Standardisation (IOS). The ISO series includes three denominiations - A, B, and C. The 'A' series is used to denote paper sizes for general printing matter, 'B' is primarily for posters and wall charts and 'C' is specifically for envelopes. It is the only system in use in the machine-made paper trade, though these denominations are not necessarily applicable to newspapers or books.

Den.	mm	inch conversions
A0	841 x 1189	33.111 x 46.82
A1	594 x 841	23.39 x 33.11
A2	420 x 594	16.54 x 23.39
A3	297 x 420	11.69 x 16.54
A4	210 x 297	8.27 x 11.69
A5	148 x 210	5.83 x 8.27
A6	105 x 148	4.13 x 5.83
A7	74 x 105	2.91 x 4.13
A8	55 x 74	2.05 x 2.91
A9	37 x 55	1.46 x 2.05
A10	28 x 37	1.02 x 1.46
4A0	1682 x 2378	66.22 x 93.52
2A0	1189 x 1681	44.81 x 66.22

B SERIES
Trimmed sizes falling between A sizes designed for large items, eg wallcharts, posters.

B0	1000 x 1414	39.75 x 55.6
B1	707 x 1000	27.80 x 39.40
B2	500 x 707	19.60 x 27.80
B3	353 x 500	13.80 x 19.60
B4	250 x 353	9.80 x 13.80
B5	176 x 250	7.00 x 9.80
4B	2000 x 2828	78.75 x 111.
2B	1414 x 2000	55.00 x 78.00

C SERIES
Envelopes and folders to take A series contents.

C0	917 x 1297	36.20 x 51.00	
C1	648 x 917	25.50 x 36.20	
C3	324 x 458	12.75 x 18.00	
C4	229 x 324	9.00 x 12.75	takes A4 sheet flat
C5	162 x 229	6.40 x 9.00	takes A5 sheet flat
C6	114 x 162	4.50 x 6.40	takes A5 folded once
C7/6	81 x 162	3.25 x 6.40	takes A5 folded twice
C7	81 x 114	3.25 x 4.50	
DL	110 x 220	4.40 x 8.60	takes A4 folded twice

ISO SERIES UNTRIMMED STOCK SIZES

The untrimmed paper sizes of the ISO 'A' series which are intended to be trimmed to 'A' sizes after printing are made in the following additional denominations, used mainly in machine-made paper designations.

The 'RA' series (addition of an 'R' to the 'A' series) is for non-bled printing and includes approximately an extra 10 - 20 mm onto the 'A' size which is trimmed off after the printing has taken place.

The 'SRA' series (addition of an 'SR' to the 'A' series) is used when printed work is bled off the edge of trimmed size and an extra 30 - 40mm is allowed on the 'A' size for trimming after printing is completed, e.g.

A2   420 x 594 mm
RA2   430 x 610 mm
SRA2   450 x 640 mm

METRIC PREFIXES

mega   million times (M)
kilo   thousand times (k)
hecto   hundred times (h)
deca   ten times (da)
deci   a tenth part of (d)
centi   a hundredth part of (c)
milli   thousand part of (m)
micro   a millionth part of

METRIC CONVERSION FACTORS

LENGTH

1 in   2.54 centimetres (cm)
12 in   30.48 centimetres
36 in   0.9144 metres

1mm   0.0394 in (1/25 in)
1 cm   0.3937 in (13/32 in)
1m   39.3 in (1.0936 yd)

AREA

1 sq in 6.45 sq cm (cm2)
1 sq ft 0.093 sq m (m2)
1 sq yd 0.84 sq m (m2)

1 sq cm   0.15 sq in
1 sq m 1.20 sq yd

WEIGHT

1 oz   28.3 grammes
1 lb   450 grammes
1 ton   2240 lb

1 gramme   0.3 oz
1 kilogramme 2.2 lb
1 tonne   1000 kg = 2204.6 lb = 0.98 ton

SOME DEFINITIONS

The symbols and terms most commonly used by the paper industry in making calculations are:

g = gram
gsm = grams per square metre
kg = kilogram (1000 grams)
tonne = 1000 kilograms
mm = millimetre
cm = centimetre (10mm)
m = metre (1000 mm)
m^2 = square metre

GLOSSARY OF PAPER TERMS

'A' Series
International ISO range of paper sizes reducing from AO (841 x 1189 mm) by folding in half to preserve the same proportions of 1:√2 at each reduction.

Absolute humidity
Quantity of water vapour in a unit volume of atmosphere.

Absorbency
The degree in which paper takes up contact moisture measured by a standard test.

Acid free
Paper that is free from any acid content or other substances likely to have a detrimental effect on the paper or its longevity.

Air dried
Dried with hot or cold air; it can include loft drying or machine drying. Used for high-quality production.

All-rag paper
Paper made from rags as the basis for the pulp. Today this can alsomean cotton linter pulp.

Alum
A complex salt, most commonly aluminium sulphate added with rosin to the pulp while it is in the beater as a sizing agent to impart a harder and more water-resistant surface to the finished sheet; also acts as a preservative and a mordant for fixing colours. If not removed from the fibre, its high acidity will cause irreversible damage to the paper.

ANSI
American National Standards Institute. Standards co-ordinating body similar in constitution to the British Standards Institution.

Antique
A printing paper with a rough finish but good printing surface, valued in book printing for its high volume characteristics.

API
American Paper Institute. US co-ordinating body for the paper industry.

Archival paper
A paper with long-lasting qualities, acid free, ignin free, usually with good colour retention.

'B' series
International ISO range of sizes designed for large items (wallcharts, posters) and falling between A series sizes.

Bast fibre
The inner bark of such plants as flax, hemp, ramie, *gampi*, *mitsumata*, *kozo*, which when separated out from the outer bark provide fibres suitable for papermaking.

Beater
A machine which alters or modifies the properties of fibres.

Beater-sized pulp
Paper-making furnish to which the size is added during beating rather than at a later stage in the process. Also caled internal-size pulp; engine-sized pulp. *See* Sizing

Beating
Hand or mechanical maceration of fibres to prepare them for pulp. Part of paper-making process where fibres are mechanically treated to modify their characteristics to those required by desired paper quality in manufacture.

Bonding strength
The ability of fibres at the surface of the paper to adhere to one another and to the fibres below the surface.

Brittleness
The property of paper to crack or break when bent or embossed.
Brightness
The paper's ability to reflect white light.

Broke
Damaged or defective paper often discarded during manufacture and usually re-pulped. When for sale marked XXX. *See also* Retree

Broken ream
Part of a ream of paper left after use.

BSI
British Standards Institution

Buffering agent

Also termed alkaline reserve, it is an alkaline substance, usually calcium carbonate or magnesium carbonate, occurring naturally in a water supply or purposely added by the papermaker to help protect the paper from acidity in the environment.

Bulk

Paper term used to describe the degree of thickness of a paper. Measured by caliper, volume or ppi (pages per inch) (USA).

'C' series

Range of sizes for elvelopes in the ISO series. To accommodate stationery in the A series sizes.

Calcium carbonate

A pigment used as a filler in some papers and as a white coating substance, and a buffering agent.

Calendering

A pressing process used to smooth or glaze a sheet of paper during the finishing process. A set of rollers on a paper machine which give a smooth finish to the web as it passes through by applying pressure. Calendered paper has a smooth, medium-gloss finish. *See also* Supercalender

Caliper

The thickness of a single sheet of paper measured in 1/1000in or in millimetres; measured with a micrometer. Also an instrument used for such measurements.

Cartridge

Printing or drawing paper with good dimensional stability, high opacity and good bulk. Often used in bookwork.

Cellulose

The main part of the cell wall of a plant.

Chain lines

The watermark lines which run at right angles to laid lines on the laid surface of the mould.

Coated paper

Paper coated with china clay or similar to give smooth surface suitable for half-tone reproduction. Coating slip is the coating mixture. Coating binder is the part of the coating mixture which ensures adhesion to the body stock. Coat weight is the amount of coating on base stock, expressed as dry weight on a given area.

Cockling

Wavy edges on paper caused by unstable atmospheric conditions. *See* Relative humidity

Cold Pressed (C.P.)

The surface quality of a sheet of paper. The same as the Not surface.

Contraries

Unwanted pieces of materials which have become embedded in a sheet of paper.

Copier paper

Paper used in photocopying machines.

Cotton fibre/ linters/rag

The soft white filaments attached to the seeds of the cotton plant. Cotton fabric is made from long fibres removed from the seeds by the ginning operation. Short fibres called linters, unsuitable for cloth but good for papermaking, are left. There are three grades of cotton fibres used in the papermaking process - first cut or lint; mill cut and second cut. Cotton is the purest form of cellulose produced in nature and it requires the least amount of processing before it can be used. Pulp can be produced from either cotton linters or rags. *See also* Rag

Couch (*Pron.* Cooch)

The action of transferring a sheet of wet fibres from the mould onto a damp felt.

Curling tendency

A curl can develop a.when the moisture content of the paper is changed by conditioning it to the studio atmosphere before printing or b. when the paper comes into contact with the process moisture, i.e. in lithography during offset or direct printing.

Custom making

A paper made specially for a client; opposite to a standard range.

Cylinder-mould

The type of papermaking machine most commonly used today in the production of mouldmade papers.

Dandy roll

Large cylindrical roll used on a Fourdrinier machine which impresses the watermark onto the paper.

Deckle

A wooden frame that fits over a paper mould to prevent the pulp from running off the edges. It also establishes the size of a handmade sheet during making.

Deckle edges

The wavy, feathered or ragged edges of a sheet of handmade paper on four sides caused by the deckle frame where pulp thins towards the edge of the mould. Also found on cylinder mouldmade papers on the two outside edges of the web.

Dimensional stability

The dimensional stability of a paper is the percentage of elongation or shrinkage caused by a given change in the relative humidity or moisture content in the air. It is a measure of the paper's tendency to misregister especially by becoming wavy (waxy) or tight-edged.

Dyes

Water-soluble colouring agents which usually penetrate and become attached to the fibre. Types of dyes include:- direct dyes, organic dyes usually derived from coal tars; fibre-reactive dyes, that form a chemical bond with the fibres; and natural dyes, derived from natural sources such as indigo and onion skins. Since some types of dyes require an acid mordant to set or fix the dye to the fibre, care must be used in their selection.

Embossed finish

Surface pattern pressed in paper.

Endpaper

Strong paper used for securing the body of a book to its case.

Engine sized

Paper sized in the beating machine rather than at a later stage in manufacture. *See* Sizing

Fastness

Resistance of colour to fading.

Felt

A rectangular sheet of absorbent material, usually of wool, cut in a larger size than the paper sheet required. It is utilised during the Western making process when newly formed sheets of paper are couched or transferred from the mould. Wet sheets are couched onto individual felts and stacked together. Also applies to cylinder-mouldmade papermaking, in which the felts are sewn together to form a continuous loop. Various grades of felts exist to give various surface to wet sheets; differing in hand- and mouldmade production.

Felt finish

A finish to top surface of the paper created by the texture of the felts; often with special weaves.

Felt mark

Paper may be naturally dried after pressing and may acquire the texture of the surface of the felt covering the paper.

Felt side

Top side of paper formed on a paper machine wire, distinct from wire side.

Fibres

The basis of a sheet of paper. Papermaking fibres are hollow tube-like structures with walls made up of three-like 'fibrills'.

Fibrilla

Part of cellulose fibre separated during the refining process.

Fibrillation

Shredding and bruising of fibres walls during beating process.

Filler

A material generally added to the beater to fill in the pores of a fibre, making a harder, more opaque surface. Pigments added to the furnish of paper to improve the printing characteristics and appearance of printed image.

Fine papers

High quality papers.

Finish

A general term for the various surfaces given to papers and boards. The type of surface on a particular grade of paper.

Finishing

The practices of drying, sizing and looking over sheets of paper when making processes are completed.

Formation

In papermaking this refers to the fibre distribution in a sheet of paper as it appears when held up to the light.

Fourdrinier

The name of a type of paper machine in which paper is made at high speed in a continuous web - machinemade paper.

Free

Pulp from which water will drain easily when on the mould.

Free sheet

American term for 'woodfree' paper. As distinct from 'groundwood'.

Furnish

The ingredients in the beater, which, when added together, give a specific type of paper.

Gelatine

A type of size obtained from animal tissues applied to the surface of paper to make it impervious to water and to aid resistance to bleeding during printing. Also imparts surface strength to watercolour and drawing papers.

Ginning

Separating the seeds from cotton. (Gin, the machine used to separate the seeds.)

Glazing

The terms used to denote a smooth surface given to a sheet of paper often made by running dried sheets through steel rollers or between polished zinc plates.

Gloss

The light reflectance from the surface of a paper, a shiny or lustrous appearance.

Grain

Direction of fibres in a sheet of paper. Long grain describes fibres running parallel to the longest side of a sheet; short grain running parallel to the shortest side.

Grain direction

The alignment of fibres in a sheet of paper caused by the flow of the web of wet paper in cylinder or Fourdrinier machines only (cross grain and machine grain).

Grammage (gsm/gm^2)

The weight of paper and board expressed in metric terms.

Groundwood

American term for mechanical pulp.

gm^2 / gsm

Grams per square metre.

Half-stuff

Half-beaten stock, often commercially prepared.

Handmade

Paper made by hand operation.

Hardwood pulp

Pulp made from hardwood (deciduous) trees, eg. oak, beech, birch, eucalyptus.

Hot Pressed (H.P.)

A term used to denote the smooth surface of a sheet of paper achieved by passing sheets through hot, heavy metal plates or rollers.

Humidity

Quantity of water vapour in the atmosphere. *See also* Absolute humidity and Relative humidity

Hydration

A process occurring during beating in which the bruised fibres begin to accept water more readily.

Hygrometer

An instrument for measuring humidity in the air.

Hygrometry

Measurement of humidity.

Hygroscopic

A hygroscopic material is one which tends to take up the moisture content of the atmosphere or to become moist.

India paper

Very thin, high-qaulity, opaque rag paper often used for printing bibles.

Internal Sizing

See Sizing

ISO sizes

Formerly DIN sizes. International range of paper and envelope sizes, comprising A series, B series and C series.

Laid mould

A wooden frame for the forming of pulp into sheets of paper in which the characteristic of closely spaced parallel lines (20-40 per inch) can be seen (in dry paper when it is help up to the light) held in place by wire worked in the perpendicular direction to the strips. Opposite of 'wove' mould.

Laid Paper

Paper that is made on a laid mould. It is customary for the laid lines to run across the page's width and the chain (linking) lines from head to foot.

Layer

The person who takes wet sheet of handmade paper and hangs them up to dry.

lb.

The weight of 500 sheets (a ream) of paper of a given size.

Lignin

The fibre bonding material found mainly in woody plants; it rejects water and and resists bonding and therefore must be removed from the fibres before the paper making process.

Linters

See Cotton linters

M weight

Weight of 1000 sheets of any given paper size (American).

Machine direction

The direction in which fibres lay on the wire of a paper machine, ie along the web. As distinct from cross direction.

Mature

1. To allow paper to settle after it has been made. 2. To acclimatise paper to printing room or studio humidity.

Mechanical pulp

Pulp produced mechanically, by grinding, rather than chemically. Usually with reference to machinemade papers.

Moisture content

Amount of moisture in paper, expressed as a percentage of weight.

Mould

The basic tool of a Western hand papermaker which consists of a (mahogany)frame and removable deckle. Varying designs exist in different countries.

Mouldmade

Paper made on cylinder-mould machine.

Not

The slightly rough, unglazed surface of a paper (i.e. Not Hot Pressed).

Opacity

The quality of opaqueness in a paper, e.g. the paper's ability to hide the printing on the reverse side or of sheets underneath.

pH

The pH value is a measure of the strength of the acidity or alkalinity of a paper. The measure of availability of free hydrogen ions representing, in lay terms, the balance between acid and alkaline components of a material. 0 pH is very acid, 14 pH is very alkaline, 7 pH represents a balance between the acid and alkaline components and is a neutral solution.

Picking

A property of paper to release surface fibres during printing operations- a lifting of small clumps of fibres out of the paper surface which can stick to the blanket in e.g. lithography and mar the printing on suceeding sheets. Picking can also cause blistering of the paper surface often on solid areas in a lithograph.

Ply

Layer of paper or board joined to another for strength, thus: 2 ply, 3-ply, 4 ply, 5ply etc.

ppi

Pages per inch. American method of specifying the thickness of paper.

Pulp

The 'stuff' used in papermaking process. Chemical pulp contains many fewer impurities than mechanical pulp.

Purity

The degree of chemical purity of a paper.

Quire

A quantity of 25 sheets of paper, a twentieth part of a ream. This is a peculiarly English measure, possibly relating to a time when counting was done in dozens (x12; old quire = 24 sheets).

Rag

Formerly the principal raw material used in the making process; often meaning cotton rags. Rag content describes the amount of cotton fibre relative to the total amount of material used in the pulp. 'Rag content' is not widely used (or is a misnomer) today as more and more high-quality paper is made not from rag but from linters. *See* Cotton.

Rattle

The sound produced by shaking a piece of paper indicating the hardness of the sheet.

Ream

Traditionally 480 sheets (equal to 20 quires of 24 sheets). Now taken to refer to 500 sheets of good paper.

Recovered fibres

Fibres from waste paper.

Recycled fibres

See Recovered fibres.

Relative humidty (RH)

Amount of water vapour present in the atmosphere expressed as a percentage of saturation. The moisture content of paper is governed by the relative humidity of the surrounding atmosphere. Research (and experience) has shown that paper perhaps has its best dimensional stability in the range of 40-55per cent relative humidity.

Retree

Slightly damaged paper sold at a reduced price and often marked XX. *See also* Broke

Rosin

One of the most commonly used internal sizing agents for paper. Occasionally used as a tub size. Introduced around the early 1800s, it is acidic in nature and detrimental to the permanence of paper.

Rough

A term used to describe the surface texture of a sheet of handmade or cylinder-mould made paper.

Salle

Traditionally a room where the sorting of paper took place.

Seconds

The term for imperfect sheets of paper (other terms - Retree and Outsides).

Security paper

Paper incorporating features which make counterfeiting difficult.

Shadow watermark

A watermark in which portions of the paper appear as light tones in a sheet of paper; the opposite to a line watermark; also called chiaroscuro.

Short grain

Paper in which the grain is parallel to the shorter edge of the sheet.

Smoothness

Smoothness of a paper is essentially the flatness of its surface. It is not the same as 'gloss' which is an optical property, nor porosity.

Size

1. Chemical or chemicals used in papermaking to control the water or ink absorbency of the paper. 2. The description of the measurement of a sheet of paper.

Sizing

A solution used to make the paper moisture resistant in varying degrees. Size can be added at two stages of the papermaking process (see below). The degree of sizing of paper determines their resistance to the penetration of moisture. *Internal sizing, Engine sizing, Beater sizing* describes moisture-resistant pulps which receive sizing treatment in the beater. *Tub Sizing* - After manufacture, when the paper has been dried, some papers are passed through a solution of gelatine (or other size) traditionally contained in a bath or tub. Other surface sizes include glue, casein and starch. *Animal Tub Sizing* - Refers to the papers that are tub sized and for which the gelatine used is obtained from a solution of parings and skins of animals.

Soda pulp

Pulp produced from hardwood chips cooked in caustic soda.

Softwood pulp

Pulp made from softwood (coniferous) trees, e.g. fir, pine, spruce.

Special furnish

Papers made from a special mixture of pulps for a specific purpose.

Standard range

This name indicates the normal range of papers produced by a manufacturer; as opposed to a special or custom making.

Stampers

Hammers (often wooden) used traditionally to beat rags to pulps.

Stock

Suspension of fibres in water.

Stuff

The materials from which paper is manufactured, the stock.

Substance

The weight or grammage of a sheet of paper expressed in lb per ream or gsm.

Surface finish

The surface character of a sheet of paper, eg. 'C.P., H.P., NOT', burnished, hammered etc.

Surface sizing

See Sizing

Technical Association of the Pulp and Paper Industry

(TAPPI) American professional organisation.

Texture

The rough surface of a paper. Can be a natural result of pulp and processing or a contrived impression.

Tooth

Characteristic, rough texture of a paper surface.

Vat

A tub or vessel that holds the wet paper stock.

Vatman

A person engaged in the scooping of pulp from the vat to form a sheet of handmade paper.

Vellum

The prepared inner side of calfskin; the term vellum can be used as an imitation of this type of surface in another paper.

Virgin fibre

Fibre used for the first time to make paper (i.e. not recycled).

Waterleaf

Used to describe a paper that contains no sizing and is generally very absorbent.

Watermark

A translucent design in a sheet of paper that can be viewed as a lighter part of a sheet only when held up to the light.

Waxy/wavy edges

Caused in paper by moisture absorption due to environmental conditions.

Web

A continuous length of paper (i.e. a roll or reel) as distinct from a sheet.

Weight

See Substance

Wireside

Surface of the pulp in contact with the mesh during during making.

Wove mould

A mould in which the covering screen is made by woven wire (similar to warp and weft in a cloth). Opposite to a laid mould.

Wove papers

Paper made on a wove mould.

XX

Mark indicating Retree.

XXX

Mark indicating Broke.

beggars make rags

rags make paper

paper makes money

money makes banks

banks make loans

loans make beggars

FINE PAPER ADDRESS LISTS

This is a conglomerate list of the many of people and companies that make, manufacture, import, trade and deal in fine papers.

To avoid unnecessary repetition, the terms that are used to describe the companies are explained in detail below. **retailer** : most likley a shop or mail order business selling direct to the public **trade counter** : retail sales at a paper merchant **supplier** : an outlet for paper sales **consultant** : a firm/individual who has a lot of knowlegde/able to look at a particular enquiry in an advisory capacity **merchant** : a paper wholesaler or paper distributor who carries stock in bulk **agent** : a company that acts for one or several specific paper manufacturers, mills, or makers **distributor** : a company that is able to trade in large quantities of paper, usually trade sales as opposed to retail sales **exclusive or sole distributor** : ususally a foreign mill will appointed a particular company to sell their product/s **representative** : a company that represents a manufacturer **importer** : a company that imports papers to resell **manufacturer or mill** : usually a large paper mill where a range of fine papers are made in large quantities; these mills can vary in size from one machine mill to huge conglomerates with many different mills and many machines **handmade papermakers** : an individual, or small group of indivuals, involved in making paper in relatively small amounts; occasionally includes various other end products besides sheets - paper courses, prepared pulps, hire of studios, custom makings, paper projects, etc. **mail order** - a company, large or small, who sells products by post.

The addresses in *italics* are retailers - i.e. people and companies that usually sell direct to the public.

Aart de Vos
Klosterport 4
8000 Århus
Denmark
Fine paper merchant

Abio Art Materials
41 Ilidos Street
115 27 Athens
Greece
Fine paper merchant

ACT Papers (Aus) Pty Ltd.
10 McGlone Street
Micham, Victoria 3132
Australia

ANW Crestwood Paper Inc.
315 Hudson Street
New York. NY 10013
USA
Paper manufacturer, importer and distributor

Art Stretchers
Queensbury Place
Carlton. Victoria
Australia
03486 1877
Paper merchant and distributors

Artetré
Via Arrigo Davila 63
00179 Roma
Italy
06 78 00 814
Paper merchant and suppliers

Artist Home Supplies
Unit 40 + 41
Temple Farm Industrial Estate
Southend on Sea SS25RZ
UK
Paper retailer

Arches see **Papeterie Arches**

Arjomari-Prioux
3, Impasse Reille
75104 Paris
France
Major mould- and machine-made paper manufacturers

Atlantis Paper Company Ltd.
2 St. Andrew's Way
London E3 3PA
UK
Fine paper importer, merchant, agent, distributors plus retail shop. Founded in 1977, Atlantis aim is to supply a complete range of paper to artists.Expanding to develop a whole range of archival and museum papers and boards, it now also provides in its Art Warehouse a paper desk for retail and mail order supplies. Special hand-, mould- and machinemade makings. Telephone 071 537 2727, paper desk 071 537 2299. Fax 071 537 4277.

Atlantis France
26 rue des Petits-Champs
75002 Paris
France
Restoration papers

Barcham Green & Co. Ltd.
Hayle Mill, Maidstone
Kent ME15 6XQ
UK
Paper merchant

Basler Papiermühle
Schweizeriches Papiermuseum
St Alban-Tal 37
CH-4052 Basle
Switzerland
Papermill and museum making handmade paper

Berrick Bros. Ltd.
Unit 1, Deptford Trading Estate,
Blackhorse Road
London SE8 5HY
UK
Paper importers, merchant s and distributors

Estb. de Beuger
rue Louis Hap 226
1040 Brussels
Belgium

Birchbank Art Materials
41 Smithbrook Kilns
Horsham Road (A281)
Cranleigh Surrey GU6 8JJ
UK
Fine paper by mail order and retail

British Paper and Board Industry Federation
3 Plough Place
Fetter Lane
London EC4A 1AL

British Waste Paper Association
Highgate House
214 High Street
Guildford GU1 3JB

R.K. Burt & Co. Ltd.
57 Union Street
London SE1
UK
Fine paper importers, merchants, agents, wholesale distributors; Information and samples supplied. Papers include the ranges of Arches, Canson, Lana, Hahnemuhle, Zerkall, St Cuthberts, Fabriano, plus cartridges, papayrus, blotting, tissue, repair papers and many other papers and boards. Telephone 071 407 6474.

Papeteries de Canson et Mongolfier SA
BP 139
07104 Annany
France
Fine paper mill

Museo Moli Paperer de Cappellades
Barcelona
Spain
Paper museum and small mill

Carriage House Handmade Paper Works
1 Fitchburg Street, C207
Somerville, MA 02143
USA
Papermakers, handmade paper mill, retailer, studio, mail order

Cartiere Antonio Cavalière
Via Fiume
84011 Amalfi
Italy
Old papermaking mill now makes recyled paper

Catherine's Rare Papers
7064 E. 1st. Ave, Suite 103-104
Scottsdale AZ 85251
USA
Fine paper retailer

Columbia
Artists' Supplies Division
Chatham, NY 12037
USA

Compton Marbling
Tisbury, Salisbury
Wilts SP3 6SG
UK

Conservation Papers
228 London Road,
Reading, Berks RG6
UK

Conté (UK) Ltd
Park Farm Industrial Estate
Park Farm Road
Folkestone. Kent CT19 5GY
UK
Fine paper importers, merchants and exclusive distributors

L. Cornelissen & Son Ltd
105 Gt Russell Street
London WC2B 5BH
UK
Artists' materials retailer including fine papers

Corners
19 Gibson Street
Kelvinbridge G12 8NU
UK
Artist material retailer including fine papers

William Cowley
Parchment & Vellum Works
97 Caldecote Street
Newport Pagnell. Bucks
UK
0908 610038
Real parchment and vellum skin makers, distributors and retailers

Cowling and Wilcox Ltd.
26-28 Broadwick Street,
London W1V 1FG
UK
(071) 734 5781
Artist and graphic materials retailers including fine papers

The Crafts Link
1221-Oyada Minoshi
Gifu-ken T 501 37
Japan
Retailer for fine papers from Gifu papermakers

(ANW) Crestwood
315 Hudson Street
New York. NY 10013
USA
Paper manufacturer and distributor

James Cropper plc
Burneside Mills
Kendal. Cumbria LA9 6PZ
UK
Machinemade paper manufacturer. Trade enquiries only.

Crescent Cardboard Co
PO Box XD
100 West Willow Road
Wheeling. IL 60090
USA
Paper manufacturer and distributor

Curtis Paper Co.
Papermill Road
Newark. Delaware 19711
USA
Paper manufacturer and distributor

St.Cuthberts Mill
Inveresk Ltd.
Wells. Somerset BA5 1AG
UK
Specialist fine mouldmade papers; manufacturer of Saunders Waterford Series, Bockingford Watercolour paper and Somerset Printmaking paper. Special makings of 1 tonne minimum available. Full overseas agents list available from the mill direct.

Daler Board Co. Ltd
East Street,
Wareham. Dorset BH20 4NT
UK
Paper manufacturer

Daler-Rowney Ltd
PO Box 10
Bracknell. Berks RG12 4ST
UK
Artists' materials manufacturer, distributor and retailer; some fine papers

Daniel Smith Inc
4130 1st Ave. South
Seattle. WA 98134
USA
Fine paper retailer

DEKO
Ludvigsbergegatan 5
S-117 26 Stockholm
Sweden
Paper retailer

Denver Art Supply
1437 California
Denver. CO 80202
USA
Fine paper retailer

Dieu Donné Press and Paper
3 Crosby Street
New York. NY 10013
Handmade mill, papermakers

Dinsion e Paramatti Arte
10036 Settimo c/c
Postale 2/123
Torinese
Italy

Direct Art
Dept. A. P.O. Box 18,
Alresford. Hants SO24 9NT
UK
Artists materials by mail order including fine paper

Docklands Art Warehouse
2 St. Andrew's Way
London E3 3PA
UK
Retail outlet for Atlantis Paper Co. plus artists' material shop

Drissler & Co
Interburger Str. 16
600 Frankfurt am Main 90
Germany
Specialist Japanese paper importer and distributor

Duntog Papermill
301 Ambuklao Road
Baguio City, Benguet Province
Philipines
Hand papermill

Earthwrite
Unit l6, Carlisle House
Carlisle Street East
Sheffield S4 7QN
UK
Recycled paper agents and suppliers

L'Ecritoire
61 rue Saint-Martin
75004 Paris
France
Fine paper retailer

Enso-Gutzeit Oy
Tervakoski Mills
Tervakoski
Finland
Handmade and mouldmade paper manufacturers

Espace Japon
12 rue Sainte-Anne
75001 Paris
FRance
Fine paper retailer in Japanese papers

EuroGraphics
Templar House, Temple Way
Bristol BS1 6HG
UK
Paper merchant, agent and distributors

Cartiere Miliani Fabriano spa
PO Box 82
60044 Fabriano
Italy
Fine hand-, mould- and machinemade manufacturers

Friends of the Earth Recycling Unit
26-28 Underwood Street
London N1 7JQ
Information on recycling

Falkiner Fine Papers Ltd.
76 Southampton Row
London WC1B 4AR
UK
Fine paper retailers. Specialist handmade, mouldmade and machinemade papers for artists and designers including European, Japanese and Indian. Large retail shop. Mail order catalogue. Competitive on large quantities. Hours of business 9.30-6.00 Mon-Sat. Tel. 071 831 1151. Fax 071 430 1248. Enquiries welcome.

Fibreplus
2716 Riverside Lane
Cayce. SC 29033
USA
Mail order company supplying
fibres for papermaking

Finbrook Papers
20 East 9 Street
N. York. NY10003
USA
Paper manufacturers

Fine Arts Articles Ltd
539 La Guardia Place
New York. NY10012
USA
Paper suppliers

Forende Paper Mills
Strad Straedo 18
1255 Copenhagen
Denmark
Paper manufacturers

Frisk Products Ltd.
4 Franthorne Way
Randlesdown Road
London SE6 3BT
UK
Paper merchants and retailers

GB Papers
Index House
Ascot.
Royal Berks 5LS 7EU
Paper merchants

John Gerard
Falckensteinerstrasse 5
D-1000 Berlin 36
Germany
Hand papermaker, studio,
custom makings

Anton Glaser
Postfach 939
Theodor Heuss Strasse 349
7000 Stuttgart 1
Germany

Green & Stone
259 Kings Road
London SW3 5EL
UK
Artist materials retailer plus fine
papers

Greenscene Co-operative
112 Fore Street
Exeter. Devon EX4 3JQ
UK
Recycled paper manufacturers and
suppliers

Gold's Artworks Inc.
2100 N.Pine Street
Lumberton .NC 28358
USA
Specialist mail order plus retail
shop, everything for papermaking

James F.Gormley Snr.
97 Spier Falls Road
Gansevoort. NY 12831-9631
USA
Mail order; new and used
papermaking equipment

Griffen Mill
Old Manor Farmhouse
Stawell. Nr Bridgwater
Somerset TA7 9AE
UK
Handmade paper mill, retailer

Peter van Ginkel
Kunstenaarsbenodigdhe. 6v
Nieuwe Kade 2
6011 LN Arnhem
Netherlands
Large fine art materials manufac-
turers and retailers, including
printmaking supplies and
equipment. Bases in Arnhem,
Amsterdam, Utrecht and Gronin-
gen. Fine paper merchants and
retailers with wide range of papers.
Mail order. Telephone 085
423334. Fax 085 435493.

Frank Grunfeld
32 Bedford Square
London WC1
UK
Paper merchant and agent

Guarro Casas SA
PO Box 2427
08080 Barcelona
Spain
Mould- and machinemade
paper manufacturer

Buttenpapierfabrik
Hahnemühle
Postfach 4
D 3354 Dassel
Germany
Mouldmade manufacturer

Handmade Plant Papers
Romilly, Brilley
Herefordshire HR3 6HE
UK
Handmade papermaker, custom
makings, courses, mail order

ICOSA Studio & Papermill
Route 4, Box 279
Ellensberg. WA 98926
USA
Papermaker

Intaglio Printmaker
15 Corsica Street
London N5 1JT
UK
Printmaking materials retailers
plus fine papers

Impex
Impex House, Paper Mews
Dorking.
Surrey RH4 1QX
Paper agents

Jackson Drawing Supplies Ltd
103 Rokeby Road
Subiaco 6008. Perth
W. Australia

JvO Papers
15 Newll Street
London E14 7HP
Paper merchant, distributor and
supplier specialising in old papers.
Telephone 071 987 7464

Kakimoto Japanese Papershop
54 Tokiwagi Teramachinijyo-
Agaru
Nakagyoku
Kyoto
Japan
Japanese fine paper retailer

Kate's Paperie
8W 13th Street
New York NY10011
USA
Paper retailer stocking large range
of decorative papers. Over 800
handmade and machinemade
papers. Specialities include
printing on handmade and
unusual commercial papers.
Sample swatches sold individually.
Extensive stationery.Telephone 212
6330570 or Fax 212 3666532
with any inquiries.

Khadi Handmade Papers
11 Tregarth Road,
Chichester. Sussex PO19 4QU
UK
Paper importers, distributors and
retailers specialising in handmade
papers from India, Nepal,
Thailand and Bhutan. Khadi
have developed a range of over fifty
papers in close collaboration with
Asian printmakers. Special
makings can be ordered. Consul-
tancy available. Main UK retailers
Atlantis, Falkiner, Purcell. Dis-
tributors in Europe, USA,
Australia and Japan. Telephone
0243 527783. Fax 0243 511373

Robert J. King
3304 Riverside Drive
Port Huron. Michigan 48060
USA
Importer and distributor small
range of handmade papers

Kimonoya
11 rue du Pont-Louis Phillipe
75004 Paris
FRance
Fine paper retailer for calligraphy
and Japanese papers

AB Klipans Finpappersbruk
Lessebo Bruk
S-360 50 Lessebo
Sweden
Paper manufacturer, hand-
made papermill

Odin Kunst
Goennegt 94
2300 Hamar
Norway
Fine paper retailer

Groupe Lana
BP 191
92305 Levallois-Perret Cedex
France
Mouldmade and machinemade
paper manufacturer

Lapis
12 Flask Walk
London NW3 1HE
UK
Fine art materials retailer; wide
range of fine papers plus specilises
in antique hand- and mouldmade
papers

T. N. Lawrence & Son Ltd.
119 Clerkenwell Road
London EC1R 5BY
UK
Paper and printmaking suppliers, retailers and mail order. Leading stockists of paper for over 100 years. Unique range of European and Japanese hand/mouldmade papers for printmaking, bookbinding, etc. Telephone 071 242 3534. Fax 071 430 2234.

Lesaffre nv
Tuinstraat 21-23
B 85 Kortrijk
Belgium
Fine paper merchants
also at
Onderbergen 76A
B 9000 Gent
Belgium
Fine paper merchants

Lessebo Bruk
5 360 50 Lessebo
Sweden
Handmade paper mill

London Graphic Centre
107-115 Long Acre,
London WC2 9NT
UK
Retail outlet for graphic artists including some papers

Cartier Enrico Magnani SpA
Piazza Mateotti 11
51017 Pescia
Italy
Hand- and mouldmade papermakers, paper mill

W.V. Marchant Ltd.
Orchard House
Mutton Lane
Potters Bar. Hertfordshire
UK
Paper agents including Zerkall papers

Maria Maeldo
Rua Rixhhuelo 1305/1501
Porto Alegre
Rio Grande do Sol CEP 90 000
Brazil
Handmade papermaker, paper mill

Lee S. McDonald Inc.
Fine Papermmaking Equipment
PO box 264
Charlestown. MA 02129
USA
Equipment and supplies for handpapermaking. Mail order

Papel hecho a mano Meirat
Veronica 13
28014 Madrid
Spain
Handmade paper mill, papermaker

Melbourne Etching Supplies
44-46 Greeves Street
Fitzroy Victoria
Australia
Art materials supplier including fine papers

Morita Japanese Paper
298 Oogizakae-Cho Bukkoj-Agaru
Higashinotoin Shimogyoku
Kyoto
Japan
Japanese paper retailer

Moulin de Fleurac
16440 Nersac
France
Handmade paper mill, papermaker

Moulin de Larroque
2411150 Couze
France
Handmade paper mill, papermaker

Moulin du Pombie
Cuzorn
47500 Fumel
France
Handmade paper mill, papermaker

Moulin de Pen Mur
BP28
56190 Muzillac
France
Handmade papermill, paper maker

Moulin Vallis Clausa
Chemin de la Fontaine
848000 Fontaine-de Vaucluse
France
Handmade papermill, papermaker

Moulin du Verger
Puymoyen
16400 La Couronne
France
Handmade paper mill, papermaker

Nautilus Press & Paper Mill
77 Southern Row
London W10 5AL
UK
Hand paper mill, paper arts, book arts, bookbinding, printing and related photography studio

New York Central Art Supply Inc.
62 Third Ave
New York City 10003
USA
Artists material suppliers including large range of fine papers -importers and retailers

Nigel Griffiths
8 Castleview Road
Strood. Rochester
Kent ME22 3PP
Handmade paper maker, paper mill

One Nine Four Paper Suppliers
PO Box A13
Huddersfield W.Yorkshire HD3 4LW
UK
Paper merchant and retailer, mail order

Oram & Robinson Ltd.
Cadmore Lane
Cheshunt. Waltham Cross
Herts EN8 9SG
UK
Art materials suppliers; some fine papers

Osborne & Butler
Hartlebury Trading Estate
Hartlebury, Nr. Kidderminster
Worcs DY10 4JB
UK
Art material suppliers; some fine papers

Paper Nao
1-29-12-201 Sengoku
Bunkyo-ku
Tokyo-112
Japan
Retail outlet for fine quality Japanese handmade papers

Paper Source, Ltd.
1506 W.12th Street
Los Angeles. CA 90015
USA
Mail order and retail outlet for papermaking supplies

The Paper Workshop
Gallowgate Studios
15 East Campbell Street
Glasgow 15DT
UK
Artists' papermaking workshop

Papers Etc.
510 Broome Street
New York. NY 10013
USA
Fine paper retailer

Paperback Ltd.
Unit 2 Bow Triangle Business Centre
Eleanor St
London E3 4NP
UK
Specialist recycled paper merchants

Paperchase
213 Tottenham Court Road
London W1
UK
General retailers, cards, art materials etc.; some fine papers

Papersource Inc
730 N.Franklin, Suite 111
Chicago. Il 60610
USA
Fine paper retailers

Papeteries d'Arches (Arjomari Prioux)
88380 Arches
France
Mouldmade manufacturer

Papeteries de Lana
8846 Docelles
France
Mouldmade manufacturer

Papeteries Canson et Mongolfier S.A.
BP 139
07104 Annonay Cedex
France
Paper manufacturer

La Papeterie St Armand
110 rue Young
Monteal, Quebec H3 2E7
Canada
Handmade paper mill

Papier +
9 rue de Pont-Louis- Phillipe
75004 Paris
France
Fine paper retailer

Papierfabriek Schut bv
Kabeljauw 2, Postbus 1
6866 ZG Heelsum
Netherlands
Mould- and machinemade paper manufacturers

Papper för konstnärer
Upplandsgatan 37
S-113 28 Stockholm
Sweden
Fine paper suppliers

Pappersgruppen AB
P.O. Box 90113
S-120 21 Stockholm
Sweden
Fine paper merchants and retailers

Papyrus Institute
3 Nile Avenue
Giza, Cairo
Eygbt
Papyrus paper makers and retailers

Paris-papiers
54 Bd Pasteur
75015 Paris
France
Fine paper retailer

H.W.Peel & Co Ltd.
Norwester House
Fairway Drive, Fairways Estate
Greenford, Middsx UB6 8PW
UK
Art materials supplier plus some fine papers

Ditta di Poggi
Via del Gesa 74
00186 Roma
Italy
Fine paper suppliers

John Purcell Paper
15 Rumsey Road
London SW9 OTR
UK
Fine paper importer, exclusive distributor, merchant and retailer with trade counter. Range of over 1000 papers, handmade, mouldmade and machinemade papers from all over the world. Special makes constantly. Carries special makings in stock. Telephone 071 737 5199. Fax 071 737 6769.

Michael Putman
151 Lavender Hill
London SW11
UK
Artists' material retailer plus some fine papers

Relma
3 rue des Poitevins
75006 Paris
France
Fine paper retailer

Reeves
PO Box 91
Wealdstone, Harrow
Middx HA3 5RH
UK
Artists' materials manufacturers and retailers plus fine papers

Reeves Dryad
P.O. Box 38
Leicester OE1 9BU
UK
Artists' materials manufacturer and retailer by mail order plus some fine papers

Moulin a papier du Val de Laga à Richard de Bas
63600 Ambert, Puy de Dome
France
Handmade paper mill and museum

Rising Paper Company
Division of Fox River Paper
Company
Housatonic
Mass 01236-0565
USA
Manufacturer of fine art papers

Rougier et Plé
13-15 bd des Filles du Calvaire
75003 Paris
France
Fine paper retailer

Otavio Roth
Handmade PApel, Texto E Arte
LTDA
Rua Das Palmeiras 103 AP 2
Santa Cecilia CED 01226
Sao Paulo
Brazil
Hand papermaker, paper mill

George Rowney & Co. Ltd.
PO Box 10
Bracknell
Berks RG12 4 ST
UK
Art materials manufacturers and suppliers plus some fine papers

Papierfabrik Schoellershammer
Heinr. Aug. Schoeller Söhne
GmbH & Co. KG
Postfach 101946
D 5160 Düren
Germany
Mouldmade paper manufacturer. Manufacturers of specialities in the range of technical drawing, graphic design, fine art, superior writing and printing papers as : Drawing- and painting papers, drawing boards, fine art papers and boards, natural tracing papers, a variety of drawing and painting blocks a plus sophisticated writing and printing materials. UK suppliers -West Design Products.

Vicki Schober Co. Inc.
2363 North Mayfair Road
Milwaukee. WI 53226
USA
Fine paper retailer

Papierfabrik Schut bv
Kabeljauw 2
Postbus 1
6866ZG Heelsum
Fine mould-and machinemade paper manufacturer

Jennifer Scott
Coach Hill House
Burley Street
Ringwood. Hants BH24 4HN
Materials, papers and services for Chinese brush painting. Mail order supplier of Chinese papers and all other materials for traditional Chinese (brush) painting.

Sea Penn Press and Paper
Mill
2228 N.E. 46th Street
Seattle, WA 98105
USA
Manufacturer of custom-made pulps for hand papermakers, custom watermarks

Sennelier
3 Quai Voltaire
75007 Paris
and
4 bis, rue de la Grand-Chaumiere
75006 Paris
France
Artist materials retailer; some fine papers

Sheepstor Handmade Papers
Covert House, Yelverton
Devon PL20 6DF
UK
Hand papermaker, papermill

Fred Siegenthaler
Stockerstrasse 2
CH 4132 Muttenz
Switzerland
Hand papermaker, papermill

Sihl
Zurich Paper Mill on Sihl
Giesshübelstrasse 15
PO Box 8021
CH Zurich
Switzerland
Mouldmade and machine-made paper manufacturers

G.H.Smith & Partners Ltd
Berechurch Road
Colchester Essex
CO2 7QH
UK
Paper merchants, and distributors, some fine papers

Smith Anderson & Co Ltd.
Fettykil Mill
Leslie, Fyfe
Scotland
Machinemade paper manufacturers

Gillian Spires Handmade Paper
4 Fore Street,
Ugborough, Ivy Bridge
Devon PL21 ONP
UK
Hand papermaker, custom making

Strathmore Paper Company
Westfield
Mass 01085
USA
Fine machinemade paper manufacturers. Full range of artists' papers and boards. Special cotton papers.

Louie Stuart
Sareiaya, Quezon City
Manila
Philipines
Fine paper retailer

Svenskt Papper AB
Box 553
S-136 25 Hanninge
Sweden
Fine paper merchant

Len Tabner
High Barlby, Eastington
Nr. Saltburn on Sea
Cleveland
UK
Fine paper retailer by mail order

Takao Co. Ltd
3-12-6
Nishiki-cho kanda,
Chiyoda-ku,
Tokyo 101
Japan
Paper retailers

Tempera OY
Uudenmankatu 16-20
Helsinki 12
Finland
Fine paper retailers

T.U.K.A. Ltd.
St. John's Place,
Banbury, Oxon OX16 8HP
UK
Paper agent and distributor

Tumba Bruk AB
S-147 00 Tumba
Stockholm
Sweden
Mouldmade and machine-
made paper manufacturers

Twinrocker Handmade Paper
PO Box 413
100E Third Street
Brookston. IN 47923
USA
Hand papermakers, paper mill,
retailers, mail order

Two Rivers Paper Co.
Pitt Mill, Roadwater
Watchet. Somerset
UK
Hand papermakers, paper mill,
mail order

Utrecht Manufacturing
Corporation
33 35th Street
Brooklyn. NY 11232
USA

Van Gelder Fijn Papier
Eendrachtstraat 18
Postbus 210
7300 AE Apeldoorn
Netherlands
Mouldmade manufacturer

Vitrex (Austr.) Pty Ltd
P.O. Box N2
Grosvenor Street
Sydney 2000
Australia

I.B. Wahlstrom
Kungsgatan 27
S-111 56 Stockholm
Sweden
Fine paper retailers

Dirk Weber
Kaiserstrasse 16
5300 Bonn 1
Germany
Fine paper retailers

West Design Products Ltd.
684 Mitcham Road
Croydon CR9 3AB
UK
Paper agents and merchants.
UK suppliers of Schoellersham-
mer papers

Whatman Ltd.
Springfield Mill,
Sandling Road,
Maidstone ME14 2LE
UK
Manufacturers of mouldmade
Whatman papers. For list of all
distributors contact the Alan
Witt at the mill direct.
Telephone 0622 692022. Fax
0622 691425.

Wiggins Teape Paper Ltd.
Gateway House
34 Marshgate Lane
London E15 2NT
UK
Machinemade paper manufac-
turers

Wiggins Teape Fine Papers
Gateway House
PO Box 88
Basingstoke Hants RG21 2EE
UK
Machinemade paper
manufacturers

Winsor & Newton
PC Box 91
Wealdstone, Harrow
Middsx HA3 5QN
UK
Artists' materials and fine art
paper manufacturer, distribu-
tor and retailer

Winsor & Newton (US)
555 Winsor Drive
Secaucus
NJ 07094
US
Artist materials manufacturers
and retailers; some fine papers

Wookey Hole Caves & Mill Ltd.
Wookey Hole, Wells,
Somerset BA5 1BB
UK
Handmade paper mill

Woolfits
39 Dupont Street
Toronto M5R 1VP
Canada
Fine paper retailers

Yorkshire Printmakers and
Distributors Ltd.
1 Windmill Hill Lane
Emley Moor
Huddersfield.W.Yorks HD3 9TA
UK
Specialist printmaking materials
retailers and distributors; extensive
range of fine papers

Zecchi
Via Dello Studio 19/R
50122 Firenze
Italy
Fine paper retailers

Zen Art Paper
Box 192
S-144 43 Stenungsund
Sweden
Fine paper retailers

Papierfabrik Zerkall Renker
& Sohne GmbH & Co KG
5165 Hürtengenwald
Zerkall
Germany
Fine mouldmade paper
manufacturer. Papers for
lithography (including offset
litho), screenprinting,
intaglio, relief printing, letterpress and bookmaking plus a
fine stationery range. Special
makings. Telephone
492427244. Fax 4924271079.
Agents in UK W. V. Marchant
Ltd. UK Distributor John
Purcell Paper. USA Distributor ANW Crestwood.

Zöchling Papier
2120 Wolkersdorf bei Wein
Austria
Fine paper retailers

FINE PAPER INDEX

(Listed alphabetically by name of paper)

LISTS OF PAPERS

INDEX

About estamp

estamp is a small, independent publishing
company producing books in the specialist
areas of fine art printmaking, the craft
and art of papermaking and bookmaking.
Many of the titles are surveys of a what is
going on in a particular field,
for example, 'Which Paper?' looks at the
whole range of fine papers for artists and
'A Printmakers Handbook' looks at workshops,
galleries and professional practice in printmaking. They are all well researched books, docu-
menting various aspects of the art professions
and contain a wealth of practical information.
estamp books are unqiue providing a valuable
source of reference for what is happening in
these fields both in Britain and abroad today.

estamp also runs a mail order bookshop
selling other specialist titles from around the
world.

Write direct to estamp for a catalogue.

estamp titles include
A Printmaker's Handbook
PrintSafe- A Guide to Safe, Healthy and Green Printmaking
British Printmaking Suppliers
**Which Paper ? - A review of fine papers for artists, craftspeople
and designers**

Future titles include
Europe 1992 - A legal guide
Exhibiting Prints - A guide to print galleries in Britain
British Print Workshops - a working survey
A Guide to Hand Papermaking

Pamphlets include
Printmaking in British Art Schools - a survey of courses
Contemporary British Artists Books

**204 St Albans Avenue
London W4 5JU**